PLATO'S
SYMPOSIUM

Continuum *Reader's Guides*

Continuum's *Reader's Guides* are clear, concise and accessible introductions to classic works of philosophy. Each book explores the major themes, historical and philosophical context and key passages of a major philosophical text, guiding the reader towards a thorough understanding of often demanding material. Ideal for undergraduate students, the guides provide an essential resource for anyone who needs to get to grips with a philosophical text.

Reader's Guides available from Continuum

Aristotle's Nicomachean Ethics – Christopher Warne
Aristotle's Politics – Judith A. Swanson and C. David Corbin
Berkeley's Principles of Human Knowledge – Alasdair Richmond
Berkeley's Three Dialogues – Aaron Garrett
Deleuze and Guattari's Capitalism and Schizophrenia – Ian Buchanan
Deleuze's Difference and Repetition – Joe Hughes
Derrida's Writing and Difference – Sarah Wood
Descartes' Meditations – Richard Francks
Hegel's Philosophy of Right – David Rose
Heidegger's Being and Time – William Blattner
Heidegger's Later Writings – Lee Braver
Hobbes's Leviathan – Laurie M. Johnson Bagby
Hume's Dialogues Concerning Natural Religion – Andrew Pyle
Hume's Enquiry Concerning Human Understanding – Alan Bailey and Dan O'Brien
Kant's Critique of Aesthetic Judgement – Fiona Hughes
Kant's Critique of Pure Reason – James Luchte
Kant's Groundwork for the Metaphysics of Morals – Paul Guyer
Kuhn's The Structure of Scientific Revolutions – John Preston
Locke's Essay Concerning Human Understanding – William Uzgalis
Locke's Second Treatise of Government – Paul Kelly
Mill's On Liberty – Geoffrey Scarre
Mill's Utilitarianism – Henry West
Nietzsche's On the Genealogy of Morals – Daniel Conway
Plato's Republic – Luke Purshouse
Rousseau's The Social Contract – Christopher Wraight
Sartre's Being and Nothingness – Sebastian Gardner
Spinoza's Ethics – Thomas J. Cook
Wittgenstein's Tractatus Logico Philosophicus – Roger M. White

PLATO'S *SYMPOSIUM*

A Reader's Guide

THOMAS L. COOKSEY

continuum

Continuum International Publishing Group
The Tower Building 80 Maiden Lane
11 York Road Suite 704
London SE1 7NX New York, NY 10038

www.continuumbooks.com

© Thomas L. Cooksey 2010

All rights reserved. No part of this publication may be reproduced or transmitted in any form or by any means, electronic or mechanical, including photocopying, recording, or any information storage or retrieval system, without prior permission in writing from the publishers.

British Library Cataloguing-in-Publication Data
A catalogue record for this book is available from the British Library.

ISBN: HB: 978-0-8264-4067-9
PB: 978-0-8264-4417-2

Library of Congress Cataloging-in-Publication Data
A catalog record for this book is available from the Library of Congress.

Typeset by Newgen Imaging Systems (Pvt) Ltd, Chennai, India

CONTENTS

1. Context 1
2. Overview of Themes 13
3. Reading the Text 19
4. Reception and Influence 133

Notes 156
Further Reading 162
Index 171

CHAPTER 1

CONTEXT

Dear one, come to the tavern of ruin
And experience the pleasures of the soul.
What happiness can there be apart
From this intimate conversation
With the Beloved, the Soul of souls?
                    Jalal al-Din Rumi (2000, p. 49)

The deepest insights spring from love alone.
            Friedrich Nietzsche (Friedländer 1958, p. 50)

Symposia were drinking parties in the ancient Greek world, the noun *ē symposia* meaning literally "the drinking together," and the noun *to symposion*, "the drinking party" or the place where the drinking party occurred. They were convivial occasions for passing the cup, reciting snatches of poetry, singing songs, telling jokes, and performing pantomimes. These were also essentially masculine affairs, wine, song, but no women, the occasion for male bonding, the initiation of boys into the masculine world of citizens, and a vehicle for the transmission of its cultural traditions.

Plato's *Symposium* takes the form and spirit of the traditional *symposon* as his starting point, but proceeds to transform it. It is ostensibly based on the recollection of a *symposon* hosted by Agathon, the tragic playwright on the occasion of his victory in the Lenaean Festival. Among the guests is Socrates and the comic playwright Aristophanes; later in the evening a drunken Alcibiades joins the group. Because everyone is still feeling the effects of the previous day's drinking, the guests decide to contest their rhetorical skills rather than their capacities to imbibe wine, each delivering an extemporaneous speech praising love (*Eros*). Among many memorable moments are Aristophanes' myth of the androgynes, Socrates' account of a wise woman named Diotima, whom he calls his erotic teacher, his recollection of Diotima's "Ladder of Love," and finally Alcibiades' comparison of Socrates with the satyr king Silenus, as well as his confession about trying to seduce Socrates. What emerges from Agathon's party is one of the most engaging masterpieces of philosophical literature. With the possible exceptions of the *Republic* and the *Phaedrus*, the *Symposium* is the most influential of Plato's dialogues, affecting not only on philosophy, but literature, the arts, and theology. Instead of the transmission of cultural traditions, the succession of speeches turns these traditions on their head. Plato uses the occasion of a *symposion* as a literary device that allows him to explore the power and nature of the erotic, and how it relates to issues of ethics, epistemology, and ontology. Perhaps most fundamentally, it also provides him with a means of dramatizing the nature of the philosopher, what it means to be a *philo-sophos*, a *lover* of wisdom.

Plato (427–347 BCE) was born in or near Athens, to a wealthy aristocratic family. He grew up during the turbulent last stages of the Peloponnesian War (431–404 BCE) and its aftermath. His stepfather, Pyrilampes, was a friend of Pericles and an important advocate of democracy, while his uncle, Charmides, was a member of the oligarchy known as the Hundred, and his uncle, Critias, was a leader of the infamous Thirty. Early in his life Plato met and came under the spell of Socrates (ca. 470–399 BCE), whom he later described in a letter as "the most just man of his time" (*Letters* 324e). After the restoration of democracy in 403, Socrates was arrested on dubious charges of impiety. This was largely because of his association with many of the figures connected with Athens' defeat, perhaps most notably the brilliant but unscrupulous Alcibiades (ca. 450–404 BCE). Found guilty, Socrates was executed in 399 BCE, by a toxic infusion made of hemlock. Disgusted, the young Plato withdrew from Athens to Megara and then traveled around the Mediterranean, eventually making the first of three visits to the court of Sicily, meeting the tyrant Dionysus of Syracuse. There, according to some accounts, he intrigued with Dionysus' son, Dion, and was imprisoned, ransomed, and eventually returned to Athens. Plato was silent about the details, but kept up a correspondence with Dionysus, Dion, and later Dionysus II, nursing the futile hope of creating a philosopher-king. Back in Athens, Plato founded a philosophical school, the Academy, whose most famous student was Aristotle.

CONTEXT

Plato's philosophical and literary activities extend over a 50-year period. Diogenes Laertius indicated that in his youth Plato applied himself to painting and poetry, composing dithyrambs, lyric poetry, and tragedies. Not irrelevantly, when he was about to compete for the prize in tragedy, he was dissuaded upon listening to Socrates in front of the theater of Dionysus (Diogenes 1972, p. 281). In addition to a series of 12 letters, we have 26 extant philosophical dialogues that are attributed to him. An exact chronology cannot be established, and Plato himself had the reputation of revising and polishing them throughout his life, leading the Greco-Roman critic Dionysus of Halicarnassus to quip that "Plato, even at the age of eighty, never let off combing and curling his dialogues and re-plaiting them in every way" (1985, p. 225). In turn, distinguishing the Socratic from the Platonic in the dialogues remains a matter of debate. That said, the scholarly consensus, focusing on thematic and linguistic features, divides the dialogues into three broad groupings, pivoting around Plato's three voyages to Sicily. Thus the *Apology, Crito, Laches, Lysis, Charmides, Euthyphro, Hippias minor, Protagoras, Gorgias, Ion*, and perhaps *Hippias major* fall into an early period from before his first trip in 388/387 BCE. Their original impetus was to defend the reputation of Socrates, featuring him in debate with the eponymous antagonist. They tend to focus on moral or ethical issues, deploying a strategy in which the interlocutor makes a statement and is interrogated by Socrates. These represent the purest instances of the Socratic method, in which Socrates moves toward some understanding of the issue in question by determining what he does not know, even if he cannot establish with certainty what he does know. The middle period from 388 to 367 BCE includes the *Meno, Phaedo, Republic, Symposium, Phaedrus, Euthydemus, Menexenus*, and *Cratylus*. Here the dialogues take on a more friendly tone, the animated and often hostile arguments of the earlier ones giving way to long stretches of exposition. Although morality and virtue remain important, they are situated in discussions of metaphysics and epistemology. The late period falls between a second trip to Sicily around 367 BCE and a third around 361, and includes the *Parmenides, Theatetus, Sophist, Politicus* (*Statesman*), *Timaeus, Critas, Philebus*, and *Laws*. The works of the third period extend and complicate the tendencies of the middle period. Plato is primarily concerned with questions of knowledge and a critical reexamination of his early ontological doctrines. The figure of Socrates moves to the background in the *Sophist* and *Politicus*, and disappears altogether from the *Law*, giving way to an interlocutor identified simply as "the Athenian."

F. M. Cornford (1950, pp. 68–69) and Léon Robin (1929, pp. vii–viii) argue that the *Symposium* was composed as a companion to the *Phaedo*, both featuring Apollodorus as a problematic disciple. R. E. Allen (1991, pp. 9–11) points to affinities with the *Protagoras*, noting that with the exception of Aristophanes, the guests at Agathon's banquet are present in the *Protagoras*. Many have noted the thematic echoes between the *Symposium* and the *Phaedrus*, both treating the power of Eros. Similarities may also be drawn between the treatment of the Good in the *Republic*, at the banquet hosted by Cephalus and his son Polemarchus, and the treatment of the Beautiful at Agathon's banquet. Such comparisons are fruitful in foregrounding various issues, but given questions of chronology, coupled with Plato's penchant for revision, it is difficult to group or sequence the dialogues, at least in the sense of a systematic exposition of ideas. Thus while it is problematic to put the *Symposium* into the context of Plato's other dialogues, at least in the sense of a systematic exposition of ideas, Plato himself carefully situates his work into an elaborate historical, cultural, and literary context against which to read it.

While the *Symposium* is probably a work of fiction, or at least a highly embellished and fictionalized account of an actual banquet, all of the participants were real, often historically significant to Plato's audience. While Plato probably composed the *Symposium* between 385 and 370 BCE, he was explicit about the time frame of the setting. The narrative frame featuring Apollodorus is set somewhere after the restoration of Athenian democracy, but before the death of Socrates (403 to 399 BCE), perhaps triggered by the then recent death of Alcibiades (404 BCE). The setting of Agathon's party itself is January 416 BCE, the date of Agathon's first victory in the winter Lenaean Festival. Plato, in other words, has set the action near the eve of the military disaster that led to Athenian defeat in the Peloponnesian War, the collapse of the democracy, and the establishment of a permanent rift between the *demos* and the aristocratic order. The Peloponnesian War, fought among Athens, Sparta and their surrogates, had by 416 stretched some sixteen years, with profound and deleterious effects on the moral health of the community. Describing this in the context of the 427 BCE Revolution on Corcyra (Corfu), the historian Thucydides noted the perversion of political rhetoric in which atrocities were described as heroic, and cowardice as moderation. "Then, with the ordinary conventions of civilized life thrown into confusion, human nature, always ready to offend even where laws exist, showed itself proudly in its true colors, as something incapable of controlling passion, insubordinate to the idea of justice, and enemy to anything superior to itself" (Thucydides 1954, p. 211). In 416 BCE, Athens was at the height of its power, but at a moral cost that had reduced social and political values to raw passions and interests. Thucydides suggested that Athens was less the victim of external enemies than its own machinations. "And in the end it was only because they had destroyed themselves by their own internal strife that finally they were forced to surrender" (Thucydides 1954, p. 135). With regard to the *Symposium*, it is important to remember that *Eros* was conventionally conceived as a passion that was potentially dangerous. In terms that anticipate Freud's *Id*, Socrates (Plato 1974) warns in the *Republic*, "that there is a dangerous, wild, and lawless kind of desire in everyone, even the few of us who appear moderate. This becomes obvious in our sleep" (572b). It is the releasing of these passions that unbalances the soul and endangers the well-being of the community.

In 415, perceiving the opportunity for glory and personal wealth to sustain what many took to be an extravagant lifestyle, Alcibiades persuaded the Athenians to send a major military expedition to Sicily against the city of Syracuse, himself part of the joint military command. But on a summer night shortly before the fleet was to sail, the *hermai* around Athens were mysteriously vandalized. (*Hermai* are phallic statues of the god Hermes, used to mark boundaries and signify fertility and luck.[1]) Such mutilations seemed not merely an act of impiety, but an omen of misfortune with regard to the impending campaign. In the hysteria that followed, Alcibiades was implicated. Many thought the destruction of the *hermai* part of an aristocratic conspiracy to undercut the moral foundations of the community. Hysteria continued even after the fleet sailed, and Alcibiades was tried and condemned *in absentia* in connection with the vandalism and on charges of sacrilege against the Eleusinian Mysteries. Learning of his condemnation, he escaped, traveling to Sparta. His subsequent aid to the Spartans contributed to the eventual Athenian defeat. In addition to Alcibiades, Debra Nails points out that other guests at Agathon's banquet were also implicated in the affair of the *hermai* (Lesher 2006, p. 202). Phaedrus was accused of sacrilege against the Mysteries, subsequently going into exile, and Eryximachus the physician was accused of desecrating the *hermai*, also disappearing.

Plato establishes a social context in the *Symposium* by situating the dialogue during a *symposion*. We should never confuse the ancient *symposion* with its dour academic descendent. Dennis E. Smith provides a nice summary of the features of a Greco-Roman banquet (Smith 2003, pp. 13–46). The institution carried a number of social and cultural associations, growing out of the civic institution of a sacrificial meal associated with archaic warrior clubs. The sacrificial meal centered on the rituals of blood sacrifice and the distribution of meat. Ritual drinking, concerned with consumption, followed the meal. The spirit of conviviality served to reinforce community identity and values. Given their origins in warrior clubs, *symposia* were all-male societies, composed of adult men and boys, who would serve the wine. Women were present, if at all, only in the role of entertainers—flute girls, dancers, and jugglers, or if the services of a *hetaera* (courtesan) were procured. In a ritualized drinking contest, the wine cup, toasts, and songs would move around the table from left to right. Aside from a libation of unmixed wine drunk to the "good god (Dionysus) [*agathos daimōn*]," the participants drank wine mixed with water placed in a krater (mixing bowl) at the center of the table.[2] A group leader was appointed, the *symposiarch*, charged with mixing the wine and directing the movement of toasts and conversation, the guardian of social order. Central to the tradition are the themes of education and initiation, involving the transmission of cultural memory through the performance of poetry and songs, memorized and performed by the boys. Much Archaic lyric, choral, elegiac, and iambic poetry was composed and transmitted for such occasions. Initiation often centered on homoeroticism and pederasty. (I will return to the role of ancient Greek homoeroticism below.)

In its transition from the Archaic to Classical period, the *symposion* shifted from the practice of the drinkers sitting around a table to the practice of reclining on couches. This had the social effect of limiting the number of participants and creating an intimate "synoptic" space, the "men's room" (*andrōn*), a place apart where seven or so couches could be distributed comfortably around the room. The typical *symposion* hosted seven to fifteen guests, usually two per couch. As a result, it also tended to be an aristocratic gathering, limited to those with the economic means sufficient to provide the special space. It also tended to become a more intimate gathering, bringing together like-minded people who shared common aims and interests. To many commoners, (*demos*), these elite *symposia* often represented a center for aristocratic misdeeds, whether it be mayhem caused by its drunken participants, or a venue where the aristocracy might conspire against the democracy. The desecration of the Mysteries or the destruction of the *hermai* had the hallmarks of a post-sympotic prank.

Manuela Tecuşan points out that in other dialogues, Plato reveals a problematic relationship with the institution of the *symposion* (Murray 1990). While the *Protagoras* attempts to describe what a good *symposion* might look like, Socrates is mostly concerned that they simply become occasions for drunkenness. For Cephalus, in the *Republic* (Plato 1974), sympotic memory serves primarily to underline the loss of youth and its pleasures rather than the transmission of traditional values. "[Old men] recall the pleasures of sex, drink, and feasts, and some other things that go with them, and they are angry as if they were deprived of important things, as if they then lived the good life and now were not living at all" (329a). In the *Laws* (Plato 1961), the Athenian expresses ambivalence. "Rightly controlled fellowship over our cups affords a disclosure of our native disposition, but is this its sole recommendation?" (652). Socrates goes straight to the point in *Phaedrus*: true lovers of wisdom (*philodoxoi*) can find little enjoyment in *symposia*. Contrasting those who seek to nourish a healthy soul with others (Plato 1995), he says, "And when others turn to different amusements, watering themselves with drinking parties [*symposios*] and everything else that goes along with them, he [the wise person] will rather spend his time amusing himself with the things I have just described" (276d). Phaedrus agrees with this, glossing Socrates' "amusements" as telling edifying stories of justice (276e). Socrates, however, prefers to take this a step further. The pedagogical goal is not about transmitting stories, even edifying ones. "But it is much nobler to be serious about these matters, and use the art of dialectic. The dialectician chooses a proper soul and plants and sows within it discourse accompanied by knowledge . . ." (276e). Distinguishing *philosophoi* (lovers of wisdom) and *philodoxoi* (lovers of belief or opinion) in the *Republic*, Socrates points to the irresolvable ambiguities in sympotic "wisdom." Such wisdom, he says, "is like those double meanings one is entertained with at banquets, and the children's riddle about the eunuch and his throw at the bat" (439c).[3] Only by going beyond amusements through the interrogation of dialectic does one truly seek wisdom.

Plato's reservations about the traditional institution of the *symposion* are readily evident in the *Symposium* itself. Thus, at an early stage the interlocutors decide to pass speeches praising love (*Eros*) around the table instead of the wine cup. In turn the *encomia* center on the role of love in moral development, rather than the occasion for erotic or ribald amusements. Finally Socrates introduces the practice of dialectical interrogation, first questioning Agathon about his speech, and then recounting Diotima's interrogation of Socrates himself.

Plato develops a literary context in the *Symposium* by having Agathon's guests decide to deliver a series of *encomia*.[4] There are several factors of importance to be considered here. First, the *encomium* or *panegyric*, a speech devoted to the praise of some person or thing, represents a standard category in classical oratory, entailing distinct elements and progression. While precise rules were not formalized until later (for instance the *Rhetoric to Alexander* which appeared around 316 BCE) a conventional *encomium* typically began with the *prooimion*, a greeting and introductory prologue. This was followed by the *genos*, an account of the subject's origins and family, which might include his or her birth, upbringing, and education. This might also include an *anstrophê*, a listing of the subject's notable companions. Central to the *encomium* was the *praxis*, the subject's various deeds and achievements. Then there was the *synkrisis*, a listing of the followers of the subject. Finally it concluded with the *epilogos*, a summary and exhortation to praise the subject.

Second, because oratorical skill was crucial for participation in public life in the ancient world, rhetoric was central to pedagogy, and rhetorical exercises in which students prepared and delivered set speeches on assigned topics were an important means of training, as well as a way of displaying one's abilities. In the *Symposium*, the first five speakers deliver set pieces (*epideixeis*), largely following the rhetorical conventions of the *encomium*. In turn, while each speaker adheres to the general rules of the *encomium*, each frames his speech in a style and manner that reflects his individual character. Phaedrus will couch his speech in general popular terms. Pausanias the legal authority will praise *Eros* in legal terms. Eryximachus the physician will offer a technical scientific account. By contrast Aristophanes the comic playwright will paint *Eros* in comic mythopoetic terms, while Agathon the tragic playwright will use a highly ornamented style. In this way, Plato offers five different discourses on love. There is a third factor, however, pertaining to the relationship between pedagogy and wisdom. The rhetorical formula may be applied to any person or thing without consideration of whether the praise is deserved.

Writing in the wake of Plato, Aristotle asserts in his own study of rhetoric, "we bestow *encomium* upon men after they have achieved something. Yet the deeds themselves do but indicate the moral habit, and we should praise a man even if he had not done a thing, if we were sure he was capable of doing it" (Aristotle 1960, p. 52). Aristotle assumes that the praises are warranted, that good acts point to an underlying good character. While this is commendable, the praise may not always be justified. A skilled and persuasive orator can indeed make the good seem bad and the bad good. It is exactly this potentially dangerous possibility that informs Plato's long-standing polemic against the sophists. In Plato's not unbiased account of Protagoras, Gorgias, Thrasymachus, and Hippias of Elis, among others, the sophists claim to offer wisdom (*sophia*), but really teach the skills of rhetoric and the techniques of persuasive speaking. They are more concerned with achieving victory than seeking wisdom. The *Encomium of Helen*, an extant speech by Gorgias, is illustrative of Plato's concern. In a virtuoso set piece, Gorgias argues that Helen should not be held guilty of the adultery that precipitated the Trojan War. If destined by the gods, then how could things have been different? If she was overcome by force, passion (love), or the power of words, how could she be held responsible, because her will had been overcome? "The persuader, as constrainer," Gorgias declares, "does the wrong, and the persuaded, as constrained, is wrongly blamed" (Gorgias 2003, p. 81). In terms that seem to anticipate a number of themes in the *Symposium*, he adds, "The effect of speech upon the structure of soul is as the structure of drugs over the nature of bodies; for just as different drugs dispel different secretions from the body, and some being an end to disease, and others to life, so also in the case of speeches some distress, others delight, some cause fear, others embolden their hearers, and some drug and bewitch the soul with a kind of evil persuasion" (Gorgias 2003, pp. 81, 82).

Plato plays on the theme of sophistry and wisdom in the *Symposium*. Stanley Rosen rightly describes Socrates as entering into the camp of sophistry at Agathon's banquet (Rosen 1987, p. 6). With the exceptions of Aristophanes and Socrates himself, each of the interlocutors had been a student of a sophist, and the dialogue *Protagoras* portrays all of them except Aristophanes, at the feet of Hippias. While the tone of the *Symposium* remains convivial throughout, and there is no deep concern for victory, Plato does cast a look at the power of rhetoric. The *encomia* delivered by the guests (except Aristophanes) reflect sophistical displays. Each is trying to impress with his oratorical skills, to achieve victory, and only incidentally come to a true appreciation of *Eros*.

By way of conclusion, I will say a word about the *words* for "love," and something about Greek homoeroticism. (See also Vlastos 1981, p. 4n4; Plato 1980, pp. 1–4; Plato 1998, pp. 5–7.) The Greek noun *erōs* and its cognate verb *eran* signify "love" and "to love" in the strongest sense of passion or desire. It may or may not have a sexual connotation, depending on the context. As a proper noun it also names the winged god, son of Aphrodite. *Philia* and *philein* are used to express a milder affection or friendship. It is conventional to translate *philia* in Aristotle as "friendship." In the *Lysis*, Plato distinguishes between *erōs*, characterized by an asymmetric passion of the lover for the beloved, without the assumption of reciprocity, and *philia*, characterized by a symmetrical reciprocity between friends (Kaln 1996, p. 259). The noun *agapē* and its verb *agapaō* are used to signify love in modern Greek. In the classical Greek of Plato it is used to describe general affection or liking. In the

CONTEXT

Septuagint, the Greek version of the Hebrew Bible, it is the word typically used to translate the Hebrew *'ahăbâ*, and in the New Testament, it is used variously to signify "love for all," love in the sense of discipleship, or "love is God [*Theos ein agape*]" (1 John 4:8). The King James Bible translates *agapē* as "charity" (1 Cor. 13:1–8). (The KJB draws on the Vulgate, *charity* deriving from the Latin *caritas*, meaning "affection," "love," or "esteem.") For a fuller discussion of the differences between *agape* and *erōs*, see Armstrong (1980), and especially Nygren (1953, pp. 160–181). Plato's *Symposium* is most fully about *erōs* and the end or object of desire or longing (*epithymia*), though he is not always rigorous in his vocabulary.

Homoeroticism is a basic given in the *Symposium*. That said, we must be careful with our terminology. Socrates was married and Alcibiades was infamous for his numerous female lovers and mistresses. While Agathon and Pausanias and probably Phaedrus and Eryximachus could be understood as homosexual in a modern sense of the term, it is problematic to apply modern conceptions of homosexuality or gayness in any normative or substantive sense to Classical Athens without falling into a *nunc pro tunc* fallacy (presentism). Sexual identity was understood in terms of penetration and phallic stimulation, whether the partner was male or female. The masculine, as distinct from the male, was defined as the active penetrator, and the partner as the passive penetrated, whatever bodily orifice might be involved. The masculine norm was understood in terms of a shifting binary between masculine and non-masculine rather than male and female. The non-masculine partner was anyone "inferior" to the masculine, whether in age, gender, or social status. Thus normal masculine behavior might focus on a younger man, a woman, or a slave. A boy might assume the passive role with an older man, but the active role with a younger boy.

Pederastic relationships in Classical Athens should be understood in terms of a highly patriarchal society, and as part of a practice of male bonding and initiation. Marriage between men and women was first and foremost about social stability, the transfer of property, the order of the household, and the production of children. Women and girls were largely supposed to remain in the confines of the household, and not venture outside without suitable male escort. While there is abundant evidence of loving relationships among men and women, and the comedies of Aristophanes and others attest to women's sexual power, the erotic ideal focused on boys who could circulate in society. An Athenian gentleman would marry for the sake of property and propagation, but seek intellectual or romantic companionship elsewhere with a younger man, his proper "equal." Some analogies might be drawn with medieval *amour courtois*, recalling the words of Andreas Capellanus from the *Art of Courtly Love*, that "marriage is no real excuse for not loving." Physical passion belongs to the spouse, while love belongs to the spiritual beloved.[5]

By boys, Athenians meant adolescents between the onset of puberty and the development of a full beard. The older man, the *erastēs* (lover), was subject to desire (*eros*), while the boy, the *erōmenos* (beloved) was the object of that desire, supposedly motivated by a mixture of admiration, gratitude, and affection. Athenian society had an ambivalent response to pederasty, both approving and disapproving. Demosthenes' *Erōtikos* (*The Erotic Essay*) celebrates the "honorable rewards" accruing from the proper relationship between lover and beloved (Demosthenes 1949, p. 47). Plato's *Laws*, on the other hand, condemns such behavior as unnatural, arguing that if taken to its logical extreme, it would destroy the race (636b–c, 838–841). Xenophon's version of the *Symposium* is critical of the effeminate Pausanias, attributing to him the argument about armies recruited from lovers that Plato puts into the mouth of Phaedrus (178e–179a): "For these, he said, would in his opinion be most likely to be prevented by shame from deserting one another—a strange assertion, indeed" (Xenophon 1923, 8.32–33). In a proper relationship the boy was to assume a rigorously passive role, unmotivated by his own sexual desires or self-interest. For an "inferior" partner to assume an active role was to be stigmatized as *katapugones* or *kinaidoi*, words difficult to translate into English, but carrying associations of being lewd, promiscuous, pathetic, and effeminate.[6] Bringing all of this back to the tradition of the *symposion*, the ideal pederastic relationship involved the education and initiation of the boy into the masculine world, a domain of male bonding in which the erotic undercurrents were permitted to become overt.

CHAPTER 2

OVERVIEW OF THEMES

Speech is a powerful lord, who
With the finest and most invisible body
Achieves the most divine work.
                    Gorgias of Leontini (2003, p. 79)

Whoever, whatever he is, we will, if it please him,
Address him as Zeus, a name we speak in awe, . . .
                    Aeschylus (1998, p. 16)

Plato's dialogues are about essential questions, not systems. For this reason they remain vital and fresh, stimulating to a wide range of readers and thinkers down to the present, while other works of philosophy, employing more systematic kinds of discourse, find themselves relegated to history and specialists. Plato uses the form of the dialogue to dramatize the process of thinking, the ferment and struggle to move from *endoxa* (popular beliefs) to *episteme* (knowledge). More fundamentally, he uses these formal features to engage the reader in that ferment and struggle. In turn, one topic tends to link with another in an elaborate network of interconnections. This does not mean that the dialogues are a hodgepodge, unfolding in a random fashion. Quite the contrary, Plato has composed them with the care of a sonneteer, with close attention to the interplay of themes, voices, tonalities, and form. He always rewards a close and attentive reading. That said, each of the dialogues tends to revolve around a cluster of themes.

The broad thematic center of Plato's *Symposium* is *eros* and the nature of love, how love shapes our moral character, informs our ethics, raises questions of being, contemplates the forms (especially the Beautiful and the Good), and drives the philosophical enterprise. Whether or not Plato had it in mind, we can read the *Symposium* as the dialectical counterpoint to the

Republic, the drinking party of Agathon with the banquet of Cephelus and Polymarchus, both beginning at twilight and ending at dawn, both devoted to the upward journey of the soul. By dialectic, I do not mean that one contradicts or cancels the other, but that each supplements and completes the other. While the *Republic* focuses on the political dimensions of the individual, the reciprocal relationship between the structure and "health" of the soul and that of the community, the *Symposium* focuses on the private dimensions, on the fundamental drives of the individual.

In turn, both works explore what it means to be a philosopher, a "lover of wisdom." But while the *Republic* dwells primarily on grasping the nature of "wisdom," the *Symposium* shifts to the other side of the equation, seeking to understand what "love" means and how it relates to the pursuit of wisdom.

In the *Republic* Socrates rehearses "the ancient quarrel between philosophy and poetry" (607b), famously banning the poet from the ideal community. But in the *Symposium*, Socrates is clearly more sympathetic. Indeed, the work as a whole vividly dramatizes the role of poetry in philosophical discourse. Underlying this sympathy for the possibilities of poetry is a corresponding awareness of the limits of reason.

From a methodological perspective, Diotima's "Ladder of Love" is an analog to the *Republic*'s "Parable of the Cave." Both treat the process of enlightenment or understanding, broadly the movement from individual appearances to something increasingly more abstract that goes beyond the individual to the ideal. But while Socrates' cave dweller must be externally compelled to make the journey of ascent, Diotima's initiates into the mysteries of love are internally motivated by their own desires up the "Ladder of Love." Related to this, the attention on love foregrounds an issue hinted at in the *Republic*, namely that the philosophical process is not easy, that the rational method by itself is inadequate for reaching the truth by itself. It is a guide, a discipline, and a preparation, but finally, it is only through unstinting effort that "all of a sudden he [the lover pursuing Beauty] will catch sight of something wonderfully beautiful in its nature" (210e). As Socrates explains in the *Phaedrus*, it involves a sort of madness or mania. The *Symposium* looks more closely into the nature of this madness.

OVERVIEW OF THEMES

In the close reading that follows in Chapter 3, I will examine the narrative and dramatic elements of the *Symposium* in addition to the explicitly philosophical, arguing that these contribute to the philosophical content. This includes a consideration of the role of the elaborate narrative framing and how it functions to deliberately complicate the picture of what we read, foregrounding the philosophical process. It also includes some awareness to characterization and the interplay of personalities, dramatizing the dialectical development of the philosophical themes. With this in mind, I will now briefly sketch the "plot" and indicate the major themes that emerge from it.

The *Symposium* is built around the recollection of a drinking party hosted by the playwright Agathon. An unidentified interlocutor has asked Apollodorus if he had attended. Apollodorus explains that it had been held many years earlier when he was still a child, but that he will recite the account of the party that he learned from one Aristodemus. Narratively, the *Symposium* is Apollodorus' recollection of Aristodemus' recollection. Thematically this raises questions about the authority of any "written" text, not subject to the dialectic of interrogation. The various narrative ambiguities compel the attentive reader to engage the dialectic indirectly by a process of interpretation and rereading.

Still feeling the aftereffects of the previous day's drinking, the partygoers decide that it would be expedient to pass "speeches" around the table, instead of the wine cup. Thus following a hint by Phaedrus, they decide that each will present an extemporaneous speech praising Eros, the god of love. While the speeches represent a rhetorical performance on the part of their speakers, each also reflects the character, profession, and values of their speakers, as well as responding to the previous speakers. The content and rhythm of the speeches and the character dynamics of the speakers serve to divide the *Symposium* into three acts.

I will examine the first act in Section 3.1. The first to speak is Phaedrus, the beloved, who praises love for the way that it morally improves the beloved, especially in homoerotic relationships. Next to speak is Pausanias, a legal authority, concerned to sharpen definitions and clarify terms. Distinguishing between a heavenly Aphrodite and a worldly one, he discerns the difference between an elevated love and a base one, praising the higher love for its moral improvement of the lover. He is followed by the physician, Eryximachus, who sees love in natural terms related to harmony and concord. Love is not only about moral improvement but the establishment and preservation of health and well-being in general. The comic playwright, Aristophanes, next takes up the topic. True to his character and profession, he offers up a comic myth of how humans were once spherical. Zeus cut them in half in order to keep them under control. Love is about people seeking their lost half, driven by the desire to heal their wounds and become whole again. Agathon the host now delivers a speech, reflecting his background as tragic playwright and devotee of sophistry. For him, the god Eros is young and beautiful, consorting with the beautiful, and therefore source of all beautiful virtues. Thematically this first "act" introduces questions of moral psychology and the way that our erotic passions contribute to the virtues. It also raises the question of the foundation of virtue. Is it a traditional or social phenomenon, as Phaedrus and Pausanias seem to suggest? Does it point to something about nature in general, or human nature, as Eryximachus and Aristophanes contend, or do we move to a concept of the moral good that transcends nature, as Agathon suggests? In broad terms this part of the *Symposium* also raises the question of the relationship between collective wisdom, the *endoxa*, and Platonic knowledge and wisdom: is there a fundamental gap, or does Socrates' position grow out of the *endoxa*, in some way regrounding it?

The second act, Section 3.2, marks a dramatic and thematic turn. Socrates convinces the group that he would like to praise love in a different way. He first interrogates Agathon about his speech, compelling him to conclude that what he has said about love makes no sense, that love is not about the possession of beauty and virtue, but in fact the drive to satisfy their absence. Socrates now changes tack, offering an account of love he had once been taught by one Diotima of Mantinea, a woman wise in many things, who had also taught him the art of love. From the perspective of narrative, Plato now adds Socrates' layer of recollection to those of Aristodemus and Apollodorus. First Diotima interrogates Socrates in a manner similar to Socrates' questioning of Agathon with similar results. Diotima explains that love is like a *daimôn*, a being neither divine nor mortal, but a spiritual intermediary. Next at Socrates' request, she offers up her own account of love, first giving the mythical account of Love as the child of Penia (need) and Poros (plenty). For this reason, Love is always seeking the beautiful and virtue. Love is about our desire for immortality, either on the physical level, through reproduction, or on the mental level, through the performance of enduring acts or the creation of great works. "What Love wants is not beauty," she says enigmatically, but "reproduction and birth in beauty" (206e). She proceeds to describe an erotic movement that progresses from a love of beautiful bodies, to beautiful works, to beautiful institutions, to beautiful knowledge, and finally to a glimpse of Beauty itself. She summarizes this ascent in what has become known as "Diotima's Ladder of Love." Socrates' critique of Agathon and Diotima's speech translate the ethical concerns of the first speeches to ontological ones. The *daimônic* posits a metaphysical realism in which Socrates or the erotic initiate is seized or directed by forces outside his direct control. In turn eros becomes the driving force that leads us to the forms or ideas, especially that of the beautiful, drawing parallels between the philosopher and the erotic initiate.

The third act, Section 3.3. presents another dramatic turn. The party is now suddenly interrupted by the arrival of a drunken Alcibiades. He has come to praise Agathon, but is shocked to discover Socrates there, for whom he feels a potent mixture of love, anger, and jealously. He is prevailed upon to deliver his own speech, praising Socrates rather than love. He begins with the famous metaphor of the silenus, comparing Socrates with a statue of the satyr king, ugly on the outside, but beautiful when opened to the interior. He then confesses how he tried unsuccessfully to seduce Socrates, then describes Socrates' various acts of virtue: "But, as a whole, he is unique; he is like no one else in the past and no one in the present" (221c). Thematically Alcibiades' speech illustrates the nature of love and erotic ascent described by Diotima, translated into the human realm.

The arrival of additional revelers soon disrupts Agathon's party, bringing it to a conclusion. Aristodemus' last recollection is of Socrates at dawn, in close conversation with Agathon and Aristophanes over whether or not a playwright should be able to write both comedy and tragedy. When Socrates realizes that his interlocutors have themselves fallen asleep, he gets up, goes out, and proceeds to his day as usual. This final "act" both provides a concrete illustration of the earlier parts, and raises thematic issues with regard to interpretation and the nature of written texts.

2.1. A NOTE ON TEXTS AND TRANSLATIONS

There are many translations of the *Symposium* readily available from the venerable Victorian version of Benjamin Jowett to the recent modern one of Christopher Gill (Plato 1999). As a matter of convenience, I have primarily relied with on the translation by Alexander Nehamas and Paul Woodruff (Plato 1989), a solid workhorse among philosophy students, checking it against the Greek and commentaries of Kenneth Dover (Plato 1980) and the Greek, translation and commentaries of C. J. Rowe (Plato 1998). Occasionally I have made slight changes or adjustments in the translation where I judged it clarified matters. Following scholarly conventions, I have cited passages from Plato using the standard Stephanus pagination of parenthetical numbers and letters, which will be key to all modern translations and editions.

CHAPTER 3

READING THE TEXT

3.1. IN PRAISE OF LOVE

This world is but a school of inquiry. The question is not who will spear the ring but who will make the best charges at it. The man who says what is true can act as foolishly as the one who says what is untrue: we are talking about the way you say it not what you say. My humor is to consider the form as much as the substance, and the barrister [l'advocat] *as much as his case, as Alcibiades told us to.*

(Montaigne 1991, p. 1051)

3.1.1. Prologue

Before turning to a close examination of the text of Plato's *Symposium* it is useful first to set it in context with two other Socratic discussions of love, Xenophon's *Symposium*, and Plato's *Phaedrus*. In different ways each may be read as a companion or complement to Plato's *Symposium*.

3.1.1.1. Symposium *of Xenophon*

Xenophon of Athens (ca. 431–355 BCE) was a soldier of fortune as well as a friend and contemporary of Socrates. He claimed that the political art learned from Socrates better prepared him to discipline soldiers than the rhetoric of Gorgias (Strauss 1978, p. 23). The bane of second-year students of classical Greek for the *Anabasis*, his account of a campaign in Mesopotamia, Xenophon left a series of important writings about Socrates, including the *Memorabalia*, the *Oeconomicus*, the *Symposium*, and the *Apology*. There are a number of striking similarities as well as differences between the *Symposium* of Plato and that of Xenophon. Whether Plato wrote in response to Xenophon or Xenophon to Plato is a matter of controversy, though the current consensus favors the latter view (Kahan 1996, p. 393).

However, even if Xenophon was inspired by Plato to offer his own account of a Socratic *symposion*, he has largely eschewed the idealized Socrates of Plato for something showing "great and good men" in their "lighter moods" (Xenophon 1923, 1.1). Indeed the seemingly casual and desultory rhythms of Xenophon's conversations, comfortably mingling "raillery and seriousness" (4.28), underscore Plato's careful artistry.

Emphasizing that he was appealing to his own experience (contrary to Plato), Xenophon offers a recollection of Socrates' attendance at a *symposion* hosted by Callias in the Piraeus, on the occasion of the Panathenaic games. In an opening reminiscent of the *Republic*, Callias sees and invites Socrates and several others, who "would present a great deal more brilliance if my dining-room were graced with the presence of men like you, whose hearts have undergone philosophy's purification"(1.5). The festivities include an acrobatic hoop dance performed by a girl and the extemporaneous remarks of one Philip the Buffoon. True to the conventions of a *symposion*, conversation circulates around the table from left to right. On one round the discussion centers on the question: In what do you take pride? Critobulus answers that he takes pride in beauty (3.7), later explaining: "since we handsome men exert a certain inspiration upon the amorous, we make them more generous in money matters, more strenuous and heroic amid dangers, yes, and more modest and self controlled also . . ." (4.15). Though different in tone, his argument resembles that of Phaedrus and Pausanias in Plato's *Symposium*. Often clowning, Socrates says that he is proud of the "trade of the procuring [*mastropeia*]" (3.10), later explaining that since a good procurer will make his clients attractive to everyone, he will be highly rewarded (4.57–61). Rona Burger points to the connection between Socratic midwifery and procuring as furtive activities that, like the philosopher, facilitate something for others (2008, p. 255n60). See also Ranasinghe (2000, pp. 151–152).

On the topic of Critobulus' beauty, Socrates responds with mock incredulity: "you boast as though you actually thought yourself a handsomer man than me" (4.19). Critobulus insists that if he is not, he would be the ugliest of the satyrs, an image that leads Xenophon to remind his readers that Socrates physically resembled the satyrs (4.20). Socrates challenges Critobulus to a contest in order to prove that he is more handsome. Punning on the Greek *kalos* whose meanings range from "beauty" to "excellence," especially in the sense of function, Socrates contends that his bug eyes are more beautiful than the Critobulus' because he has a wider field of vision, that his flared nostrils allow him to pick up more scents, that his snub nose makes it easier for him to spy on people with a sidelong glance, that his large mouth allows him larger mouthfuls (5.3–10). Picking up the satyr motif, Socrates concludes, "do you not reckon it a proof of my superior beauty that the River Nymphs . . . bear as their offspring the Sileni, who resemble me more closely than they do you?" (5.7). Silenus is the king (and father) of the satyrs (or silens), part human, part goat, and the companion of the god Dionysus. In Plato's *Symposium*, Alcibiades will play on both the motif of the satyr and Silenus.

The eighth section of Xenophon's *Symposium* is the most interesting with regard to reading Plato's version. Socrates describes Love (*Eros*), as "a mighty deity [*daimonos*] that is coeval with the eternal gods, yet youngest of them all in appearance, in magnitude encompassing the universe, but enthroned in the heart [*psyche*] of men" (8.1). This description reads like a conflation of the various accounts of Love presented in Plato's *Symposium*. Love is a *daimôn*, like one of the gods, but not. His influence both encompasses nature, yet also the human soul or psyche. In order to illustrate the ubiquitousness of Love, Socrates observes that he cannot find a time when he was not in love. He then notes that Charmides has gained many lovers (and even occasionally feels some passion), that Critobulus, though still a beloved, is beginning to feel passion for others, that Niceratus is said to actually love his wife (and even be loved in return!), and that Hermogenes is in love with nobility of character (8.2, 3). Finally, when Socrates asks Antisthenes if he does not love anyone, he receives the answer: "I am madly in love with you" (8.4). Again this seemingly random succession is similar to the progression in Plato's *Symposium*. Thus in Charmides and Critobulus we see the love of lover and beloved, similar to that represented by Pausanias and Phaedrus. In Niceratus' love of his wife and its reciprocation, we can see parallels with the love described by Eryximachus and Aristophanes, who both see love in heterosexual as well as homoerotic terms, love forming a harmony or unity in its reciprocity. Hermogenes' love of nobility and character echoes in its way the love described by Agathon and Socrates/Diotima. And finally Anisthenes' love for Socrates parallels that of Alcibiades.

Pulling together this answer with the fact of his physical ugliness Socrates praises Antisthenes' discernment of virtue. "I see that you are in love with a person who is not marked by dainty elegance nor wanton effeminacy, but shows to the world physical strength and stamina, virile courage and sobriety" (8.8). He then notes that he does not know if there be one Aphrodite or two, one "Heavenly" and one "Vulgar," but conjectures that the different kinds of love come from different sources. Thus carnal love would come from the "Vulgar" Aphrodite, and spiritual love, love of friendship and of noble conduct, would come from the "Heavenly" goddess (8.9–11). He further argues that the soul becomes more lovable the longer it progresses toward wisdom, noting that while a taste for physical beauty will eventually reach a point of surfeit, "the affection for the soul, being pure, is also less liable to satiety" (8.15). Pausanias introduces the same distinction in Plato's *Symposium*.

Speaking frankly, he claims under the influence of the wine, Socrates compares the two kinds of love to the man who rents a farm and the man who owns one. The former, like the man who is only interested in the physical appearance of the beloved, cares only about an immediate short-term profit, not increasing its value. By contrast the latter, like the man who seeks friendship, is interested in cultivating and enhancing his farm, a process that also entails improving himself. "For one cannot produce goodness in a companion while his own conduct is evil" (8.27). True love, then, is ennobling and mutually improving. His position strongly resembles Aristotle's notion of true friendship (*philia*) in the *Nicomachean Ethics*: "they seem to become still better from their activities and their mutual correction. For each molds the other in what they approve of, for 'what is noble is from noble people'" (1172a10).

The *symposion* draws to an end when the performers stage an erotic pantomime about the marriage of Dionysus and Ariadne. The kissing is so genuine that many of the banqueters are aroused, excusing themselves from the party to hurry home to wives or lovers, while Socrates and others go for an evening stroll.

3.1.1.2. Phaedrus *of Plato*

One of the greatest of the Platonic dialogues, the *Phaedrus* is in many ways a companion piece to the *Symposium*, centered on the passionate love between Socrates and the young Phaedrus. Plato's *Phaedrus* seems to have been composed about the same time as the *Symposium*, though some argue that its introduction of a tripartite soul makes it a later work (Kahn 1996, p. 260), grouping it more closely with the *Republic*.

Phaedrus and Socrates are walking together outside the city walls in a woodland precinct holy to the river god Achelous. Phaedrus praises an *encomium* on love composed by the sophist Lysis. At Socrates' request, Phaedrus recites the speech (Plato 1995, 230e–234c). In brief, Lysis distinguishes between actions motivated by erotic love (*eros*) and those motivated by friendship (*philian*), arguing that the young man should grant his favors to an older suitor who is *not* in love with him. The suitor acting out of erotic passion will say or do anything to satisfy his desire, and eventually abandon the beloved when the passion has cooled. By contrast, the actions of dispassionate friends are voluntary, and so devoted to the long-term interests and well-being of the beloved.

Humoring Phaedrus, Socrates expresses his ecstasy over the speech, though it is more from enjoying the enthusiasm of the young man's reading than with the content of the speech itself. Ironically, his words of praise seem more in the spirit of the erotic lover than the friend. He shifts tone, however, when Phaedrus goes on to claim that Lysis has omitted nothing about his subject. Socrates disagrees: "If, as a favor to you, I accept your view, I will stand refuted by all the people—wise men and women of old—who have spoken or written about this subject" (235b). When pushed, he cites the lyric poets Sappho and Anacreon. We might also make a space here for Diotima. Phaedrus cajoles a reluctant Socrates to offer his own speech. In the end, Socrates will offer two, followed by a long discussion about rhetoric and writing.

Socrates begins his first speech (237a–242a) by asking that they establish a clear definition of love (*erōs*) and its effects. He then claims that we should be aware that we are ruled by two principles, one an inborn desire for pleasure, the other an acquired judgment for the pursuit of what is best. "Now when judgment is in control and leads us by reasoning toward what is best, that sort of self-control [*sôphrosunê*] is called 'being in your right mind'; but when desire takes command in us and drags us without reasoning toward pleasure, then its command is known as 'outrageousness [*hubris*]'" (237e–238a). Eros, then, is a dangerous madness, a forceful drive that overpowers the impulse to do right (238c). Shifting to highly rhetorical, rhymed phrases, Socrates jokes he is the grip of something divine, declaring, "I'm on the edge of speaking in dithyrambs" (238d). Here Socrates seems to be sarcastic, poking fun at the overwrought rhetorical flights characteristic of the sophist Gorgias, and similar to the climax of Agathon's speech in the *Symposium* ("I am suddenly struck by a need to say something in poetic meter" [197c].).

With his definition of love established, Socrates outlines an argument similar to that of Lysis. The lover, motivated by a madness that can destroy body and soul, will not benefit the beloved, but more likely harm him in order to satisfy his desire for beauty in human bodies. "You should know that the friendship of a lover arises without any good will at all. No, like food, its purpose is to sate hunger" (241c). Unlike Lysis, however, Socrates does not suggest that the boy should therefore grant his favors to a dispassionate friend.

When Socrates brings his first speech to a conclusion, Phaedrus notices that it is exactly noon, the sun directly overhead, and the two start to leave. Socrates suddenly stops, and declares that he has just been taken with "the familiar divine sign" (242c), the famous *daimôn* (see below 3.2.): "I thought I heard a voice coming from this very spot, forbidding me to leave until I made atonement for some offense against the gods. In effect, you see, I am a seer [*mantis*], and though I am not particularly good at it, still . . . I am good enough for my own purposes" (242c). We may take this possession as real, unlike the mock ecstasy earlier. He renounces his speech as horrible, claiming that his words were offensive to the gods, especially Eros, son of Aphrodite. To atone, he will deliver a second speech, which he says came from Stesichorus of Himera, son of Euphemus. While Stesichorus was an important name among the archaic Greek poets, and Socrates opens his speech quoting Stesichorus' palinode, "There's no truth to that story" (244a), Plato may also be playing on his name: Stesichorus, son of "Good Speaker [*Eu-phemus*], from the Land of Desire [*Him-era*]" (Plato 1995, p. 27n56).

READING THE TEXT

Socrates' second speech (244a–257b) is a veritable hymn to the essential nature of eros in human life. It is the driving force that makes human life possible. Further, while eros is a madness, it is one that enables the rational life. The argument is too complex to discuss in detail here, but it is important to touch on several points.

First, while the earlier speeches had rejected all madness (*mania*) as harmful and dangerous, Socrates makes amends by suggesting that there are four positive kinds of madness: First and most important is the prophetic madness that comes from Apollo and is the province of figures such as the *pythia* of Delphi, the Sibyl, and the priestesses of Dodona. Next is the madness associated with "mystic rites" and the expiation of guilt that comes from Dionysus. Examples of this might be found in the insanity of Orestes in Aeschylus' *Orestia*, or that of the Bacchants described by Euripides in the *Bacchae*. The third kind is the Bacchic frenzy associated with poets, a gift of the Muses. Good poetry, Socrates suggests, is not just about skill or craftsmanship, but inspiration. The fourth is erotic madness, the madness of the love that comes from Aphrodite. In the context of the Phaedrus, this is what Socrates is most interested in elaborating. To do this he must first describe the structure and nature of the soul.

In basic terms, the soul is immortal: "That is because whatever is always in motion is immortal, while what moves, and is moved by, something else stops living when it stops moving," so the soul is a self-moving mover (245c).[1] To say what the soul *actually is*, Socrates quips, would require a god, but he can say "what is like [*eoiken*]" (246a). He then unfolds the famous parable of the charioteer, an elaborate extended simile in which he likens the soul to "the natural union of a team of winged horses and their charioteer" (246a). In humans one horse is purebred and obedient to the reins, while the other is wild and disobedient, constantly struggling against the reins. We see here Plato anticipating the tripartite model of the soul that he develops in the *Republic* (439a–e), composed of the reason, will, and appetites. Originally the soul had wings and traveled the circuits of heaven where it saw and was nourished by beauty, wisdom, and goodness of reality as it is. When the soul gives in to the heaviness of the bad horse, it descends from heaven toward earth and the wings atrophy. Some souls remember the divine and others do not: "Many souls are crippled by the incompetence of the drivers, and many wings break much of their plumage. After so much trouble, they all leave the sight of reality unsatisfied, and when they have gone they will depend on what they think is nourishment—their own opinions" (248b). The souls eventually enter physical bodies, giving them animation. We need not here go into the details about the reincarnation of souls.

Returning to the question of erotic madness, Socrates says that lovers choose their beloved after their own fashion, the noble person drawn to the nobility of the beloved, while those of a base disposition are drawn to baseness in the beloved. (We might draw a comparison with Aristophanes' androgynes seeking their lost halves.) In effect, the philosophically inclined lover has an intimation of the heavenly nourishment within the beauty and nobility of the beloved. Erotic madness is a complex mixture of agony over the lost vision of the divine, coupled with the joy of recollecting it. Correspondingly, the beloved is slowly awakened to love the beauty within and beyond, nourishing and initiating him into the love of the good. Bringing it all back to Lysis' speech and the benefits of love, Socrates concludes that the madness of the true lover offers the beloved the possibility of divine gifts, while the rewards of the companionship of the non-lover can only be human benefits (256e).

We can read the *Phaedrus* as a miniature version of the *Symposium* with a succession of speeches on love, first by the sophist, then to Socrates himself, and finally by Socrates ostensibly recollecting some authority (Stesichorus/Diotima). In both dialogues the movement of the speeches is dialectical, preserving, reworking, and transcending the previous. Thematically, both dialogues affirm the importance of the irrational, expressed in the erotic, seemingly at odds with the usual Platonic privileging of the rational over the irrational. In turn each in his way affirms the value of the true poet, despite the convention that Plato bans the poet from the ideal community. In the deepest sense, both works are concerned with what it really means for a philosopher to be the lover of wisdom.

3.1.2. Narrative frame

We are now ready to turn to Plato's *Symposium* itself. It is contained in an elaborate two-level narrative frame, the first featuring the narration of Apollodorus, and the second the narration of Aristodemus. A sort of prologue or overture, it serves to set the scene and introduce the major themes, but in a subtler fashion, to dramatize and subvert them. First it draws attention to the formal properties of the *Symposium*, pointing to how they also carry philosophical significance with regard to authority and the transmission of knowledge. Second, and closely related, it hints at the recurrent Platonic concern about memory. Third, it introduces the issue of love and passion.

3.1.2.1. (172a–174a)

"*[D]oxō moi,*" "[I] believe I'm not unrehearsed]" (172a), are the opening words of the *Symposium*. In a rhetorical gesture of understatement, Apollodorus indicates that he *believes* that he is not unprepared to answer the question addressed to him by an unnamed friend. The word choice is also ironic, given Plato's classification of *doxa*, beliefs or opinions below *epistemē*, true knowledge with regard to the Forms. At the same time the understatement seems to affirm a definite certainty. Apollodorus is certain about his belief in his ability, but is that the same as knowledge? This ambiguity informs the conversation that follows. A friend, whom we can equate with the reader or auditor of the dialogue, has apparently just asked Apollodorus about a dinner hosted by the tragedian Agathon and attended by Socrates and Alcibiades. The exchange commences with the jesting Apollodorus responding that he is well rehearsed in the matter, having recently given an account of it to Glaucon. Glaucon had explained that he had received a garbled account of the dinner from a man who had in turn heard it from one Phoenix, son of Philip. He had also asked if Apollodorus had actually been present at the dinner. To this Apollodorus explained that the dinner occurred many years earlier, part of the celebration occasioned by Agathon's winning the prize for his first tragedy, reminding Glaucon that Agathon has not lived in Athens for many years. Apollodorus indicates that he would have been a child at the time, that his own passion for the wisdom of Socrates was relatively recent, and that his source was the same as that of Phoenix, one Aristodemus of Cydatheneum who *had* actually been present. He also indicates that he had checked with Socrates on some of the details. He also admits at the end of the *Symposium* that Aristodemus had fallen asleep and missed much of a conversation among Socrates, Agathon, and Aristophanes on dramatic writing (223d). In other words, we are offered an authoritative account that turns out not to be all that authoritative.

In the manner of a good textual critic, Plato establishes a line of textual authority and transmission by means of Apollodorus' immediate conversation with the unnamed friend, and the earlier one with Glaucon. The report of the garbled version of Phoenix underlines the relevance of obtaining an unmediated line of transmission and getting the facts straight. The immediate effect of all of this attention to accuracy seems to validate the authenticity and trustworthiness of Plato's account. But having done that, Plato's Apollodorus says that neither he nor his source could remember everything, so he will tell only what he recollects to be the most important. The unmediated line of transmission back to Socrates is suddenly contingent upon the memories and interpretive judgments of first Aristodemus and then Apollodorus, in effect the memory of a memory or the interpretation of an interpretation. On one hand, this is a perfectly normal rhetorical and literary convention. Most of the speeches recorded in the histories of Thucydides, for instance, represent idealized reconstructions, not transcripts; yet on the other, it foregrounds a recurrent tension in Plato's writings.

Plato plays an analogous game in the *Republic*, at the end of Book 3. Here we have the famous argument about banning or expelling the poet from the ideal community. For Socrates, since the empirical world of appearances is merely a shadowy approximation of the world as it actually is, its claim to represent reality is false. Similarly any realistic representation of the world of appearances is itself a contingent approximation of its object, and also therefore false. Thus mimetic or representational works of art are false representations of a false representation. In other words, it would seem that artists are doubly dishonest, and should therefore be removed from any healthy community seeking to instill virtue, a move that would also expel the poet and topple the authority of Homer. Astounded by this proposal, Glaucon asks Socrates how one could implement a cultural and social program so radical that it would mandate the elimination of all mimetic art, ostensibly including painting, poetry, dance, sculpture, drama, narrative, and even much music from the ideal community because these were guilty of lying about lies. Tongue in cheek, Socrates declares that they might persuade people by *lying*, by telling a "noble lie [*gennaion ti en pseudomenous*]" (*Republic*, 414b–c). Indeed, despite the stated hostility to fiction, the *Republic* unfolds its arguments through a succession of fictions, including the famous "Ring of Gyges," the "Parable of the Cave," and the concluding "Story of Er." In a telling move, Plato's Socrates wonders, if people "in our time," could be so persuaded by such fables. By this gesture of doubt, Plato winks at his own audience, at the same time diverting them from the fact that this figure of the doubting Socrates is itself a noble lie, a textual game created by Plato as a vehicle for his philosophy. In a similar sleight of hand, the doubts raised about the memories of Aristodemus and Apollodorus both seem to lend credence to Plato's ostensible concern for accuracy, while at the same time distracting us from the fictional character of the entire *Symposium*.

The fact that the *Symposium* is set at a *symposion*, at a drinking party celebrating the triumph of a playwright is significant. First, it raises the issue of tone, and how we are to take the speeches offered by each of the interlocutors. In the context of a *symposion* as both social practice and literary convention, the various contributions are generally meant to be entertaining rather than profound. Much in the spirit of a celebrity roast, each participant speaks in a tone of self-parody and exaggeration, poking fun at himself and the other. While the various contributions may express popular or traditional wisdom (*endoxa*), they are not necessarily meant to be taken as serious arguments. We cannot demand of them logical rigor, since by definition that was never part of their intention. That would be to judge them by a standard they never claimed. That said, Agathon's concluding assessment of his speech: "part of it in fun, part of it moderately serious as best I could manage" (197e), underscores the interpretive problem both with regard to how to take his speech and that of the others. Part of what he says is meant as a game, but part is something he seriously believes.

Second, the context of playwright Agathon's party reminds us that the dialogue form itself is a sort of play, and as we shall see, that Plato parodies the conventions of the theater. But at a more fundamental level, Plato reiterates and repeats the relationship between performer and audience. We as auditor or reader are the audience for the performance of Apollodorus, who emphasizes himself that he is well-rehearsed in his lines. In turn, Apollodorus was the audience for the performance of Aristodemus. In his turn, he was the audience (witness) to the various speeches performed by Socrates and the others at Agathon's party. Finally, Socrates, in his recollection of the wisdom of Diotima, stands as a willing audience to her performance. In other words, the truth or wisdom articulated or represented by Diotima is five removes from us, five mediating filters. A microcosm that anticipates later developments, these vertical stages of removal echo the vertical progression up the rungs on the metaphorical "Ladder of Love" that Diotima describes in her speech. It also echoes the horizontal progression around the banquet table as each interlocutor delivers his speech.

The interconnected motifs of theater and performance closely link to the themes of authority and memory. Thus, when the performer recollects and recites a speech, does he understand what he says, or does he mechanically recite words that he has merely memorized? This concern recurs in many guises throughout Plato's dialogues. In the *Ion*, for instance, Socrates compels a famous rhapsode to admit that while he is skilled at moving people's emotions during his recitals, he is ignorant of the meaning of his speeches. Socrates will make an analogous complaint in the *Symposium* (198d–e). This also relates to Socrates' ongoing debate with the Sophists who are long on persuasive skill, but perhaps short on wisdom. So too, do Apollodorus or Aristodemus really understand the speeches they remember and recite? Do we, for that matter?

Also relevant is the use of authority, particularly the practice of supporting a position by citing a poet or some line of verse to make a case or clinch an argument. Can Homer be taken as an absolute authority in all matters? Can a line of poetry taken out of context and not subject to interrogation make a compelling argument? Throughout the speeches of the *Symposium* the various speakers draw on the poets or allude to myth to support their claims. That said, they are not hesitant to alter, "correct," interpret, or even invert their authorities, when the traditional wisdom seems to get in the way of what they want to say. Thus, for instance, Love will be the youngest of the gods, the oldest of the gods, the most beautiful, the most ugly, or not a god at all. Is a mutable authority an authority at all?

To more fully appreciate the issues of memory, transmission, and knowledge implicit in the *Symposium*, it is useful to return again to Plato's *Phaedrus*, which treats these concerns explicitly. In the course of their discussion of love, Socrates and Phaedrus turn to the issue of memory, especially as it relates to the role of writing. Here Socrates complains that written texts destroy human memory. Writing, he contends, is like painting, merely offering a resemblance of something. Far from being a *memory*, it is merely a *reminder*. More to the point, a written text is unresponsive and can neither explain nor defend itself. In turn, I cannot immediately question or challenge an absent author. To such would-be interrogation, the written text maintains a "majestic silence." I can only reread the text, and it can only repeat itself. "[W]ritten words," says Socrates, "go on telling you just the same thing forever" (*Phaedrus* 275c). I may certainly achieve some insights, but it is an asymmetrical dialectic. On one side the reader can never be entirely sure that she has taken away what she was meant to receive, thus losing certainty. Nor on the other, can the author be certain that potential readers will take away what was intended, thus losing control over his words. The written act is not merely a representation, raising problems of imitation or what the representation actually represents, but also problems of reading and interpretation.

This goes to the heart of the philosophical project of seeking wisdom in order to achieve a good life. It points to a divided loyalty or split identity. Insofar as it remains true to its roots as a mode of life that seeks the cultivation and enlightenment of the soul, philosophy is still concerned with the nature of the good life. But at the same time, insofar as it becomes self-conscious of its activities, seeking and examining its basic assumptions, philosophy refocuses onto a meta-discourse, concerned with the analysis of concepts and the clarification of terms.

All of this underlies the apparent philosophical bind in which Plato finds himself with regard to literature. As a repository of traditional wisdom in the Hellenic world, the poetry of Homer and the lyric poets have the authority of tradition. The mnemonic repetition central to the transmission of the oral tradition fixes its form, while precluding the possibility of clarification or modification. The oral expression therefore becomes unstable in relation to interpretation. It is exactly the cognitive power of writing that draws attention to this instability, exposing flaws and contradictions that can neither be resolved nor ignored. Early in the *Republic*, a character named Polemarchus tries to argue a point of ethics (about the nature of justice, or what it means to be a just person) by appealing to the authority of the lyric poet Simonides. After a series of arguments deploying the ambiguities of Simonides' words, Socrates demonstrates that this ethical position seems to lead to a contradiction. "[I]t follows," says Socrates "that justice, according to you and Homer and Simonides, appears to be a craft of thieving, of course to the advantage of one's friends and the harm of one's enemies. Is that not what you meant?" (*Republic* 334b). Flustered, Polemarchus can respond only, "No, by Zeus . . . I don't any longer know what I meant, but this I still believe to be true, that justice is to benefit one's friends and harm one's enemies." Unable to respond to Socrates' logic and unable to resolve the ambiguities with the long-departed poet, Polemarchus finds himself in the position described in the *Phaedrus*, and can only endlessly repeat himself, but never advance his position.

While Plato might address the problem by claiming to favor the dialectical give and take of an actual conversation, it is really the cognitive power of writing that drives his philosophical enterprise and shapes the rules of engagement. His frustration, like that of Polemarchus, is that of an oral culture confronting the linguistic self-awareness of a written one. Despite his stated reservations, Plato must resort to the strategies of writing and by extension literature. The Platonic dialogues as a whole are a written literature that play on the fiction of oral tradition and dialectic. He may complain how the written text creates false realities, but he is using exactly those resources of the written text to evoke an absent speaker in order to force the reader to read and reread, to think and rethink. The written word may lack the tone of voice, facial features, and gestures of the speaker, but a good writer can suggest them, providing a fuller, albeit not foolproof interpretive context. In turn, the power of the text to create worlds or evoke emotions offers the philosopher a powerful set of tools to stimulate insight. This is the impetus behind Socrates' appeal to "noble lies" (*Republic* 414b), or to the use of parables throughout the *Republic*. It is also part of the impetus behind Plato's parodies of the theater and various types of *encomia* in the *Symposium*. Each figure is evoked and exemplified by his language.

Having considered the thematic concerns for authority, memory, and transmission implicit in the narrative frame, we may turn to the central issue of love and passion. Underlying Apollodorus' recollection of the speeches at Agathon's party is an obsession for Socrates, which he likens to madness. "I'm a maniac and I'm raving! [*mainomai kai parapaiō*]" (*Symposium* 173e). (In the *Phaedo* [117d], Plato's account of Socrates' execution, Apollodorus breaks down with such profuse and loud weeping, that everyone but Socrates himself loses control.) Apollodorus explains that before he had come into contact with Socrates, his life had been at loose ends. Now he prefers philosophical conversation. "After all, my greatest pleasure comes from philosophical conversation, even if I'm only a listener, whether or not I think it will be to my advantage" (173c). By contrast the talk of businessmen bores him, with the paradoxical result that though he is considered a failure in material terms, he considers himself spiritually rich. This ironic turn anticipates the perennial discussion of Socrates' legendary physical ugliness against the beauty of his person, echoing the deeper theme of the contrasting relationship between the realm of appearances and some underlying truth or reality. On an ethical level, material success does not necessarily correspond to moral goodness. In a society that values power and wealth, Apollodorus' desire for wisdom would appear to be madness, another instance of the infamous charge that Socrates makes the good seem bad and the bad seem good.

3.1.2.2. (174a–178a)

We are now at long last ready to commence an examination of Apollodorus' account. "Well, the speeches went something like this—but I'd better tell you the whole story from the very beginning, as Aristodemus told it to me" (174a). Here the narrative voice shifts to Aristodemus who tells how he once came upon Socrates dressed in his best sandals, having just come from the baths. This opening description itself hints at another irony. Aristodemus is himself a Socratic maniac, so obsessed that he goes around barefoot in emulation of the master (173b). Apollodorus himself recalls Aristodemus as "a real runt of a man" (173a), and in a surviving fragment of the play, *The Banqueters*, Aristophanes speaks of one Aristodemus who had been defiled and buggered (*katapugōn*) so often, that even his anus *(proktōs)* was named Aristodemus. For him philosophic life seems to relate to a dress code, to be a philosopher is to appear as one. Socrates explains the occasion of his unusual attire by saying that he is on his way to the victory dinner party hosted by Agathon. Playing on the fact that Agathon is famously good-looking, even pretty, he quips that he has "prettified [*ekallōpisamēn*]" himself so that his "beauty [*kalos*]" might match that of Agathon (174a).

Here the English strains to catch the Greek wordplay. The word *kalos* signifies the "beautiful," but also "good" in the sense of auspicious, and "noble." In turn the name Agathon derives from *agathos* which means variously "good," "gentle," and "noble." In a ribald double-entendre, Socrates characterizes his pursuit of the good within the beautiful in terms of his pursuit of the handsome young man (Agathon). With this in mind, we should add the deeper wordplay. The word "philosophy," derives from the Greek *philo-sophos*, literally the "love of wisdom." The word *philia* signifies "love" in a general sense in Greek, including feelings of affection for friends, parents, and children. By contrast *erōs* signifies "love" in the sense of intense desire, usually with sexual connotations. As the proper noun *Eros* (classical Greek script does not have capitals), is the young winged deity, the son of the goddess Aphrodite (he is Cupid in the Roman/Latin context). The common noun *ta aphrodisia* signifies "sexual intercourse." Further, Kenneth Dover (1980, p. 2) notes that eros can be understood as "desire doubled," which was also conceived as "madness." With this in mind, Apollodorus' mania for Socrates and philosophy can be conceived as an erotics of wisdom (an *eros-sophos*), an intense desire rather than merely a *philo-sophos*. All of this is characteristic of the wordplay typical of the institution of *symposia* in general and Plato's *Symposium* in particular. It also offers the first hint at the central theme of how intense desire becomes the vehicle for the pursuit of wisdom.

Socrates invites Aristodemus to join him, and they proceed to the party. Soon abstracted, however, by some philosophical problem, Socrates falls behind, telling Aristodemus to go ahead, that he will follow. In an awkward position Aristodemus must proceed to Agathon's house, an uninvited guest. The playwright is nevertheless gracious, and in the spirit of hospitality characteristic of the traditional *symposion*, invites him to join the party, though Aristodemus remains chiefly a silent witness of what unfolds. Functionally, Aristodemus the uninvited guest and would-be-lover of Socrates marks the opening of Agathon's party, much as Alcibiades, another gatecrasher and would-be-lover marks its close.

Several times Agathon sends a servant to fetch Socrates, who has withdrawn to the porch next door, just standing there unresponsive to calls. When Agathon instructs the servant to persist in calling Socrates, Aristodemus intervenes, saying, "that is his way; he sometimes stops and stands wherever he happens to be" (175b). This interlude of intense abstraction seems to be an instance of Socrates' periods of *daimonic* possession. I will go into more detail below. Later in the *Symposium*, Alcibiades will offer another anecdote about Socrates standing in rapt concentration (220c–d). About halfway through the meal, Socrates finally arrives, and is invited by Agathon to sit by him. Taking his place, Socrates quips that it is a pity that wisdom were not like water, flowing from the full cup to the empty. That way he might be overflowing with Agathon's wisdom. He adds in his characteristic manner, and perhaps a hint of irony, "[m]y own wisdom is of no account—a shadow in a dream—while yours is bright and radiant and has a splendid future" (175e).

Agathon's party observes the religious conventions of a *symposion*. "When dinner was over, they poured a libation to the god [Dionysus], sang a hymn, and—in short—followed the whole ritual" (176a). Given Dionysus' double identity as god of wine and god of the theater, the ritual focus is appropriate. The guests quickly decide, however, that since many were still suffering from the effects of the previous day's drinking bout that they might pass a speech around the table instead of the cup. Taking a hint from Phaedrus that there are no proper hymns to Love (*Erōs*), Eryximachus proposes that each deliver a speech praising Love. Eryximachus also suggests that the flute-girl (*aulētris*) be sent off to play to herself or over to the women's section of the household (176e). During the course of a conventional *symposion*, she would provide musical entertainment for the company on the pipes (something like a recorder), and in some circumstances provide sexual entertainment as well. Socrates approves this proposal, declaring himself an "expert in things erotic [*deinos ta erōtica*—literally *erotics*]" (177d). (He makes a similar self-characterization in *Lysis* 204c and 206a.) Because he suggested the topic, Eryximachus is appointed *symposiarch*, the master of ceremonies. Phaedrus is designated the first to speak.

3.1.3. The speech of Phaedrus (178a–180c)

The historical Phaedrus of Myrrhenus (ca. 444–393 BCE) is in his mid-twenties at the time of the *Symposium*, and closely linked with Eryximachus (Nails 2002, p. 282). In addition to the *Symposium* he appears in the *Protagoras* and the *Phaedrus*. The comment attributed to Phaedrus that there were no adequate hymns praising Love recalls a jest by Socrates in the *Phaedrus*. Teasing the young man, he says, "I'm sure you've brought into being more of the speeches that have been given during your lifetime than anyone else, whether you composed them yourself or in one way or another forced others to make them" (242a–b). It is not important here to ask whether Phaedrus was simply interested in sophistic rhetoric, tempted by the persuasiveness of Lysis, or using the speech as an indirect means of offering himself to the dispassionate Socrates. It does, however, set the context for his speech in Agathon's *symposion*, especially with regard to the moral benefits of love. It also hints at the irony that for him the benefits of love and beauty are chiefly beautiful speeches.

Still a young man, Phaedrus' contribution to the *symposion* shows the hallmarks of the journeyman, closely adhering to the conventions of an *encomium*. After a brief *prooimion*, praising Love as a great god, he turns to the *genos*, regarding Love's parents and origins: Erōs is the most ancient of gods, the proof of this being that his parents are not mentioned in either legend or poetry.[2] In support of this, Phaedrus quotes a passage from Hesiod's *Theogony* that after the birth of Chaos, Earth and Love simply appeared. In a non-sequester, Phaedrus then argues that since Love is the oldest, he also gives the greatest goods. He then turns to the *praxis*, describing the benefits of Eros.

Love benefits both the lover (*erastēs*), and especially the beloved (*erōmenos*), for it is the affection of the beloved for the lover that reinforces the guidance of the lover. In other words, the beloved feels pride in the lover's approval, and shame in his disapproval, a motivation more powerful than the benefits of public honor, wealth, or family loyalties. For that reason, the beloved will seek what is most honorable and noble. Similarly the lover desires to live up to the expectations of the beloved, and is ashamed to fail those expectations by doing something shameful. If only the army or a community were composed of lovers, Phaedrus laments: "Theirs would be the best possible system of society, for they would hold back from all that is shameful, and seek honor in each other's eyes" (188e). (Xenophon attributed this argument to Pausanias [8.32, 33].) Phaedrus' favorable description of warrior lovers hints at the social practices of Spartan society (the Lacedaemon), which combined the martial, social, and erotic, a social cohesiveness based on male bonding and *esprit de corps*. More immediately the idea of warrior lovers protecting each other anticipates Alcibiades' story of how Socrates had saved him on the battlefield.

Phaedrus now turns to the *synkrisis*, showing the noble followers of Love, and how their noble actions in turn enhance Love's reputation. First noting that only lovers would be willing to die for each other, incredulously even if the lover were a woman, he cites the case of Alcestis' willingness to take the place of her husband Admetus in Hades, in order to save his life. He also points to the case of Orpheus and Euridice, and finally to Achilles and Patroclus. Phaedrus' erotic ideal is thoroughly homoerotic, and though he grants that the moral force of love can also apply to women, he privileges the moral power of male bonding. Rejecting the portrayal of Achilles in Aeschylus' play, *The Myrmidons*, he contends that it is wrong to say that Achilles was the lover of Patroclus and not his beloved. There is a double thrust here. First he implies that it was his status as beloved that motivated Achilles to live up to the heroic ideal, the only hero to bear the epithet "best of the Achaeans [*aristúein*]." In doing this, he suggests, "[The gods] are more impressed and delighted, however, and are more generous with a loved one who cherishes his lover, than with a lover who cherishes the boy he loves" (180b). Thus Achilles' love from the perspective of the beloved is greater than that of Alcestis as lover. The reason for this, he suggests by way of analogy, is that the relationship between the beloved and the lover is like that between humans and gods.

Summing up in the *epilogos*, he concludes, "I say Love is the most ancient of the gods, the most honored, and the most powerful in helping men gain virtue and blessedness, whether they are alive or have passed away" (180b).

At one level, Phaedrus' speech can sound like an incoherent hodgepodge of unsubstantiated generalities and *non-sequesters*. Many comment on the way he muddles his examples (e.g. Allen 1991, pp. 12, 13). Much of what he says about the moral superiority of the beloved is self-serving, reflecting his own status as beloved, and perhaps even a beloved who is getting a bit old for the role. That said, many of his comments look back to earlier themes in Plato, and look forward, anticipating what develops in the *Symposium*. Thus Love should be understood as a powerful drive. It has the power to ennoble, to bring out our better qualities. At the same time, Phaedrus introduces the idea of a hierarchy of loves, when he suggests that the love of the beloved is greater than that of the lover. In turn, this relates to the divine nature of love, that the horizontal relationship between lover and beloved is a form of worship that is connected to the vertical relationship between the gods and humans.

He also couches the moral good or bad in terms of the shame (*aischron*). E. R. Dobbs (1951, pp. 28–63), Dover (1974, pp. 230–242), and Anderson (1993, pp. 21–22) speak of the difference between a "shame culture" and a "guilt culture."[3] Phaedrus' focus on the relationship between Achilles and Patroclus seems to echo on several counts, Socrates' indictment of the Athenians from the *Apology* (Plato 1961). There, Socrates recalls the case of Achilles, who when warned that he would be killed if he sought to kill Hector in order to avenge the death of Patroclus, dismisses the danger. "When he heard this warning, he made light of his death and danger, being much more afraid of an ignoble life and of failing to avenge his friends" (28d).

Phaedrus also echoes the *Apology* when he suggests that the desire for the lover's approval or shame at his disapproval has a stronger influence on us than public honor, wealth, or family loyalties. Socrates indicts Athens for the perversion of its values: "Are you not *ashamed*," Socrates asks the jurors, "that you give your attention to acquiring as much money as possible, and similarly with reputation and honor, and give no attention or thought to truth and understanding and the perfection of your soul?" (28e). This passage also underscores the limits of Phaedrus' *encomium*.

There are two problems: first, while the beloved does not wish to be shamed in the eyes of the lover, it does not follow that the lover automatically represents a model for universal emulation, aside from the judgment of a naive and credulous young man. To appear not shameful to a shameful lover is no guarantee of virtuous behavior, especially as Phaedrus suggests, if the beloved eschews the normalizing values of family and community. Second, while Phaedrus argues that the beloved will seek to be virtuous in the eyes of the lover, he remains fixed on physical beauty of the body rather than the soul. This underscores an asymmetry in the relationship between the beloved and the lover. The beloved certainly seeks to improve himself and not be shamed in the eyes of the lover, but in this the lover must stand as the established embodiment of *kalos*: "the lover is more divine than the beloved: the god is in him and he is inspired" (180b). It assumes that the lover possesses some divine possession, the *daimonic*, or that he has already achieved some ideal. One might ask if the elderly Gustav von Aschenbach in Thomas Mann's 1912 novella, *Death in Venice*, has achieved some ideal of *kalos* when he has his hair dyed in order to appear younger and more attractive to the young Tadzio.[4] While the beloved may certainly become morally improved according to Phaedrus' formulation of love, the lover is left no room for growth. Paradoxically, because the lover has no room for growth, both the lover and the beloved remain fixed at the same level. It is these problems that Pausanias tries to rectify in his speech, by reversing the vector with regard to the moral improvement of the lover/beloved.

Apollodorus indicates that according to Aristodemus, there were several speeches after that of Phaedrus that he did not recall well, so skipped over them, turning next to that of Pausanias.

3.1.4. The speech of Pausanias (180c–185e)

The historical Pausanias of Cerameis is the lover of Agathon, and will later accompany the poet when he moves to the court of Macedon (Nails 2002, p. 222). He also appears in the *Protagoras*, sitting with the sophist Prodicus. His speech in the *Symposium* responds to that of Phaedrus, or the line of thought opened by him. R. G. Bury describes his skills as those of a practiced pleader with a "lawyer-like" style of argumentation (Plato 1973, p. xxvi). Thus he begins by wanting to clarify the definition of love. Love is inseparable from the goddess Aphrodite, but mythic accounts identify two Aphrodites: the motherless daughter who emerged from the severed testicles of Uranus (we might recall the famous painting by Botticelli, featuring Venus, the Roman version of Aphrodite, standing on a scallop shell), and the daughter of Zeus and Dione. The first is named Urania or Heavenly Aphrodite, the second Pandemos or Common Aphrodite. Since there are two Aphrodites, there must be two Loves, Heavenly Love and Common Love. The object of his praise, therefore, is Heavenly Love. (Xenophon attributed this argument to Socrates [8.9–11]; see above 3.1.1.1.)

Pausanias then asserts the ethically interesting proposition that no action is inherently good or bad in itself. Rather, it is how the action is performed that makes it good or bad, or the disposition motivating the action. The same, he contends, applies in love: "Love is not in himself noble and worthy of praise; that depends on whether the sentiments he produces in us are themselves noble" (181a). In other words, it is a question of the motive or disposition. The act is "beautiful" if done beautifully or for beautiful reasons, but shameful if done shamefully, for shameful reasons. Common Love is opportunistic, seeking immediate gratification, especially of a sexual nature. Heavenly love, by contrast, is attracted to the noble, strong, and intelligent. Pausanias attributes the differences to the fact that Common Love is younger, so immature in his tastes, while Heavenly Love is older. Further, he suggests that Common Love has a mixed nature because his parents are male and female, while Heavenly Love has only a father, partaking only of the single (and from his point of view), superior male nature. He goes on to argue that there should be laws that forbid relationships with young boys who have insufficiently mature judgment. "These vulgar lovers are the people who have given love such a bad reputation that some have gone so far as to claim that taking *any* man as a lover is in itself disgraceful" (182a).

While Phaedrus had drawn his examples of love from mythology, Pausanias draws from history and social customs. The absolutist Persian empire, as well as tyrants in general, fear men bound together by the bonds of noble love. Such lovers will work and die for each other, making them effective tyrannicides. Fear and condemnation of such lovers shows a lust for power on the part of the ruler, and cowardice on the part of the ruled. Conversely, the Athenian and Spartan acceptance of male love relationships shows their ethical superiority. The lover is encouraged, and the conquest is considered noble.

Athenian custom, he claims, separates the wheat from the chaff, allowing us to distinguish the Heavenly from Common Love. First we consider it shameful for the beloved to yield too quickly to the lover, since resistance over time testifies to constancy. Second, we consider it shameful to be seduced by the temptations of money or power, rather than attracted by nobility and character. Such behavior shows a taste for corruption. Summarizing, Pausanias argues that the ideal love relationship represents the coincidence of two principles. First, the lover's willing subjugation to the beloved is neither servile nor reprehensible. He is not motivated by lust or sexual gratification, but sees a potential for virtue in the beloved that points to the possibility of a lifelong relationship. Second, the beloved seeks the subjugation of the lover for the pursuit of wisdom (*philosophian*). He is not seeking material gain or power, but senses that the lover can make him wise and virtuous.

Much in Pausanias' Heavenly Love is reminiscent of Oscar Wilde's famous account of the "Love that dare not speak its name," and Wilde's words could read as a gloss: "There is nothing unnatural about it. It is intellectual, and it repeatedly exists between an elder and a younger man, when the elder man has intellect, and the younger man has all the joy, hope and glamour of life before him" (McKenna 2005, p. 391). The younger beloved receives the benefits of the lover's maturity and experience, while the older lover vicariously enjoys the vitality and enthusiasm of youth. We might also draw a parallel with the deep affection of the young man mentored by the older, as for instance in the case of the young athlete for the coach, in effect the feelings of love and gratitude of the younger for an older, other than a parent, who has shown interest in the personhood of the younger.

Returning to his proposition that acts are not inherently good or bad, but rather a function of the disposition behind them, Pausanias suggests that even if the lover or beloved is deceived, and that the partner turns out to be corrupt, nevertheless, because the deceived partner was operating from a virtuous disposition, he remains honorable. In short, according to Pausanias all of this demonstrates the value of Heavenly Love to the community and its citizens, "for he compels the lover and his loved one alike to make virtue their central concern. All other forms of love belong to the vulgar goddess" (185b).

Pausanias' speech forms a sort of pair or complement with Phaedrus'. Both see love in homoerotic terms, and both are centered on the relationship between individuals. Both also agree that love has the power to make us better, though Phaedrus privileges the moral superiority of the beloved, while Pausanias favors the lover. For Phaedrus it is the dread of the lover or the beloved appearing shameful to the other that motivates virtuous actions. Pausanias takes this a step further. Instead of framing the motivation negatively in terms of the fear or avoidance of shame between the lover and beloved, he turns things around, framing the relationship positively in the coincidence of the proper virtues of the lover and beloved. Unlike Phaedrus, Pausanias realizes that not all "love" is disposed to virtue. Thus he distinguishes the higher Love from the lower, the older Love focused on the soul and moral improvement, from the younger Love centered on the body and sexual gratification.

It is easy to agree with the broad outlines of Pausanias' claim that the Heavenly Love seeks wisdom. We may also agree with him about disposition and performance of acts beautifully (or not shamefully), but what exactly does this mean? What is the standard of deportment and where does it come from? Here Pausanias falls back onto a conventionalist mode of thought, privileging the given customs and norms (*nomoi*) of Athenian and Spartan society. Although both Pausanias' and Phaedrus' reading of the norms are self- serving, neither seriously questions what Athenians would consider normatively virtuous or shameful, aside from their own homoerotic relationships.

Daniel E. Anderson points out that despite Pausanias' criticism of Phaedrus for claiming that the beloved pursues Eros for the sake of reward, both finally praise Love for Love's benefits, rather than for itself, as a means, and not as an end in itself (Anderson 1993, p. 28). In this regard, it is useful to recall that piety in the Greco-Roman world was predicated on cultic practice rather than creed, in the proper performance of prayers and sacrifices independent of what one understood them to be, or even believed about them. Agathon's party commenced with a perfunctory sacrifice to Dionysus: "they poured a libation to the god, sang a hymn, and in short followed the whole ritual. Then they turned their attention to the drinking" (176a). As I indicated in the first chapter, historically, the upper-class coterie represented at Agathon's party was considered among some circles of Athenian society disrespectful of the religious mystery cults and other traditional religious practices.

Most important, however, to fully appreciate the universalizing move that Eryximachus will make, it is important to keep in mind the moral relativism of Phaedrus and Pausanias, grounding love as they do in the individual and the moral standard in the conventions of the community. Philosophically we also see a transition from a moral psychology grounded in the relationship between the individual and his community, to a moral "physics," grounded in a relationship with nature, ultimately pointing to a moral metaphysics, grounded in transcendent forms.

At this point Aristodemus reports that Aristophanes was next in line to speak. He however is suffering from hiccups, presumably because he had eaten or drunk too much. He turns, therefore, to Eryximachus the physician (who is reclining with Aristodemus on an adjoining couch), demanding either that he cure him, or take his place in the sympotic sequence. Ultimately Eryximachus does both. First he prescribes a cure in which Aristophanes is to counter the hiccups by tickling his nose with a feather in order to induce sneezing. Second, he offers up his own speech praising Love. The exact significance of this comic interlude and the switching of places have raised extensive speculation. From a narrative perspective, it breaks up the action, and reminds Plato's readers of the convivial atmosphere of a *symposion*, contributing to the verisimilitude of the scene. It also points to the physicality in Attic Old Comedy, which frequently played on the comic possibilities of bodily functions. It also serves to foreground a contrasting pairing or correspondence between Eryximachus and Aristophanes, and then between Aristophanes and Agathon. In the first case we can notice the connection between the sober Eryximachus, a physician devoted by definition to the god Apollo, and the possibly drunken

Aristophanes, devoted to Dionysus, god of both intoxication and theater. In the second case, we may note the obvious connection between Aristophanes, the comic playwright, and Agathon, the tragic playwright. Whatever the explanation, the exchange of positions with Eryximachus and Aristophanes marks a clear division in the *Symposium*.

3.1.5. The speech of Eryximachus (185e–189d)

Like his father Akumenus, the historical Eryximachus of Athens (ca. 448–415 BCE) was a physician. At the time of the *Symposium* he would have been about thirty-two years old, and is portrayed as the lover of Phaedrus. In addition to the *Symposium*, he appears in the *Protagoras*. Implicated in the desecration of the hermai, the historical Eryximachus disappears from the scene after 415, either exiled or executed (Nails 2002, p. 143).

Eryximachus' speech in the *Symposium* is written in a plain, unornamented style, couched in the professional jargon and conceptual framework of the physician, and we might say without being too anachronistic, the scientist. It is important to note that while Phaedrus and Pausanias envisioned Love as a god, at least figuratively speaking, Eryximachus from the start conceptualizes love in naturalistic terms, subject to scientific observations and manipulation. This reflects a universalizing move to counter the cultural conventionalism of Phaedrus and Pausanias. It also reflects the naturalistic tendencies of Hippocratic tradition, which rejected divine explanations for the cause of disease. In the case of "Sacred Disease" (i.e. epilepsy), for instance, Hippocrates declares that though the disease is called "sacred," it "but has a natural cause, and its supposed divine origin is due to men's inexperience . . ." (Hippocrates 1, p. 139).[5]

Thus Eryximachus concurs with Pausanias' distinction between the two types of Love, but contends that he needs to take it further. Love does not merely belong to the human soul in relation to beautiful individuals, but represents a broader natural phenomenon that influences animals, plants, and even the gods. "In fact, it occurs everywhere in the universe" (186a). In the domain of medicine, he notes that in all bodies (human and animal) there are two species of Love, the principle that relates desire to its objects. Thus the healthy constitution seeks healthy love and the diseased constitution seeks unhealthy love. The task of the physician is exactly to distinguish the Love that is noble from the Love that is ugly in order to transform the body's desires and affect its health. He can implant good love when it is absent, and diminish bad love when it is present.

Framing matters in cosmological terms, Eryximachus describes the world as the tension between opposing elements. The physician must reconcile and establish concord and love between these elements: hot to cold, bitter to sweet, wet to dry. Underlying his medical views is the cosmology of the Presocratic philosopher, Empedocles of Acragas (ca. 493–433 BCE), who argued that the universe was a dynamic steady state composed of the shifting recombination of the elements earth, air, water, and fire. The elements come together or separate under the influence of repulsion (Strife) and attraction (Love). "At one time they are brought together by Love to form a single order," Empedocles declares in an extant fragment, "at another they are carried off in different directions by the repellant force of Strife; then in course of time their enmity is subdued and they all come into harmony once more" (Wheelwright 1966, p. 131). Here Konstan and Young-Bruehl note the influence of Hippocratic doctrine, citing the first book of the *Regimen*, where the body is understood as a system or *harmonia* of opposites (1982, p. 42).

Eryximachus proceeds to assert that the same pattern of achieving a harmony between opposites also informs physical training (gymnastics), agriculture, poetry, and eventually astronomy. He cites, and proposes to correct a line by another Presocratic philosopher, Heraclitus of Ephesus (d. ca. 480 BCE), known for his paradoxical and often obscure sayings: "being at variance with itself is in agreement with itself, like the attunement of a bow or a lyre" (186e). He glosses these lines to really mean that the musician creates a harmony by resolving between high and low notes. "Naturally, it is patently absurd to claim that an attunement or a harmony is in itself discordant or that its elements are still in discord with one another. Heraclitus probably meant that an expert musician creates a harmony by resolving the prior discord between high and low notes" (187a).

Extrapolating from the musical metaphor, Eryximachus argues that medicine, like music, creates agreement by producing concord and love between the various opposites. Taking up and refining Pausanias' division between Heavenly and Earthly

Love, he speaks of the Honorable Love produced by Urania, the Heavenly Muse. The other is produced by Polyhymnia, the muse of many songs. As with the case of enjoying a fine meal without becoming a glutton, the challenge is how to enjoy the pleasures of Earthly Love without falling into debauchery. In all matters human and divine, we must take into account the two types of love and be attentive to their harmony. When the gods and elements of nature are in harmony, conditions will be temperate, harvests will be plentiful, and men will enjoy health. When out of harmony, there are storms, plagues, and disease among plants and animals. "All of these are the effects of the immodest and disordered species of Love on the movements of the stars and the season of the year" (188b).

Taking this cosmology a step further, Eryximachus suggests that the art of divination (*manike*), reading the will of the gods from various signs, is really the science of monitoring the balance between the two loves, making adjustments if possible to keep things in harmony. In this way the diviner mediates between the gods and humans by being aware of the signs of harmony or disharmony, the effects of love, and a physician, who tried to produce loving affection between gods and men. Summing up, he grandly declares that Love, directed toward the good by temperance and justice, whether Heavenly or Earthly, is the source of happiness, good fortune, civil order, and concord with the gods. Such a vision of his professional skills as a physician is in fact part of the Hippocratic doctrine, which conceives medicine as the master science: "transplant wisdom into medicine and medicine into wisdom, for a physician who is a lover of wisdom [*philosophos*] is the equal of a god. Between wisdom and medicine there is no gulf fixed; in fact medicine possesses all the qualities that make for wisdom" (*Hippocrates* 1949, p. 287). In passing, we might recall that Socrates' dying words (*Phaedo* 118), allude to a debt to Asclepius, the titular god of medicine.

In *Regimen 1*, Hippocrates outlines his methodological principles: "I maintain that he who aspires to treat correctly the human regimen must first acquire knowledge and discernment of the nature of man in general—knowledge of the primary constituents and discernment of the components by which it is controlled. For if he be ignorant of the primary constitution, he will be unable to gain knowledge of their effects" (1959, 4, p. 227).

In this we see an anticipation of the concern expressed by both Agathon and Socrates for explaining the nature of love itself in order to properly understand its consequences. In the *Phaedrus*, Socrates speaks favorably of the methods of Hippocrates, noting "all great arts demand discussion and speculation about nature (*phuseōs*)" (269e). He then adds that the methods of healing are like those of rhetoric: "the one must start with an analysis of the nature of the body and the other the nature of the soul" (270b). In words that almost paraphrase Hippocrates, Socrates asks, "how do you think one can acquire any appreciable knowledge of the nature of the soul without knowing the nature of the whole man?" (270c).

Some thematic parallels may be drawn between Eryximachus' model of the healthy body and its relationship with the cosmos, and Socrates' tripartite model of the soul in the *Republic* (436a–445e, 545b–580a). (It is also useful to recall Socrates' metaphorical representation of the soul as a charioteer trying to control two horses in the *Phaedrus* [246a–256e].) In Socrates' account, the moral health of a community represents a collective norm derived from the psychic health of the individual members. When the members are predominantly in ill health, the community will also be unhealthy. Socrates imagines the soul in terms of the interaction among at least three component faculties: the reason, will, and appetites. The just or healthy soul is one in which the three faculties act in harmony with each other, acting according to their proper natures. Thus the soul is governed by the reason with the aid of the will to hold the appetites in moderation. By contrast the unhealthy soul is one that is out of balance or disharmony, the reason, will and appetites functioning outside their proper domains. We might speak of the willful person, where the will asserts authority over the reason, or the appetitive person, whose behavior is dominated by the satisfaction of appetites. "To produce health in the body is to establish the part of the body as ruler and ruled according to nature, while disease is that they rule and are ruled contrary to nature," says Socrates in terms with which Eryximachus might concur (444d).

It is not surprising that Eryximachus has a high regard for his own expertise, though there is some irony in the fact that having described a cosmic vision of Love and the practice of medicine, his medical skill is illustrated by curing Aristophanes' hiccups.

Presumably he might have explained that the discord of Aristophanes' diaphragm is resolved by creating a corresponding discord in the nose, thereby reestablishing bodily harmony. While this deflates some of his own self-importance, it does not necessarily invalidate everything he has said.

3.1.6. The speech of Aristophanes (189d–194e)

The comic playwright Aristophanes of Cydatheneum (ca. 450–ca. 386 BCE) would have been about thirty-four years old at the time of Agathon's banquet. The speech created for him by Plato is one of the most famous of the *Symposium*, and one of the most engaging and sympathetic. Many readers find this ironic, given the playwright's apparent antipathy to Socrates in the *Clouds*, where the philosopher is ridiculed as a scoundrel and sophist. In that play, the "hero" Strepsiades goes to Socrates' school, the Phrontisterion ("the wisdom-shop"), to learn how to cheat his creditors by means of persuasive speaking. (Alcibiades saw himself satirized in Strepsiades' wastrel son, Phidippides.) Socrates alludes to the play in the *Apology* (18b–19b). On the other hand Plutarch records Socrates saying that he was not bothered by the ridicule in the *Clouds*. "I'm teased in the theater as if it were a big drinking party" (Aristophanes 2007, p. 47). A surviving epigram by Plato praises Aristophanes (Aristophanes 2007, p. 109).

Aristophanes' prefaces his speech by saying that he proposes to take a different approach from the others, adding that people have missed the power of Love, for if they had realized that Love cares for humankind more than any of the other gods, and cures the ills that we would have mended, we would build temples and make sacrifices to him. Aristophanes then proceeds to unfold his talk in the manner of Old Comedy on the origins and nature of love. Whether the speech presented in the *Symposium* is based on an actual Aristophanic comedy no longer extant, or whether it is Plato's creative attempt to imagine an Aristophanic trope, is a matter of conjecture. Rabelais' and later Shakespeare's reference to "the beast with two backs" (Othello 1.1.117), an evocative metaphor for a couple in sexual union suggest the plausible inspiration for Aristophanes' (or Plato's) spherical humans. At the end of the *Symposium* Aristodemus recollects that Socrates was arguing with Agathon and Aristophanes that authors should be able to write both comedy and tragedy (223c). One way or the other, it is one of the most enduring and memorable episodes of the *Symposium*, comparable to the chariot in the *Phaedrus*.

Once upon a time, there were three types of humans, male, female, and androgynous, a combination of the male and female principle. The males derived from the Sun, the females from the Earth, and the androgynous from the moon, which shares characteristics of both the Sun and Earth. At this time all humans were completely spherical, with four hands, four legs, two faces, two sets of genitals, and other pairs of organs. Because of their multiple limbs they can walk upright in any direction, and run rapidly by doing cartwheels. They were so powerful and fast that they threatened the gods. Aristophanes explains that the Homeric reference (*Iliad* 5.385, *Odyssey* 12.308) to the assault on heaven by the giants Ephialtes and Otos was really about the human race. Zeus and the other gods find themselves confronted by a dilemma. If they destroy the human race, the gods will no longer receive sacrifices, yet they cannot let the humans run riot. In good Aristophanic fashion, Zeus comes up with a "happy idea" to solve the problem. He orders the humans cut in half, the way one cuts an egg with a hair, so that now they have only two arms and legs. Apollo turns the faces forward, and cinches up the wounds to form the navel, a reminder of our origins. Should that remedy not be sufficient, Zeus warns that he will cut them in half again, so that they must hop about on one leg.

Once the plan is executed, the severed humans desperately go about seeking their lost halves, throwing their arms around each other and trying to weave themselves together again in their embraces. In this condition the humans begin to die from hunger, preferring to cling to each other more than anything else. To solve the problem, Zeus orders that the genitals be turned to the front, forming interior reproduction, the satisfaction of sexual pleasure a consolation, thus allowing the halves to get back to their jobs and other needs. This, Aristophanes explains in "just so" fashion, is how love comes into being in every human: "it calls back the halves of our original nature together; it tries to make one out of two and heal the wound of human nature" (191d). We are all the matching half of a human whole, seeking our lost half. Those who were originally male seek male halves; those who were female seek the female; those who were androgynous, halves of the opposite gender, heterosexual.

Love, however, is different from sexual intimacy. When one meets one's other half, whatever the orientation, something wonderful or amazing happens: "the two are struck from their senses by love by a sense of belonging to one another, and by desire, and they don't want to be separated from one another, not even for a moment" (192c). Such people remain together all of their lives, and although they cannot articulate what they want from each other, they take a deep joy in being with each other. It is a relationship that endures beyond the mere satisfactions of sexual intimacy or explained by the satisfaction of interests. "It's obvious that the soul of every lover longs for something else; his soul cannot say what it is, but like an oracle it has a sense of what its wants, and wants to talk of it as if in riddles" (192d). Aristophanes imagines Hephaestus, the god of fire and blacksmiths, asking what two such lovers lying together would most desire in their hearts. He conjectures that they would probably want to be welded together, the two made one, even into death. Our true nature, says Aristophanes is wholeness, and Love is the pursuit of wholeness, our desire to be complete, to recover our original nature. Milton's Adam, having apparently read his Plato, declares in *Paradise Lost*: "Part of my Soul I seek thee, and thee claim/My other half" (4. 487, 8).

Summing up, Aristophanes warns that we should seek order before the gods, otherwise humankind might be split again. Further, we should be guided by love in order to seek wholeness, avoiding behavior that is hateful to the gods. Only then will we find the young beloved meant for us, a goal that few seem to achieve. Turning then to Eryximachus, he insists that his speech not be turned into a comedy, and that he is not referring to Pausanias and Agathon, when he refers to the male type seeking male halves, though he admits that they probably belong to that class, but to humanity as a whole, male and female. Ultimately, Love will make us blessed and happy.

R. E. Allen contends that Aristophanes' myth begins in comedy, but ends, if not in tragedy, than in a "life-denying" vision of the human condition, comparable with Epicurus, the Stoics, or even the Buddha (Allen 1991, p. 35). In the sense that the wholeness can never actually be achieved, that the ultimate object of desire is unattainable, there is certainly a tragic dimension to Aristophanes' myth. The claim of "life-denying," however, does not follow, especially when contrasted with Epicurus, the Stoics, or the Buddha. While they argue for liberation from desire, contending that it is source of suffering, Aristophanes sees the dynamic character of life in the desires. If love is not the animating principle of the cosmos that Eryximachus describes, it is certainly what animates human life. It is life affirming. More relevantly, the drive to seek wholeness in Aristophanes, though it may not be achieved, anticipates Socrates' and Diotima's characterization of Love as something needy, driven by the impulse to fill an absence. In an analogous fashion the philosopher is marked by his or her seeking of wisdom, even while admitting that any final enlightenment may only come after years of effort, if ever at all. Socrates' recurrent comparison of his philosophical vocation to midwifery is not irrelevant. The midwife serves as an intermediary, helping others give birth to children without producing children of her own. In the same way philosophers help others to give birth to ideas, even though they may not have their own.

Despite their differences of approach and tone, both Eryximachus and Aristophanes conceive love in related terms of health, whether the preserving or righting of a healthy balance, or the attempt to heal a wound. Aristophanes differs from the physician in that he has returned the erotic from the natural order in general to the domain of the human. Love and its urgency are something that belongs to humans. In turn both differ from Phaedrus and Pausanias in their move to universalize love by grounding it in nature (*phuseōs*). In the case of Eryximachus love is part of nature in general, while in the case of Aristophanes, nature is narrowed to human nature and the human condition. To understand the significance of this narrowing of the domain of love to human interactions, one might consider that in the *Phaedrus* Socrates quips that "landscapes . . . have nothing to teach me—only the people in the city can" (230d). Socrates might perfectly well agree with Eryximachus that love is related to concord and harmony in nature as a whole, but finds it hard to interrogate a landscape (unlike Sir Francis Bacon, who likened the scientific method to torturing the secrets out of nature). Socrates can learn only by questioning other people, a position that elevates the ontological status of humans and human interaction in relation to the ground of being. It is only in the human domain that love is relevant. One way or the other, they have raised the level of love and its benefits beyond the level of social conventions. The next step, represented by the dialogue between Agathon and Socrates, takes us beyond the physical to something transcendent.

Aristophanes' speech draws general approval from the group, leading to another interlude. Eryximachus praises the speeches in general, up to that point, adding that were Agathon and Socrates not such experts on love, it would be hard to imagine what more might be added to the topic. Socrates comically expresses his anxiety about following such speeches, as does Agathon. Here Socrates reminds Agathon that he seemed in command when he appeared before the theater audience. Agathon, however, responds that it is more frightening to be in front of a few intelligent men than a senseless crowd. To this Socrates quips that he is sure that Agathon would certainly pay attention to people he considered wise, but that this group, who were also part of that theater audience, surely does not qualify. Then trying to maneuver Agathon, he asks whether he would be ashamed of doing anything ugly in front of a group of wise people. Agathon answers in the affirmative, where upon Socrates asks if that meant that he would be willing to do something shameful in front of the ordinary crowd? Before he can answer, however, Phaedrus intervenes, recognizing that Socrates is trying to derail the sympotic order, and shift to his more usual mode of inquiry. Assuming the role of symposiarch he orders Agathon to proceed with his speech.

3.1.7. The speech of Agathon (194e–197e)

The tragic playwright Agathon of Athens (ca. 447–ca. 401 BCE) is at this point about thirty years old, the beloved of Pausanias. He was a student of sophist Prodicus, and appears in the *Protagoras* (Nails 2002, p. 8). He was also a target of Aristophanes in several plays, most notably the *Thesmophoriazusae* (*The Women Celebrating the Thesmophoria*), in which the playwright Euripides, learns that the women of the Thesmophoria, a festival dedicated to Demeter, want to have him condemned to death because of his legendary misogyny. To solve his problem he proposes that Agathon disguise himself as a woman and deliver a speech in his defense. The playwright refuses this "happy idea," so the role falls to a hapless relative of Euripides. Aristophanes is playing on Agathon's reputation for effeminacy and the premise that he could pass as a woman.

"I wish first to speak of how I ought to speak, and only then to speak" (194e), Agathon declares, commencing with a rhetorical flourish that echoes the extravagant and self-reflexive style of Gorgias. (There is a quality of frivolousness and theatricality in Agathon's speech that strongly resonates with Susan Sontag's 1966 account of camp.) Situating himself with regard to the earlier speeches, Agathon contends that no one has so much praised the god himself as celebrated the benefits that accrue from Love. He proposes first to speak of Love's physical character, then his moral character. Thus Love is the happiest of the gods because he is the most beautiful and the best. This is because, contra Phaedrus's view, Love is the youngest of the gods, a conclusion he infers from the fact that Love prefers the young and the beautiful and flees from the old and the ugly. Agathon self-servingly implies that the old are no longer capable of love, or certainly that the young could not possibly love the old. In this, he might easily imagine him playfully nudging the older and famously ugly Socrates, who is sitting next to him on the same couch. Agathon observes that Love is always with young people and that (contra Eryximachus) since likes are attracted to each other, Love must therefore be young. The violent passions described by Hesiod and Parmenides are the products of necessity rather than Love. On one level this proposition seems to resemble Socrates' claim in *Phaedrus* that "everyone chooses his love after his own fashion" (252d). In both the *Phaedrus* and Socrates' account in the *Symposium*, the attraction is not, of course, physical resemblance, but the intimation of an inner beauty, the recognition of similar dispositions.

Agathon next argues that Love is the most soft or delicate (*apalos*) of the gods. By way of proof, he cites a passage from Homer's *Iliad* (14.92–93) in which the delicate goddess Atē (Mischief) walks on the heads of men rather than on the ground. Quickly catching himself, he explains that he means the souls of men and gods, since of course the skulls of men are not soft. He then adds that Love is the most supple of the gods, the most graceful, the most balanced and the most fluid in his nature, with exquisite skin and coloring.

Having described the physical characteristics of Love, a portrait that strongly resembles himself, Agathon turns to Love's moral character, arguing that he is the cause of the cardinal virtues (*aretē*): justice (*dikaios*), moderation (*sofrosunē*), courage (*andreia*), and wisdom (*sophia*). His basic argument is semantic, contending that if one is doing something out of love, then one is not being forced or coursed. Rather, everyone serves Love willingly. Thus, Love neither wrongs, nor is wronged by men or gods; he is neither the victim of wrongs, nor victimizer of anyone. Conceiving the virtue of justice narrowly as a willing obedience to the "laws that are kings of society" (196b), then justice is the political condition in which all members of society agree with each other and willingly love the laws. Similarly the virtue moderation is willingly moderating the desire for pleasure. In mastering the strong emotions of pleasure and desire, Love must be moderate. To support the claim of Love's control over courage, Agathon alludes to the Homeric account of Ares and his love of Aphrodite (*Odyssey* 8.266–366), citing a passage from Sophocles's play *Thyestes* (Plato 1998, p. 164). Here the courageous god of war is moderated or controlled by his love for the goddess. Turning finally to wisdom, Agathon recalls Eryximachus' praise for his own profession. If the physician has conceived Love in terms of a physician curing discord and establishing order and harmony, the poet contends that Love is a poet, noting that Apollo was god of music and art as well as medicine. Thus Love is a poet and transforms his devotees into poets. Since he causes others to be creative, he must himself be creative, "for you can't give to another what you don't have yourself, and you can't teach what you don't know" (196e). To be skilled or creative is to love one's craft, so Love involves knowledge of the various crafts.

Agathon's characterization of Love as a poet briefly opens a conceptual door for an expressionist model of art, playing on the literal sense of *poiesis* as making, fabrication, or creation, and Diotima herself will later pick up this theme. Here a poet does not so much represent something as create its own order of being. Agathon himself, however, quickly falls back into a representational model of poetry related to the mastery of skill or craftsmanship (*techne*). We might recall Socrates' comments about poetry and poetic madness in the *Phaedrus* (245a). To be wise in one's craft is to be skilled in the knowledge of one's craft. For Agathon, the skill or knowledge required for poetry is a form of wisdom. Apollo's knowledge of medicine, prophecy, archery, and music are poetic skills, as are Hephaestus' of bronze, Athena's of weaving, and Zeus's of governance (197b). Love, then, is the guide to wisdom.

Pulling the various features together, Agathon declares that Love is the most beautiful of the gods, that Love's very presence settles discord, since out of love we pursue beauty and flee conflict. "Once this god was born, all goods came to gods and me alike through love of beauty" (197a). Inspired by his topic, he shifts to poetic meter that Love, "Gives peace to men and stillness to the sea/Lays winds to rest, and careworn men to sleep" (197d). Finally, rhapsodizing Love with rhetorical virtuosity, Agathon concludes: "Love [*eros*] cares well for good men, cares not for bad ones. In pain, in fear, in desire or speech, Love is our best guide and guard; he is our comrade and our savior. Ornament of all gods and men, the most beautiful leader and the best! Every man should follow Love, sing beautifully his hymns, and join with him in the song he sings that charms the mind of god or man" (197e). His words almost seem to anticipate the account of love in Paul's letter to the *Corinthians*, and some theologians will claim that they represent identical concepts: "Love [*agapē*] is patient and kind; love is not jealous or boastful; it is not arrogant or rude. Love does not insist on its own way; it does not rejoice at wrong, but rejoices in the right. Love bears all things, believes all things, hopes all things, endures all things" (1 Cor. 13:4–7). Paul of course signifies "love" with *agapē* rather than *eros*, though it becomes a route for later theologians who wish to frame Christianity in Platonic terms.

Relinquishing the floor to the *symposiarch*, Agathon tells Phaedrus, "Let it be dedicated to the god, part of it in fun, part of it moderately serious as best I could manage" (197e). Here Aristodemus reports that everyone burst into applause, and Socrates turns to Eryximachus, asking jokingly that does he now think he was foolish in fearing to have to speak after Agathon's speech. The physician answers that Socrates had indeed been prophetic about the quality of the speech, but doubted that he would be at a loss for words. Indeed, his prediction proves more prophetic than Socrates'.

In a series of backhanded compliments, Socrates praises Agathon's speech for its delivery and variety, adding that while the bulk of it may not have been wonderful, the ending was a marvel of beautiful words and phrases. Punning on the name of the gorgon whose head turned men into stone, he images Agathon striking him dumb with the head of Gorgias. In other words, while Agathon's speech was long on rhetorical effect, it was short on substance, more virtuosity than virtue. Socrates next bemoans his own presumption in entering into the contest of praising Love and in claiming that he was expert on matters erotic. Assuming the stance of Socratic ignorance, he insists, "I was quite vain, thinking that I would talk well and that I knew the truth about praising anything whatever" (198d). Turning to the contest as a whole, he adds ironically, "But now it appears that this is not what it is to praise anything whatever; rather, it is to apply to the object the grandest and the most beautiful qualities, whether he actually has them or not" (198e). The ability to make statements about something is independent of the truth or falsity of those statements. Rather, each speech says more about the speaker, what he loves and desires, how he would appear and be perceived, than about Love itself: "for the proposal, apparently, was that everyone here make the rest of us think he is praising Love—and not that he actually praise him. I think that is why you [plural] stir up every word and apply it to Love; your description of him and his gifts is designed to make him look better and more beautiful than anything else— to ignorant listeners, plainly, for of course he wouldn't look that way to those who knew" (198e).

It is useful to set Socrates' assessment of the speeches against Agathon's self-assessment that his own speech was part in fun, but "part of it moderately serious as best I could manage" (197e). The same might also be applied to the other speakers as well. First, true to the tone and conventions of a *symposion* the speeches do not claim to be serious. They are meant to be playful and joking, marked by exaggeration and self-parody. All of this is part of the game. Having said that, Agathon admits that he believes much of what he says about the power of love, and that he is aware of the limits of his method, that he is trying to explain himself as best as he can. In this he distinguishes himself from Gorgias, who characterized his *Encomium of Helen* to be an "amusement for myself" (Gorgias 2003, p. 84).

While acknowledging that Agathon's praise was beautiful and respectful of the god, Socrates claims to be ignorant of the methods of praise. In an apt metaphor drawn from Euripides' *Hippolytus* (612), he declares that it was by the "tongue"(*ē de glōssa*) that he had promised to deliver an *encomium* on Love, not by the "mind" (*ē de phrēn*); he therefore refuses to deliver yet another one. Instead, with the permission of the group, he will tell the truth his own way, following his own method.

Before turning to the speech of Socrates in the next chapter, it is valuable to summarize the first five speeches, and to anticipate how they relate to what Socrates will say. The speeches of Phaedrus, Pausanias, Eryximachus, Aristophanes, and Agathon survey the best with regard to the conventional or traditional wisdom on the question of *erōs* (the *endoxa*). Frisbee Sheffield nicely terms the *Symposium* "a prime endoxic forum" (2006, p. 23). The question, then, is whether Socrates' account of love builds on the picture developed by the first five speakers or rejects them? Is there an overall thematic progression and continuity running through the *Symposium*, or is Plato simply summarizing the conventional wisdom in order to dismiss it, a sort of clearing the deck? Do the various speeches represent Plato simply displaying his artistic and rhetorical skills, or could he have omitted them? In his translation of the *Symposium*, Christopher Rowe summarizes the latter view when he warns, "we should be wary of supposing that there is, or is meant to be, any sense of a gradually developing picture of *erōs* . . ." (Plato 1998, p. 8). Rowe notes that Socrates prefaced his speech with the general complaint that everyone seemed more concerned with appearing to praise Love than actually doing so, and that no one seemed to really know the truth about the matter. He then contends that Socrates will proceed to demolish Agathon's speech. Rowe concludes that "[i]t is in any case hard to construct a joint account that might emerge from the sequence from Phaedrus to Agathon. All five are essentially individual contributions, with each attempting to go one better than the one before in an apparently haphazard way" (Plato 1998, p. 8). I believe that this overstates the case. It seems counterintuitive that Plato would take such care in setting up the alternative cases simply with the intention of knocking them down.

Plato did not choose to write a treatise, but to create a work of art. He is not transmitting a doctrine that can be reduced to a series of wise maxims to be memorized and taken away as if they were offered in the spirit of traditional wisdom literature. In a similar fashion, we cannot say that we understand the Pythagorean Theorem simply because we have memorized the formula or even the steps in the proof. Knowing the steps and understanding them are quite different. Rather, by creating a work of art, part narrative, part dramatic, Plato engages us in a more visceral process, the various parts contributing to the impact of the whole. We can no more consider that we have grasped the *Symposium* by skipping over the earlier speeches and paraphrasing what Socrates or Diotima says, than we can say that we have experienced the impact of Shakespeare's *Hamlet* by skipping straight to act five. Diotima's metaphor of initiation is important. We must go through a process. Only then might we grasp what we are to understand.

Frisbee Sheffield offers the alternative view that the speeches do trace a development of some sort: "Plato could be indicating in the construction of this dialogue that philosophical understanding emerges ultimately through a process of working through the *endoxa*" (2006, p. 31). Sheffield distinguishes what he terms the strong dialectical reading and the weak version. In the strong version, the five speeches contain elements of truth and provide the grounding for the nature of the inquiry. By way of analogy, he notes Aristotle's similar use of the *endoxa*. He finds more compelling, however, the weak dialectical reading. "It could be the case that the speeches raise the right sorts of ideas and issues to be resolved for a proper explanatory account, and so they need to be attended to and worked through as part of philosophical progress. The speeches on this view could include useful falsehoods, that is views that are not true, but whose underlying puzzles prompt the inquiry in a relevant direction" (2006, p. 31). Following Sheffield's line, we might summarize the major emergent themes.

In Phaedrus' account love is the most powerful force in the acquisition of virtue and happiness. This power comes from love's ability to create feelings of happiness with regard to noble activities, and shame with regard to base ones. Key here is to explain how love has the ability to instill love of the noble beauty (*kalon*). He does not, however, distinguish true beauty, the proper object of desire from false beauty. Why, in seeking beauty, might one not just pursue sexual gratification instead of virtue?

Pausanias agrees with Phaedrus that love can lead to virtue. He is cognizant, however, that not all love seeks virtue. For this reason he distinguishes two types of love. Good Love seeks the soul over the body. We might say that while love for the body is about physical gratification, love for the soul is about spiritual gratification, the pleasure that comes from improvement, either in the satisfaction taken in the improvement of the beloved by the lover, or in the desire of the beloved to be improved by the lover. In this way love is about the cultivation of virtue, the achievement of excellence, and such excellence is also about achieving wisdom. Pausanias is not clear, however, on what exactly he means by wisdom aside from a conventional designation for some positive knowledge.

Eryximachus concurs with both Phaedrus and Pausanias that the proper goal of love is virtue. He further agrees with Pausanias' distinction between a love for the soul and one for the body. For him, however, Love is a broader phenomenon than just the attraction to a beautiful body or soul. Instead of conceiving love as something limited to humans, he makes a universalizing move, equating love with the workings of nature as a whole, and pertaining to the attraction and joining of opposing forces. He wishes to take up the issue of wisdom from the perspective of his professional expertise. As a physician he is knowledgeable about the workings of nature and possesses the skills to reestablish harmony and concord, a bringing together of opposites. For him love is very much about material nature and physical health. Part and parcel of the Hippocratic tradition, he equates this knowledge with philosophical wisdom. Just as the physician is concerned with establishing a proper harmony between opposed elements, so the expert on love is concerned with creating healthy interpersonal relationships marked by justice and moderation.

Aristophanes picks up the medical theme, seeing the benefit of love playing on the notion of healing. For him, however, love is not about the establishment of a harmony between opposites, but the reestablishment of unity or wholeness. Like Eryximachus, but unlike Phaedrus and Pausanias, Aristophanes conceives love as something general, and not circumscribed by gender, rejecting their privileging of homoerotic relationships. Similarly he does not consider love in terms of an attraction to beauty. Unlike Eryximachus, he prefers to think of love in human terms rather than the subcategory of a larger natural phenomenon. The joining together of the two halves is not so much a harmony between opposites, but a combining to create something greater than the parts. Our happiness or well-being involves seeking this wholeness or completeness. Unlike Eryximachus, however, Aristophanes thinks about healing not in physical, but in psychological or spiritual terms. The literal wounds of the androgynes are metaphors for psychic divisions. The art or expertise of love involves recognizing some quality in the other, and what we need to heal or complete ourselves. Why we should be happy in unity is not entirely clear.

Agathon agrees with Eryximachus that love involves a fundamental knowledge. Instead of nature, however, he sees it as the source of the cardinal virtues of justice, courage, moderation, and wisdom, expanding the value of love described by Phaedrus and Pausanias, but in a way that goes beyond social norms. Love is also the source of creativity. He disagrees with the earlier speakers in the sense that they have spoken of the benefits of love, but not its essential nature. Much as the tragic mask is the opposite of the comic one, he disagrees with Aristophanes that love is about healing or satisfying a need. We are not drawn to our lost halves, but to those like ourselves who possess youth, beauty, and virtue. It is not about healing the soul, but about nurturing and expanding it.

Up to this point the *Symposium* has presented five accounts of love, according to Apollodorus' recitation of Aristodemus' recollections. Love makes us virtuous. Love makes us seek wisdom. Knowledge of love provides a knowledge that allows us to achieve harmony or concord in nature. Love seeks to heal us, to make us whole. Love is beautiful and virtuous and for that reason seeks beauty and virtue. Now Socrates proposes to tell about Love in his own way.

3.2. DIOTIMA EXPLAINS

I have taken my stand at the courtyard-gate
Of a man who welcomes strangers,
And sweet is my song.

Here a fitting feast is set; not often
Is the house without guests from over sea.
                                    Pindar (Nemean *1.20*)

Blessed is the one of all the people on the earth
Who has seen these mysteries.
But whoever is not initiated into the rites,
Whoever has no part in them,
That person never shares the same fate when he dies
And goes down to the gloom and darkness below.
            Homeric Hymn to Demeter *(Homer 2003, pp. 25, 6)*

Socrates' speech on the topic of love falls into three parts. Recalling his request to "tell the truth my own way," that the "words and phrasing will take care of themselves"(199b), the first two parts offer examples of Socratic *elenchus*, the method of interrogation in which Socrates challenges his interlocutors' propositions, inducing them to refute themselves by showing how their various claims conflict with each other. In the first part, Socrates interrogates Agathon, compelling him to abandon his claims about love. In the second part, he gives an account of how he was similarly refuted by a wise woman named Diotima. In the third part, Socrates changes course and recollects an explanation of love delivered by Diotima herself. It is interesting to note that Socrates claims merely to be reciting what he was taught by Diotima, much as in the *Phaedrus*, he claims that Stesichorus had originally delivered the second speech (244a). In a curious fashion, Plato has put Socrates into a position with regard to Diotima, analogous to that of Aristodemus with regard to Socrates, and Apollodorus with regard to Aristodemus. Each in his way functions as an intermediary between the audience and the source.

3.2.1. Socrates contra Agathon (199c–201c)

Socrates' speech may be paired with Agathon's both concurring with its basic intention, while disagreeing with its particulars. Socrates opens his remarks by praising Agathon for "beautifully" saying, "one should first show the qualities of Love himself and only then those of his deeds" (199c). While he will refute Agathon's specific conclusions about the nature of love itself, he nevertheless indicates his agreement with the basic move of wishing first to establish the nature of love, that it is an essential prerequisite for understanding the benefits of love. His characterization of the speech as "beautiful," a point he later reiterates after his refutation (201b), can be read ironically, a good natured, "nice try." Yet it is possible to find more in Agathon's speech than just eloquent nonsense. Socrates' desire to "tell the truth my own way," by the conversational mode of the *elenchus* suggests that he sees some merit. We might recall that in the *Theaetetus* Socrates says that "a debate need not be taken seriously and one may trip up an opponent to the best of one's ability, but a conversation should be taken in earnest; one should help out the other party and bring home to him only those slips and fallacies that are due to himself or to his earlier instructors" (167e). Whether an *encomium* falls within the realm of debate or somewhere between debate and conversation, Socrates' move to the conversational mode (or at least the fiction of a conversation in the case of Diotima) indicates his underlying seriousness and sympathy.

Socrates' argument about the nature of love challenges Agathon's claim that Love is by nature inherently beautiful and good. To do this he develops two propositions: (A) that Love is the love of something (200a), and (B) that Love loves things of which he has a present need (200e).

Socrates first asks Agathon whether (the nature of) Love is such as to be a love of something or of nothing (199e). To clarify his question he offers several analogies. Is a father the father of something or not? The ready answer is that the father is the father of a son or daughter. Similarly, a brother, to the degree that he is a brother, is the brother of a something and not nothing, in this case he is the brother of a brother or sister. Returning to the original question, it would seem that the answer is surely that Love is (by its nature) in love with something and not nothing.

For the time being setting aside the question of what the something is (the object of love), Socrates asks whether Love desires that something it loves. Again Agathon agrees that it must. Socrates then asks: when Love desires and loves something, does he actually possess its object of desire at that time or not? Agathon hesitantly agrees that it is "likely" that he does not have what he loves and desires. Socrates, however, pushes him to say that it is necessary that he does not possess the object of his love and desire, because if he had it, he would not desire it. So, for instance, a tall person cannot desire to be tall, nor a strong person desire to be strong, because each already possesses the desired height or strength. Love, then, loves things of which he has a present need.

But isn't it common to hear a healthy person saying that she desires to be healthy, or a tall man saying he loves being tall? Anticipating such possible objections or ambiguities, Socrates clarifies that when we hear a tall man say he desires to be tall, or a healthy woman say that she desires to be healthy, what they really mean is not that they desire something that they already have at present, but that they desire something they may not have in the future. That is, "[w]henever you say, I desire what I already have, ask yourself whether you don't mean this: I want the things I have now to be mine in the future as well" (200d). We may call this proposition (C). The claim to love something one already has, therefore, does not violate the central proposition that Love loves things of which he has a present need (B). The full importance of (C) will become evident below in Diotima's speech.

Pulling the elements together, Socrates concludes, "a man or anyone who has a desire desires what is not at hand and not present, what he does not have and what he is not, and that of which he is in need; for such are the objects of desire and love" (200e). Combining this with the premise that Love loves something (not nothing), Socrates returns to Agathon's earlier contention that the quarrels of the gods were resolved by their love of beautiful things, and not ugly things (197b). If that is so, then that means that Love has a desire for beauty. But by the premise that we desire what is not present or part of our being, we must conclude that Love's desire for beautiful things implies that he does not possess beauty at all. Therefore, contrary to Agathon's original claim, Love cannot of necessity be beautiful. Recognizing the incoherence of his position, Agathon cheerily concedes: "It turns out, Socrates, I didn't know what I was talking about in that speech" (201c). Socrates amplifies his argument: Since most people agree that beautiful things are also good things, then by extension, if Love's desire for beauty implies that it is not in itself beautiful, then similarly its desire for the good implies that it is not in itself inherently good.

Thus far, Socrates has followed the usual path of the *elenchic* method found especially in the early dialogues, determining with certainty what something is not, but not conversely what it is. Thus whatever love is, we may say with certainty that it is not in itself beautiful or good. The argument leaves open, however, what love is. Now, however, Socrates proposes to make a turn, and offer an account of love in and of itself.

3.2.2. Diotima contra Socrates (201c–203b)

Rather than offer his own speech on love, Socrates declares that he will recite a speech about Love based on two conversations he has had with a woman named Diotima of Mantinea. "I shall go through her speech as best I can on my own, using what Agathon and I have agreed to as a basis" (201d). This move is paradoxical on several levels. First, in framing the speech this way, Plato puts Socrates into a narrative position similar to Apollodorus and Aristodemus. Rather than discovering and testing the truth of his propositions by means of the *elenchic* method, he has Socrates claiming to recollect and transmit a given body of knowledge. Second, Plato adds a new dimension to the *symposion*, in effect introducing a woman into the midst of an essentially masculine institution that was by its nature the consummate vehicle for the transmission of masculine traditions. Instead of the subservient position as a flute-player or juggler, a woman assumes the role of authority.

Socrates describes Diotima as "a woman who was wise [*sophē*] about many things besides this [Love]: once she even put off [*anabolēn*] the plague for ten years by telling the Athenians what sacrifices to make. She is the one who taught me the art of love [*erōtitka edidaxen*—literally 'the teachings of love'] . . ." (201d). Several points should be noted in unpacking this passage. First, her ability to put off the plague supposedly lends credibility to her authority. There are several accounts of Greek communities consulting religious authorities in matters of epidemics (Plato 1980, p. 138n201d3). Plato's *Laws* recounts the story of how Epimenides the Cretan prophesied that the Persians would not invade for another ten years, and would then be defeated. It is interesting to add that Socrates frames this authority in terms of postponing the inevitable plague, rather than preventing it altogether. Natural or divine forces can be modified, but neither transcended nor eliminated. Second, the description of Diotima as an erotic teacher may elicit a sly smile; priestesses to Aphrodite at the cult center in Corinth, for instance, functioned as prostitutes, "Corinthian girls." But that said, Socrates does not actually specify any cultic affiliation for Diotima, and more to the point, although many modern readers of the *Symposium* describe Diotima as a priestess, Socrates does not. Diotima seems to possess medical knowledge, and part of this skill relates to the mantic, her ability to read the signs of nature in order to divine the will of the gods, and to make the necessary sacrifices to preserve harmony and concord. More significantly we may see in the description of her echoes of Eryximachus, who linked the art of medicine with the mantic. Recall his words on divination. "The task of divination is to keep watch over these two species of Love and to doctor them as necessary. Divination, therefore, is the practice that produces loving affection between gods and men; it is simply the science of the effects of Love on justice and piety" (188c). She stands as a messenger between man and gods. Socrates indicates that she seems to have been successful with her skills as a diviner, and by extension her credibility as an expert on Love.

Whether Diotima is based on a real woman or is one of Plato's "noble fictions" is a matter of debate. Kathleen Wider (1986), surveys the literature arguing that she was real, and David Halperin (1990, pp. 119–130), the literature that she is a fiction. Some find a prototype for Diotima in the figure of Aspasia of Miletus (ca. 470 BCE– ca. 400 BCE), the companion of Pericles the famous Athenian statesman. Aspasia was known for her wit and intelligence, though sometimes disparaged in surviving anti-Periclean propaganda. In Plato's dialogue *Menexenus*, Socrates claims that Aspasia taught him a funeral oration. When Menexenus asks Socrates if he can remember what she said, he replies, "I ought to be able, for she taught me, and she was ready to strike me because I was always forgetting" (236c). Aside from the fact that some scholars question the authenticity of the *Menexenus*, most read it in terms of anti-Periclean satire rather than a statement about Aspasia herself. A later anti-Socratic discourse titled, "A Reply to the Admirer of Socrates," by Herodicus of Cratetean (flourished 125 BCE), claims that Aspasia was Socrates' erotic teacher (*erôtodidaskolos*) (Halpern 1990, p. 123). In the *Memorabilia*, Xenophon records a visit that Socrates made to the courtesan Theodoté, finding her posing for a painter. "My friends," Socrates tells his companions, "ought we to be more grateful to Theodoté for showing us her beauty, or she to us for looking at it? Does the obligation rest with her, if she profits more by showing it, but with us, if we profit more by looking?" (Xenophon 1923, 3.11). We might also recall that in the *Crito* Socrates tells of dreaming about "a gloriously beautiful woman dressed in white robes," with the enigmatic prophecy that "to the pleasant land of Phthia on the third day thou shalt come" (44a–b): this is perhaps the inspiration for Boethius' Lady Philosophy in *De Consolatione Philosophiae*.

Whatever the historical realities behind Diotima, Plato has integrated her and her speech so closely with themes and motifs of the *Symposium* that it is hard to separate her from narrative and dramatic fiction. (The same, of course, may be said of all of the characters in the *Symposium*, including Socrates himself.) Mantinea is a real city in the Peloponnese, and the site of a Spartan victory in 418 BCE that nearly toppled the political career of Alcibiades. There is some irony in the fact that Socrates' teacher should be linked with a place associated with Socrates' pupil's near disaster. On the allegorical side, Richard Halperin points out that the name "Diotima of Mantinea" can be translated literally: "Zeus [god]-honor from Prophet-ville" (1990, p. 121), an apt name. Further the name readily lends itself to puns on *mantikê* [seercraft] (Hunter 2004, p. 81). The Greco-Roman historian Plutarch claimed that at the time of his assassination, Alcibiades was living with a courtesan named Timandra, whose name literally means, "honor the man." If this is true, Plato might have had in mind a word play contrasting Socrates' lady "god-honor" with Alcibiades' lady "man-honor" (Nussbaum 1986, p. 167).

It is also useful to recall that in the *Theaetetus*, Socrates claims his mother, Phaenarete, was a midwife (149a), and famously compares his own philosophical task to midwifery: "My art of midwifery is in general like theirs . . . and my concern is not with the body but with the soul that is in travail of birth. And the highest point of my art is the power to prove by every test whether the offspring of a young man's thought is a false phantom or instinct with life and truth" (150b–c). Like the midwife, he does not himself give birth to truth, but helps others do so. He induces the birth of "soul-children" (wisdom) and serves to alleviate the pangs of perplexity. Anticipating the figure of the *daimon*, he serves as an intermediary, helping his patients discover the truth "by themselves from within." "But the delivery is heaven's work and mine" (150d). All of this resonates with the figure of Diotima, linking her with the vocation of the philosopher. She combines in her person the physician or midwife, the seer, and the philosopher, all three conceived in terms of the function of an intermediary between humanity and the divine. Closely related to this, Diotima couches her erotic knowledge in terms of mystery religions with their secret rituals of initiation, and sacred narratives (*hieroi logoi*) (Burkert 1985, pp. 276–304 and Eliade 1978, pp. 290–301). See also Anders Nygren, who points out that Plato's doctrine of Eros, "has previously existed independently in the context of Mystery-piety" (1953, p. 163).

Socrates begins his narrative about Diotima by explaining that she questioned him about Love in terms *remarkably* similar to those by which Socrates interrogated Agathon. Some attribute this claim to Socratic irony and others to Socrates' trying to soften the social awkwardness of contradicting Agathon at his own party, by suggesting that he too had made the same mistake. That said, Agathon seems to have taken his defeat with humor and grace. More to the point, the spirited give and take normal to a *symposion* would have meant that such routs were part of the game and not the cause for any offense. I would argue, rather, that there is no reason not to take Socrates at his word, that there is continuity between Agathon and Socrates (at least in this noble fiction), and not a fundamental break. Therefore Socrates picks up where he left off with Agathon, using the same line of argument. "You see, I had told her almost the same things Agathon told me just now: that Love is a great god and that he belongs to beautiful things" (201e). He then explains how Diotima refuted his position, showing as Socrates had shown Agathon, that Love is neither beautiful nor good.

Falling into a logical trap, the incredulous Socrates asks does this not mean that Love must therefore be ugly and bad? To this Diotima asks, if a thing is not beautiful is it therefore ugly? By way of analogy she asks, if something is not wise [*sophon*], is it therefore ignorant [*amathes*]? Is there not something between wisdom and ignorance? To Socrates' perplexity, she answers, "it's correct belief [*orthē doxa*] without being able to give reasons [*logon*]" (202a). This central position is certainly not the same as knowing in the true sense, because knowledge or wisdom cannot be unreasoning, but it cannot be ignorance either, because it would be absurd to say that belief that is correct is incorrect. Shifting her terms slightly, she summarizes that the character of "correct belief," then, is "something between prudence [*phrōnēseōs*] and ignorance [*amathias*]" (202a). Here interestingly, Diotima substitutes *phronēsis* where she had previously used *sophos*. *Phronēsis* is variously translated intelligence, practical reason, or the knowledge of the proper ends of life as distinct from more theoretical knowledge for *sophos*, though most scholars assume that here he is using them as synonyms for "wisdom" (Plato 1998, 174n). By the same reasoning, it does not follow that because Love is not beautiful and not good, that it is ugly and bad. Rather, like "correct belief [*orthē doxa*]" Love is something in between.

"Yet everyone agrees that [Love] is a great god," Socrates insists (202b). Recall that he made a similar point in the *Phaedrus* when he worried that he might have been impious in his negative remarks about Love (242d). In a gesture that underscores the problematic nature of traditional or popular knowledge, Diotima laughs at Socrates, asking him if by "everyone" he means the ignorant. She then explains that his own stated claim that Love is neither beautiful nor good contradicts his other claim that Love is a great god. Are not the gods by definition good, beautiful, and happy, a proposition that looks back to what Agathon himself had asserted (195a)? It would be impious to say otherwise. Since the gods are already good, beautiful, and happy, they have no need to desire these states. But since Love needs and desires the good and the beautiful, he must not already possess them. Lacking these, therefore, Love does not satisfy the criteria for being a god. So he is not a god, yet clearly, he is not mortal either. Rather, Love is something in between mortal and immortal (202d). Diotima calls him a "great spirit [*daimon*]. Everything spiritual [*daimonios*], you see, is in between god and mortal" (200e). Before turning to the next step in the argument, it is necessary to step back say more about the word *daimon*, its function in Greek culture, in Socrates, and in Plato.

The word *daimon* (spirit) or its adjective form *daimonios* (spiritual or pertaining to the nature of spirits) is difficult to translate, in part because the ancient Greek culture is not consistent in its usage. While the English words *demon* and *demonic* derives from *daimon* the Greek concept does not in itself imply the notion of a devil or some malevolent force. A "happy" person is one who is *eu*daimon, literally one possessing a good or fortunate *daimon*. *Eudaimonia*, Aristotle's highest realizable good, is conventionally translated "happiness" or "well being," while the unhappy person is *kakodaimon* or *dysdaimon* (Burkert 1985, p. 181). In some contexts *daimon* may be used to signify god or goddess in the general sense of deity, as distinct from god in person (*theos*). The one exception to this is the cult of the Good *Daimon* (*Agathos Daimon*) in whose honor the first libation to Dionysus was dedicated (Burkert 1985, p. 180). In the context of Plato's *Symposium*, the pun on Agathon's name is inevitable, and of course, Agathon's guests opened the banquet with a hymn and libation to the god (176a). In other contexts, it is used to signify the "genius" of the individual (the individual's spirit, so to speak); Heraclitus declared that a man's character is his guardian divinity (*ēthos anthrōpō daimōn*) (Kahn 1981, p. 80). In some cases it may also stand for the souls of the departed. For instance, in Euripides' 438 BCE play *Alcestis*, the heroine is described as a "blessed daimôn" (1003) after her death. (At the risk of stretching a point, we might recall Phaedrus' remarks on Alcestis [179d].) *Defixiones*, curse tablets made to cast magical spells, often evoked *daimones*, affiliated with the spirits of the dead, to aid the supplicant (Gager 1992, p. 101). Comparisons might also be made with the numinous in primitive religions. *Daimon* is also related to occult power, external forces that move us. In *Works and Days*, Hesiod uses *daimones* to signify the souls of the men of the golden age, between the divine gods and moral humans: "Since the earth covered up this race, they have been divine spirits by great Zeus' design, good spirits on the face of the earth, watchers over mortal men, bestowers of wealth . . ." (Hesiod 1988, p. 40). This last usage seems close to Diotima's account.

In many of the Platonic dialogues (e.g. *Euthyphro* 3b, *Euthydemus* 272e, *Phaedrus* 242b, and *Theatetus* 151a) and the *Memorabilia* and *Apology* of Xenophon, there are various references to Socrates' *daimonion*, or his "divine sign," his "customary sign," or his "little voice": "I am subject to a divine or supernatural experience a sort of voice which comes to me, and when it comes it always dissuades me from what I am proposing to do, and never urges me on" (*Apology* 31c–d).[6] Similarly in the *Phaedrus* he describes himself as a "seer [*mantis*], and though I am not particularly good at it, still, like people who are just barely able to read and write, I am good enough for my own purposes" (242c). Whatever the actual ontological character of the *daimonic*, Socrates seems to have understood it as something real, but outside the domain of rational explanation or classification. "We are dealing with active powers, not names," notes Paul Friedländer (1958, p. 35). We might say that the *daimonic* allows Plato to introduce the irrational into his account of knowledge. We might also say that it allows him to think of this knowledge in terms of forces that have an existence independent of the individual's soul. From our post-Cartesian post-Freudian perspective, the notion of hearing voices or being caught in a mania seems to exemplify subjectivity. For Socrates and Diotima, however, it is exactly being blindsided by these feelings outside of our rational control that marks their independent existence. Just as being struck by lightning indicates something outside the person struck, so being possessed by *daimons* points to something external to the self, signifying a metaphysical realism.

When Socrates asks about the function of these *daimons*, Diotima says that they are about "interpreting [*hermēneuon*]," and "conveying [*diaporthmeuon*]" prayer and sacrifice from men and gods, and conversely to men they bring commands from the gods and gifts in return for sacrifices. Filling the space between the immortal gods and moral humans, "they round out the whole and bind fast the all to all" (202e), a description that resonates with Aristophanes' speech (191d). Diotima further explains that the gods do not mingle with humans. They are remote and inaccessible, and therefore communicate with humans only through the mediation of the *daimons*. It is through them that all divination (the *mantic*) passes. The person wise in these arts is a "man of the spirit," while the person wise in other ways is "merely a mechanic" (203a). Here Diotima rehearses the Platonic distinction between knowledge in the sense of true wisdom (*sophos*), and knowledge in the sense of skill (*techne*) or information.

Among the various *daimons* is Love, Diotima says. As a *daimon*, Love (eros), possesses an existence independent of the individual soul; it is something real. Accepting this, Socrates asks about the parents of Love. "That's rather a long story," Diotima responds. "I'll tell it to you, all the same" (203b). She then unfolds an elaborate parable.

3.2.3. Diotima: lesser mysteries (203b–209e)

The beginning to Diotima's tale, or sacred narrative (*hieros logos*), plays off elements from both Pausanias and Agathon. Thus, on the birth of Aphrodite, the gods hosted a celebration. Attending the party was Poros, son of Metis. (The name Poros signifies "way" or "means" and Metis, "cunning," or together "cunning ways," or "resourcefulness"; according to Hesiod she was a wife of Zeus and the mother of Athena.) Indulging in too much nectar, Poros becomes drunk, falling asleep in the garden of Zeus. During the midst of the festivities, Penia ("poverty") comes begging at the gate. Seeing an opportunity, Penia lays next to the drunken Poros, becoming pregnant with Love (Eros). Diotima's little allegorical myth subtly echoes the scene at Agathon's party. The "poor" and "deficient" Socrates tries to conceive and become pregnant with an understanding of love by aid of the various speakers, "cunning" in their ways, "drunk" on their rhetoric.

By her account Diotima explains that because Love was conceived just after the birth of Aphrodite, he thereafter followed her, attracted by her great beauty. In this conception, Aphrodite is closely linked with Love, but not his mother. For this reason then, Love serves the goddess, but is not himself a god.

Because he is the son of Poros and Penia (resourcefulness and poverty), Love partakes of features from both his parents. Contrary to Agathon, Love is not delicate and beautiful, but rather "tough and shriveled and shoeless and homeless" (203d). Because of his mother, he is always living with Need, but because of his father, he is always scheming after the beautiful which he does not possess: "he is brave, impetuous, and intense, an awesome hunter, always weaving snares, resourceful in his pursuit of intelligence [*phronēseōs*], a lover of wisdom [*philosophōn*] through all his life, a clever enchanter [*goēs*—literally a 'howler of enchantments'], sorcerer [*pharmakeus*—the word can signify both a 'sorcerer' and a 'poisoner'], and sophistry [*sophistēs*]" (203d). We might here recall that Agathon had characterized

Love as young, supple, and beautiful, in effect, a self-portrait. Diotima, or Socrates through Diotima, however, characterizes Love in terms that suggest a portrait of Socrates, tough, shriveled, and shoeless. Recall also the description of Aristodemus (173b). Such a description applies the proposition that if Love desires beauty, intelligence and wisdom it must necessarily not possess them. That said, a closer look indicates that Diotima is painting a group portrait of Love. The list of characteristics attributed to Love can be applied without too much difficulty to all of the speakers around the table: Phaedrus, brave, impetuous, and intense; Pausanias, an awesome hunter, weaving snares; the physician Eryximachus, in his way a lover of wisdom; the comic playwright Aristophanes howling his enchantments and his poison/magic; and Agathon, the lover of sophistry.

Diotima further explains that by nature Love is neither mortal nor immortal, since he is neither human nor a god. He comes to life when he encounters the object of his desire, but dies when he does not. This conception of Love as neither immortal nor mortal is analogous to her earlier comments about something that is neither beautiful nor ugly, neither knowledgeable nor ignorant, neither divine nor human. That said, claiming Love to be neither mortal nor immortal raises a curious ontological issue, since it is hard to imagine an intermediate position, though psychologically speaking what she describes seems perfectly correct, especially when we acknowledge the often fickle nature of love, one moment springing to life, the next fading away. All of this relates back to the *daimonic* character of love and the grounding for Plato's view that love represents something real but independent of us. Recalling, for instance, the account of the soul in the *Phaedrus* (246b–d), humans possess a mortal part (their bodies) and an immortal part (their souls). Since love is neither mortal nor immortal, it is not part of the body and not part of the soul, so somehow must be separate and distinct from them.

Love is also between wisdom and ignorance. None of the gods loves or desires wisdom, because they already possess it, and returning to the earlier discussion, we desire (love) only what we do not possess. Similarly the ignorant do not love or desire wisdom because, being ignorant, they do not know what they do not possess. Love, on the other hand, is a lover of wisdom because he does not possess wisdom, but also knows that he does not possess it. By his nature then, Love is a philosopher, a lover of wisdom, because Love is always drawn to beauty, and wisdom is among the class of beautiful things. Glossing Socrates' confusion, Diotima suggests that he had thought that Love was *being loved*, the object of desire, when in fact Love is *being a lover* (the agent of desire). Confusing the means with the end, he had supposed that Love must be beautiful, because he is always associated with beauty, when in fact this desire represents an absence and a need.

Having considered the nature of Love, Diotima turns to the question (204d): what is the point of loving beautiful things? Put another way, what does the lover of beautiful things desire? Echoing the earlier discussion, Socrates answers that the lover desires to make them his own (since he does not possess them). But, Diotima further asks, what will he actually have when he possesses the beautiful things?

In order to make herself clearer, Diotima reframes the question in terms of good things rather than beautiful ones. Thus, what does the lover of good things desire? Again the answer is to make them his own. Then, when he has good things (the object of his desire), what does he have? (Or in Aristotle's famous formulation of the same question in the *Nicomachean Ethics*, what is the highest realizable good? [1095a25].) Socrates readily answers that one will have happiness (*eudaimonia*). The reason I seek what I take to be good, is because it makes me happy. Happiness, further, is the ultimate goal, since it would seem odd and pointless to ask what I would seek beyond happiness or by means of happiness (205a). In her argument, Diotima assumes and Socrates does not question, that the word happiness signifies only one thing. Happiness is a kind of love, since it is something we desire. Deploying the earlier premises, it implies either something that we do not have, and therefore desire, or something we have but want to possess forever. Diotima further adds that this desire seems to be common to all humans. In other words, all people desire happiness.

Diotima now asks: since all people desire happiness, and happiness is a kind of love, why do we not say that all people are lovers? We observe, however, that some people are in love and others are not. Does this not imply some contradiction in our premises? When Socrates indicates perplexity, she answers "it's because we divide out a special kind of love, and we refer to it by the word that belongs to the whole—'love'; and for the other kinds of love we use other words" (205b). To further illustrate, she draws an analogy with the word poetry (*poiēsis*—making, creating). Any craft or profession that is engaged in creating or making something out of nothing is literally a kind of poetry, and anyone engaged in creating and making is in the literal sense of the word a poet. Yet we do not call the plumber or farmer a poet (except perhaps when we are being hyperbolic), reserving the word to label a special class of making and creating with music and verse (*poiētes*). The same then may be said of lover. In the sense that every desire for good things or happiness is love, and everyone desires good things and happiness, then everyone is a lover. As a matter of convention, however, we reserve the words "lover," "love," and "in love" to those who devote themselves wholly to the special kind of love. There are two philosophically interesting points we should linger over.

First, Plato indicates his awareness of the limits of the lexicon. We are often careless or imprecise with our language, using the word "love," when we mean something else. For instance, the semantic field of the word "love" embraces a host of words that are connected, yet not interchangeable: love, ardor, infatuation, attraction, devotion, lust, lechery, to list a few. In acknowledging this Plato posits that when he uses the word 'love," he uses it in a special sense. This allows him to anticipate those who object to the claim that there is something universal behind words such as "happiness" or "love," by saying that the words are ambiguous or have multiple meanings. His answer is yes, we often misapply the word, but I mean it in this special sense, not to be confused with the others. We must distinguish real love from apparent love, and analogously the real good from the apparent good.

Second, Diotima's description of a love by "the name that belongs to the whole [*holou*]" (205b) resonates strongly with Socrates' attempt to define the philosopher in the *Republic* (474b–476a). Trying to get at what it means to say that a philosopher is a "lover" of "wisdom," he describes a lover as one who is a desirer of the whole. "[W]hen we say that a man loves something, it must be shown, if the word is properly applied to him, that he loves not one part of it and the other not, but that he is fond of all of it" (474c). While a lover might speak affectionately of the nose, eyes, or other parts of the beloved, it would be absurd (outside the realm of fetishism) to say that he loved the nose and eyes, but not the whole person. With regard to our previous distinction, the lover would have confused the apparent love for an apparent good for the real love of the real good. Turning specifically to the lover of wisdom, he says: "The lover of wisdom, we shall say, has a passion for wisdom, not of one part and not another, but of all of it [*alla pasēs*]?" (475b). Love, then, entails a desire for the whole of wisdom. The question then becomes for Socrates how one can grasp the *whole* or *all* of wisdom, as distinct from the *sum* of knowledge. This points to the Platonic doctrine of Forms.

In what would seem to be an anachronistic allusion to Aristophanes' speech, a point that does not escape the comic poet's notice, Diotima says that according to a certain story, lovers are people who seek their other halves (205e).[7] She explains that the lover does not seek a lost half or seek a whole unless this half turns out to be good, noting that people are willing to cut off a diseased arm or leg. Rather, we take joy in saying "something belongs to me" only if this means "good." In other words, what I desire to possess is not good because I possess it, but I desire to possess it because it is good. All of this relates back to the earlier proposition that what we really love is nothing other than the good. So we may say, applying proposition (A) that "people love the good" (206a), and proposition (B) that this is equivalent to saying that "people want the good to be theirs" (206a). Relating this back to proposition (C) about possessing the object of desire and to keep or have it in the future, we may amend our proposition to say "Love is wanting to possess the good forever" (206a). This then, according to Diotima is the object of love.

If this is what love is, Diotima asks Socrates, how do people pursue it? "What is the real purpose of love?" (206b). When he protests his ignorance, that he would not be her student if he knew the answer, she declares: "It is giving birth in beauty [*tokos en kaloī*], whether in body or in soul" (206a). There is some ambiguity in Diotima's Greek, and Socrates protests that it would take a seer to figure out what she has just said. The preposition *en* can mean "in" in the sense of "inside," literally "in (something) beautiful," in this context implying penetration during sexual intercourse. It can also mean "in" the sense of "in the presence of" (Plato 1989, p. 53n79). *Tokos* means literally "a giving birth," and can be applied to males or females. When applied to males it is conventionally translated "begetting," and when applied to females, "bearing." This is distinct from *kuein* (be pregnant), which is normally applied only to women (Plato 1980, p. 147). Also relevant is the verb *gennaō* which can be translated "to engender" or "to father." *Kalon*, as we have noted elsewhere, signifies not only beauty, but also propriety and nobility.

In general we may say that no one would desire to have an erotic union with (*in*) something ugly, only with (*in*) something beautiful. This is because giving birth is something divine. In other words, this is how something that is mortal can achieve a modicum of immortality. In the context of ancient Greek tradition, immortality is one of the fundamental features that distinguish the gods from humans. We transcend the limits of human nature through reproduction, the performance of memorable deeds, or the creation of great works. Transposing Eryximachus' treatment of harmony to the limits of nature and more specifically human nature, she says: "Pregnancy, reproduction—this is an immortal thing for a mortal animal to do, and it cannot occur in anything that is out of harmony, but ugliness is out of harmony with all that is godly. Beauty, however, is in harmony with the divine" (206c–d). Playing on a sexual double-entendre, she notes that pregnant animals and humans are joyfully disposed near beauty, while they draw back and "shrink-up" (206d), in the presence of ugliness.

Elaborating on the theme of "giving birth," Diotima explains: "All of us are pregnant [*kuousin*], Socrates, both in body and in soul, and, as soon as we come to a certain age, we naturally desire to give birth" (206c). M. F. Burnyeat notes what seems to be a curious reversal in which pregnancy causes love, rather than love being the cause of pregnancy (1977, p. 8). Elizabeth E. Pender tries to resolve this by glossing "pregnancy" (*kuousin*) to mean, "aroused," in the sense of "full of excitement," and "giving birth" (*tokos*) to be a euphemism for ejaculation (1992, p. 74). This pregnancy may also be understood as a potential that is actualized, made concrete when stimulated by beautiful thoughts.

What Love wants, then, is not beauty *per se*, but "reproduction and birth in beauty" (206e). Reproduction goes on forever, what mortals have instead of immortality. In other words, Diotima takes proposition (C), the desire to possess the good in the future, to its logical extreme, the desire to possess the good forever. Love entails the desire for both the good and immortality, or we might say that good among the various competing "goods" that are immortal. This is the fundamental driving imperative of the erotic, the powerful yearning to transcend our natural limits, even within the boundaries of nature.

On the occasion of another meeting, Diotima asks Socrates: "What do you think causes love and desire?" (207a). How do we understand the urgency and pain associated with *eros*? Clearly love is "intentional"; it is love of something or someone (see Corrigan 2004, p. 109). Does such an intention entail a rational choice? Does it represent a calculation of self-interest, positions advocated by Phaedrus and Pausanias? Is it the product of some natural force, positions advocated by Eryximachus and Aristophanes? "Human beings, you'd think, would do this because they understand the reason for it" Diotima says, "but what causes wild animals to be in a state of love?" (207c). Here Diotima wishes to take the argument a step higher. To understand love in the human context, we need first to realize that it represents a phenomenon that we see in all animals. "Footed and winged animals alike, all are plagued by the disease of Love" (207b). This is manifest first in the painful urgency related to the need for sexual intercourse. Then it is manifest in the ferocity by which animals will protect their young. Weak animals will fight strong ones, even though it may cost their lives. Animals will starve themselves in order to feed their young. The same behavior may be observed in humans. "For among animals the principle is the same as with us, and mortal nature seeks so far as possible to live forever and be immortal. And this is possible in one way only: by reproduction, because it always leaves behind a new young one in place of the old" (207d). Unpacking the arguments contained in these comments, we may draw two conclusions.

First, humans are distinguished from other animals by their exercise of reason and ability to make rational choices. However, since the erotic intention is observed in both animals and humans, it follows that it is not about reason. Humans may understand their behavior, but it is not the understanding that governs it. We have not rationally decided that *eros* is the best way to achieve immortality. Second, since both humans and animals are willing to suffer injury and death for the sake of their young, it would seem that it is not about self-interest, at least in the narrow sense of the term; indeed the behavior caused by erotic attraction can often be contrary to self-interest. Similarly insofar as we are willing to endure injury and privation and often characterize love in terms of pain and suffering, we are not acting out of a pursuit of pleasure. Paradoxically it is even sometimes necessary to sacrifice our lives for the sake of our immortality. Love is not hedonistic; love is not selfish.

So far Diotima has considered the erotic with regard to humans to the degree that they are animals. She now proposes to extend the argument to humans as humans. To get at this she begins with an analysis of human identity that sounds remarkably like David Hume's in *A Treatise of Human Nature* (1.4.6). We tend to suppose that we are alive and the same from one time to the next. "[A] person is said to be the same from childhood till he turns into an old man" (207d). Yet in reality, this is not the case: "he is always being renewed and in other respects passing away, in his hair and flesh and bones and blood and his entire body" (207d). We are not the same from one time to the next either with regard to our bodies or our souls: "for none of his manners, customs, opinions, desires, pleasures, pains, or fears ever remains the same, but some are coming to be in him while others are passing away" (207e).[8] Even more fundamental is the lack of identity of knowledge. As new knowledge comes to be, other passes away. "For what we call *studying* exists because knowledge is leaving us, because forgetting is the departure of knowledge, while studying puts back a fresh memory in place of what went away" (208a). The knowledge may seem the same, but it is not. It is constantly being renewed. Memory in this context is not the recollection of what is there, but the renewal of what has departed. "By this device . . . what is mortal shares in immortality whether it is a body or anything else, while the immortal has another way" (208b).

In other words, whether we are speaking of the animals or humans, the body or the soul, there is one fundamental mechanism or principle at play, the desire for immortality. For those centered in the body, this involves literal reproduction and a focus on the creation and nurturing of offspring; for those centered on the soul, this involves the performance of deeds or the creation and nurturing of works that will be transmitted and remembered.

Socrates is amazed by Diotima's speech, and asks if this is actually the way things are. "And in the manner of a perfect sophist she says, 'be sure of it [*eu isthī*], Socrates'" (208c). Whether Plato merely has Socrates make this remark as a playful reference to the sophistic formula, or whether he means to cast a shadow of doubt over the whole speech is a matter of debate. Compare this with similar remarks in the *Euthyphro* (274a) and the *Hippias Major* (287c). Diotima proceeds to elaborate, echoing her earlier comments on the way that animals will suffer and die for the sake of their offspring, extending them to the "offspring" of the soul. Consider, she asks, human irrationality (*alogos*) in seeking honor and in wanting to be famous. They are willing to risk danger, money, misfortune, physical risk, and even death for the sake of glory, even more than what they would endure for the sake of their children (208c). Would Alcestis have died for Admetus, or Achilles risked death for Patroclus, she asks, anachronistically echoing the examples of Phaedrus; would Kodros, a legendary king of Athens, die to preserve the throne for his sons, if they had not expected the memory of their virtue to live on after them? "I believe that anyone will do anything for the sake of immortal virtue and the glorious fame that follows; and the better the people, the more they will do, for they are all in love with immortality" (208d–e).

In this, Diotima echoes and transposes Phaedrus' argument from the individual to the universal. Instead of pursuing virtue for fear of appearing shameful in the eyes of a lover, we pursue it for the sake of being remembered as virtuous to all future generations. As in the case of the immortality of the body, the urge to achieve an immortality of the soul is governed neither by reason nor self-interest, neither pleasure nor benefit. The erotic drive for immortality is the unitary impetus for all our diverse activities. It is universal, applicable to animals and humans. It is, as Diotima says, irrational, and by her way of thinking because it is universal, and because it is outside our control, independent of our rational choices, it is therefore objective, representing something that has a real existence.

Returning to the theme of pregnancy and pulling the various elements together, Diotima proposes a hierarchy, according to the manner by which people seek to achieve immortality. "Now, some people are pregnant in body, and for this reason turn more to women and pursue love in that way, providing themselves through childbirth with immortality" (208e). Then there are others who are pregnant in soul, perhaps even more so in their souls than their bodies. These are pregnant with what is fitting, "for the soul to bear and bring to birth [*ha psuchē kuēsai kai tekein*]" (209a). And what is fitting? "Wisdom [*phronēsin*] and the rest of virtue [*aretēn*], which all poets [*poietai*] engender [*gennētores*] as well as all the craftsmen who are said to be creative" (209a). The greatest and most beautiful part of wisdom, involving moderation [*sôphrosunē*] and justice [*dikaiosunē*], deals with the ordering of the community and the household.

Summarizing the process, Diotima imagines a young man who has been pregnant with the virtues of moderation and justice since his earliest youth. He desires to beget and give birth, so he seeks a beauty in which he would beget. In other words, he is born with a potential, but must seek an object suitable to give it expression and actuality. Since he is pregnant with beautiful virtues, he is naturally drawn to bodies that are beautiful in the same way, and if he finds a soul that is beautiful and noble he will immediately be filled with "words/inward thoughts about virtue [*logōu peri aretēs*]" (209c). In terms of Eryximachus, he seeks one who is in harmony with his own beauty, or in the terms of Aristophanes, he is seeking his lost half, one who seeks a beauty akin to his own. He becomes the beloved of a virtuous lover who tries to nurture and educate his charge, causing the beloved to conceive and give birth to what he was pregnant with. If the erotic is about seeking immortality in beauty, then at the most basic level we seek immortality achieved through reproduction of the body, drawn to the beautiful body. On the next level, we seek immortality achieved by the reproduction (recollection) of the soul, through the creation of works of poetry and other creative achievements. Who, Diotima asks, would not desire to have given birth to the intellectual offspring of a Homer or Hesiod, works such as the *Iliad* or the *Theogony*, even more than merely human progeny?

Finally at the highest level, we seek immortality achieved by the reproduction of the soul, through the creation of institutions and laws. Consider the enduring honor and glory given to Lycourgos, the legendary lawgiver of Sparta, or Solon, the lawgiver of Athens. "Already many shrines have sprung up to honor them for their immortal children [civil institutions], which hasn't happened yet to anyone for human offspring" (209e).

With regard to this production of "words about virtue," C. J. Rowe asks, "but how so?" (Plato 1998, p. 191nb7–8). Ontologically this is a valid point, but metaphorically and psychologically it describes a real experience. Wherever we may say that the thoughts come from, it is not unusual for one person to be "inspired" by another. We could switch to a more contemporary metaphor and speak of the "chemistry" between two people. More seriously, Diotima's metaphor is consistent with Plato's epistemology and his model of education. The Forms or Ideas that are the basis for the production of words are already present. In turn the Socratic method elicits the interlocutor's beliefs. It assumes that there is something to be discovered and tested in the pupil. "The sophist treats his pupil as an empty receptacle to be filled from the outside with the teacher's ideas," says M. F. Burnyeat. By contrast, "Socrates respects the pupil's own creativity, holding that, with the right kind of assistance, the young man will produce ideas from his own mind and will be enabled to work out for himself whether they are true or false" (1977, p. 9). The beautiful lover, much like the Socratic midwife in the *Theaetetus*, helps the beloved bring forth the ideas that are already there, with which he is already pregnant.

3.2.4. Diotima: the greater mysteries (209e–212c)

Many scholars conventionally label what follows the "ascent" passage of the *Symposium* (209e–212a), culminating in Diotima's "Ladder" or "Stairway" of Love. Taking stock of things up to that point, Diotima tells Socrates that he might be "initiated [*muētheiēs*]" into those rites of love that she has thus far described (210a). That is, Socrates might with diligence be capable of giving birth in beauty to virtuous works or institutions. She is hesitant, however, wondering if he can achieve "the final and highest mysteries [*ta de telea kai epoptika*]" (210a), adding that it is for the sake of these final mysteries that she has taught him what she has. Diotima frames her discussion of love in the language of Mystery Religions, with their stages of initiation (*muēsis*), mysteries or revelations (*epopteia*), and secret rites performed or experienced by the initiated (*orgiazein*) (Burkert 1985, p. 324; for a fuller discussion see des Places 1981, pp. 83–98). Despite her hesitations about Socrates' aptitude, she tells him that she will give it her best try.

Diotima now shifts to the other side of the erotic equation. Instead of speaking of the beloved, pregnant with virtues, she turns to the role of the lover (*erastes*), who fathers or engenders (*gennaō*) good things by his nurturing the pregnant beloved. She outlines five stages of development. Each involves a movement from gazing at or contemplating the beauty of one item, to recognizing the family resemblance of beauty in all instances. It is always, J. M. E. Moravcik observes, "other directed" toward something independent of us; the objects of our aspiration are outside our souls (1971, p. 292). It is a process that devalues the prior stage while it enhances the latter. By extension, the lover is ultimately the lover of wisdom, the philosopher.

First (210a–b), from his youth, the would-be lover should devote himself to beautiful bodies. If the one who is leading him (the lover's lover or the teacher of erotics—*ta erotica*) has done his job properly, the lover will fall in love with one body, "and there engender beautiful ideas/words [*kai entautha gennan logous kalous*]" (210a). We might recall that Socrates earlier characterized himself as an expert on the art of love (177d and 198d). The lover soon realizes that the beauty of any one body is akin to that of any other, and since what attracts him is the "beauty of the outward form [*ep'eidei kalon*]" (210b). This leads the lover to appreciate the beauty in all bodies. Achieving that perspective, he finds it foolish to focus exclusively on one instance of beautiful bodies; "he must become a lover of all beautiful bodies" (20b).

Second (210b–c), the lover finds himself drawn to potential beloveds who possess decent souls even though their bodies are not in "bloom" (210b). By this he recognizes that it is not the beauty of bodies that moves him, but the beauty in people's souls (*psuchais kalos*), not their physical attractiveness, but the desirability of their characters. The lover will be content to love this young man and "beget ideas [*tiktein logous*]" that will make him better (210c). Since the beauty of the soul is manifest in the beautiful pursuits or practices (*epitēdeuma*), and norms or customs (*nomos*) of the behavior, what the lover loves in loving the soul are the pursuits and customs.

Third (210c–d), the lover contemplating the pursuits and customs of the beloved realizes that these are informed by beautiful knowledge (*epistēnōn*). Thus after gazing on the pursuits and norms, the lover will turn to knowledge, eventually realizing that underlying specific instances of knowledge, there is a "great sea of beauty" (210d).

Fourth (210d–e), gazing upon this "great sea of beauty," the lover brings to birth (*tiktē*), "many gloriously beautiful ideas and thoughts, in unstinting love of wisdom [*philosophia*], until, having grown and been strengthened there, he catches sight of a certain single kind of knowledge [*tis epistēmē mia*]" (210e). That is, he has moved from knowledge of specific instances to knowledge of the whole, in effect from knowledge*s* to knowledge. Recall Diotima's earlier description of "the name that belongs to the whole" (205b), and the account of the philosopher in the *Republic*, who "has a passion for wisdom, not of one part and not another, but of all of it? [*alla pasēs*]?" (475b). The lover has moved from the knowledge of loves to the science of love, the single knowledge that informs all of the particular *knowledges*. The first four stages are preparation for what is to follow.

Fifth (210e–211b), after taking a breath, Diotima admonishes Socrates to pay close attention. The lover who has gone through the proper stages in the proper way, from body to bodies, from bodies to practices (of souls), from practices to knowledge, and from knowledge to wisdom, will "all of a sudden [*exaiphnēs*] catch sight of a beauty amazing in its nature [*thaumaston tēn phusin kalon*]" (210e). That is to say, the lover has glimpsed the pure form of beauty itself. Diotima posits four predicates. First, it is eternal, neither coming into being nor passing out of being. Second, beauty is not relational or relative; that is, it is not in the proverbial eye of the beholder, beautiful to some and ugly to others. Third, it is not bound to any particular thing or instance. It does not appear in the guise of a beautiful face, beautiful words, or some kind of beautiful knowledge: "it is not anywhere in another, as in an animal, or in earth, or in heaven, or in anything else" (211a–b). In other words, the form of beauty is not limited by either the temporary or the spatial. Finally, fourth, it is immutable. It is "itself by itself with itself, it is always one in form; and all other beautiful things share in that, in such a way that when those others come to be or pass away it does not become the least bit small or greater nor suffer any change" (211b).

It is important to underline here, as F. C. White reminds us, that the form of the beautiful differs from the form of the good that Socrates describes in *Republic*, that is that there is an identity between the good and the beautiful (White 1989, p. 155). In glimpsing the beautiful the lover gives birth to good words and deeds, and the glimpse of the ultimate beauty will lead us to the good, an achievement that will assure our enduring immortality through the recollection of our good words and noble deeds. "Diotima does not say that the sight of beauty causes the beholder to bring forth beauty. The essence of her story rather is that beauty produces something beyond it—the good" (White 1989, p. 156).

Diotima summarizes what she has said in a passage later commentators call the "Ladder Love," playing on her simile. Given its importance and subsequent influence, I will quote it at length.

> This is what it is to go aright, or be led by another, into the mystery of Love: one goes always upwards for the sake of this Beauty, starting out from beautiful things and using them like rising stairs: from one body to two to all beautiful bodies, then from beautiful bodies to beautiful customs, and from customs to learning beautiful things, and from these sciences [*mathēmata*] he arrives in the end at this science [*mathēma*], which is learning of this very Beauty, so that in the end he comes to know just what it is to be beautiful. (211c–d)

(While our word "mathematics" derives from the Greek *to mathēma*, the word is better-translated "systematic knowledge" or "science" in the German sense of *die Wissenschaft*.) Expounding the significance of what she has said, Diotima says that such a vision of the beautiful would render all other measures of beauty trivial. Nor would she consider anyone who has had such a vision as living a poor life. Quite the contrary, bringing the vision of a pure, unmixed form back to the proposition of seeking immortality by giving birth in beauty, Diotima concludes that "in that life alone, when he looks at Beauty in the only way that Beauty can be seen—only then will it become possible for him to give birth [*tikten*] not to images of virtue [*eidōla aretēs*] (because he's in touch with no images), but to true virtue (because he is in touch with the true Beauty)" (212a). (The noun *eidōlon* can mean "image," "phantom," or "unsubstantial form.") We must relate this back to our hierarchy of offspring literal and figurative who have been engendered in beauty: children, works of poetry, inventions, moral and political institutions are merely images or phantoms of virtue, mere approximations in their impure form, contingent on particular things. Only those engendered in pure beauty will produce true virtues. "The love of the gods belongs to anyone who has given birth to true virtue and nourished it, and if any human being could become immortal, it would be he" (212a–b).

Here Socrates draws his narrative about Diotima to a close, and turns the floor back to Phaedrus, with the remark, "I was persuaded. And once persuaded, I try to persuade others too that human nature can find no better workmate for acquiring this than Love" (212b). Socrates' words are reminiscent of the closing to his account of the Myth of Er at the end of the *Republic*: "If we are persuaded by me to believe that the soul is immortal and that it can endure all evils and all blessings, we shall always hold on to the upward journey and we shall in every way practice justice with wisdom, in order that we may be at peace with ourselves and with the gods . . ." (621c). Socrates makes a similar proposal in the *Phaedo* as a way of eliminating any anxiety about the fate of one's soul (114d–e). In both cases, we seem to be left not so much with a proof of Socrates' propositions but with the "correct belief [*orthē doxa*]" sustained by a Pascalian wager. On the other hand, what other recourse does Socrates have available to him? How can the person who has reached a level of understanding or comprehension communicate his understanding to those who do not possess it? Socrates raises the same issue in the *Republic*, especially in the Parable of the Pilot (488b–c): To those ignorant of the skills required for the navigation of a ship the pilot seems merely to be staring off into the horizon, when in fact he is most intensely busy. Analogously, how can the uninitiated distinguish the wisdom of a philosopher from the demagoguery of a persuasive sophist? Thus, how can the Socratic philosopher impart wisdom aside from being a lover, a midwife, or a mistress of mysteries, exhorting and encouraging the beloved, the patient, or the initiate? The only way for the Socratic philosopher to impart wisdom is to guide students to discover it for themselves.

Diotima's "contribution" to Agathon's *symposion* raises a number of issues that we need to consider in more detail. These fall into three broad areas of inquiry: the first is to consider more fully the philosophical doctrine expressed in the "ascent" passage and whether or not it reflects Plato's position. The second is to consider more fully the function of Diotima. The third is to consider the relationship of "ascent" passage with the earlier speeches.

Ludwig Chen (1983) argues convincingly that there are two ontic aims and one cognitive aim expressed in the "ascent" passage (p. 66). The first four stages of ascent, the movements from body to bodies, from bodies to the practices of souls, from customs to knowledge, and from knowledge to science, represent a horizontal movement, embracing more and more instances, but remaining in the realm of the particular. It is an expansion rather than a transition, moving methodically and progressively, but on the same plateau (Chen 1983). Only "until" that point that the lover (cognitively the philosopher) has gained necessary strength and growth by contemplating the "vast sea of the beauty," will he "suddenly" behold beauty itself. Chen underlines Diotima's qualifications "until" (*heōs*) and "suddenly" (*exaiphnēs*) to emphasize the cognitive and ontic gap between the instances of beauty glimpsed through the first four stages, and the final vision glimpsed in the final stage (Chen 1983, p. 69). Ontologically the beauty of instances is different from the beautiful itself. Cognitively it represents a different way of thinking. Chen labels the process one of "deindividualization": "the object of his [the lover's] knowledge is really this or that beautiful body as deindividualized, i.e., without regard for its possessor" (p. 67). Thus the lover loves all the specific instances of the bodies indifferently, "not the beauty-in-all-bodies as such" (p. 67). Thomas Gould makes an analogous point. "If things go well, we come to value profound intelligence, real understanding, splendor of soul, and actually quite forget the individual who first quickened our awareness of these things" (Gould 1963, p. 55).

Many scholars read the process described in the first four stages of ascent in terms of abstraction and generalization, inscribing Plato's theory of ideas in terms of empirical logic. Chen rejects this view, arguing that we see neither, since abstraction moves to something common, but Diotima speaks of a "sea" of instances. Similarly, the goal of generalization in empirical logic seeks to yield a concept (Chen 1993, p. 70). Thus if I look at many instances of red apples, I might draw the generalizing concept: "all these apples are red." But what concept can I draw from "I apprehend the Form of Beauty" other than the nonsensical tautology "All beauty is beautiful"? "What does an imageless image look like?" and other analogous propositions that start to resemble Zen koans. In its absolute and unmixed purity, the form of beauty is beyond rational or empirical description. We can only point at it; we do not have the means of saying what it is. *Erōs* is a kind of orienting disposition.

Similarly, J. M. E. Moravcsik points out that the move made by Plato from one kind of beauty to another is not a matter of apprehending the common denominator within plurality (1971, p. 289). The mind turns toward the new kind of beauty by the feelings of dismissal and disdain of the older kinds of beauty at the old level, while at the same time forming positive feelings toward the instances of beauty at the new level. All of this, Moravcsik argues, raises the question of the causal relationship between the levels. He contends that there cannot be a necessary causal connection between the steps, arguing that if there were one, then nobody could appreciate the beauty of mathematics without having appreciated bodily beauty (1971, p. 289). Whatever the erotic tastes of mathematicians, Moravcsik begs the question of why in fact it is not necessary to appreciate bodies in order to appreciate the beauties of mathematics. More to the point, what is the test for the claim that one *truly* does appreciate the beauty of mathematics? Diotima's recurrent insistence on the lover's being properly "led," as well as her concern for the proper order of the rites of love suggests that Plato does believe that there is a necessary relationship between the stages. Moravcsik also argues, "we cannot suppose that the steps are sufficient conditions for our successors. Such a view would entail that once someone takes the first step on the path, he will always arrive at the terminal point, sooner or later" (1971, p. 289). Again Diotima's description of the right process in terms of "will," does seem to suggest a belief in the causal sufficiency of the transitions, especially with regard to the first four stages up the ladder of ascent, though such a claim seems more tentative. Moravcsik rightly speaks of the way that the prior stages of ascent are playing a "contributory cause" to their successors (1971, p. 289).

All of this relates to another important aspect of the "until" and the "suddenly" that we should consider, especially as it relates to the fifth and final stage of ascent. That is, we should also say that the lover/philosopher *might* behold beauty itself, but that this final vision does not represent an absolute certainty. Although Diotima expresses strong belief that when the rites of love (the first four stages of ascent) are done correctly and in the right order, the sight "will" happen, she is not offering a written guarantee. The first four stages can be understood in terms of method and progress. But the fifth stage requires a cognitive leap, or what A. J. Festugière calls a "cognitive seizure [*la saisie cognitive*]" (Festugière 1950, p. 288), though this may or may not result. A rite or ritual can lead us to the edge, but cannot necessarily give us the final nudge. The method can only prepare the lover/philosopher, put him in the proper place, the proper frame of mind, but it cannot by itself bridge the final gap. All of this goes to acknowledge the inherent limits of reason. Festugière describes this when he distinguishes between the "geometrical" method and the dialectic. The hypotheses of the former assume the validity of first principles that exist at the same level of being, while those of the latter refer to a superior order in the hierarchy of being (Festugière 1950, pp. 170, 1). Reason is a powerful tool for establishing insight in hindsight. It provides the means to distinguish the "wind egg" as Socrates describes false concepts in the *Theaetetus* from true insight, but it cannot create or discover those insights by itself. We must wait "until" the moment "suddenly" occurs. We might compare the cognitive leap or seizure to inspiration, insight, enlightenment, understanding, the "aha! moment," "little light bulb flashing on," the mystical experience, the leap of faith, the opening of one's self to the possibility of being, or to conflate Diotima's metaphor with Wittgenstein's, kicking away the ladder after we have climbed it.

The process and progress that Diotima describes resembles what Socrates says at the end of the "Parable of the Cave": "If you interpret the upward journey and the contemplation of things above as the upward journey of the soul to the intelligible realm, you will grasp what I surmise. . . . Whether it is true or not only the god knows, but this is how I see it, namely that in the intelligible world the Form of the Good is the last to be seen, and with difficulty" (517b). The upward journey is difficult, and whether it is ultimately true or not is known only to the gods. We ourselves must rely on a strong belief. Whether Socrates himself actually ever achieved the final vision is unclear. Nevertheless, it represents for him a bright hope that shapes his actions. In contrast with the *Phaedo*, where Socrates considers that the task of philosophy is the "practice of dying" (66b), in order to liberate the soul and purify us of the obscuring contamination of the body, he seems more optimistic about the possibility of grasping the Forms in the *Republic* and the *Symposium*.

There is another implication to this. If the methodical procedure cannot by itself directly cause us to glimpse the Form of the Beautiful, and if we must wait (so to speak) for it to happen (if at all) on its own time, then that glimpse represents for Plato something real, independent of our rational control, beyond our cognitive faculties. We may refer this back to Plato's conception of the *daimonic* as something external to the self, signifying a metaphysical realism. Like Virgil, the embodiment of reason in Dante's *Divina commedia*, reason can only take us so far. The final vision requires the intervention of a Beatrice, presenting herself as a divine gift, somehow outside or independent of the individual soul. Only then are we able to stretch the cognitive faculties to the point at which:

> My mind was struck by light that flashed
> And, with this light, received what it had asked.
> Here force failed my high fantasy [l'altra fantasia]; but my
> Desire and will were moved already—like
> A wheel revolving uniformly—by
> The Love that moves the sun and the other stars
> [l'amor che move il sole e l'altre stele]. (Dante 1986, 33. 140–145)

While it is likely that Dante was not directly familiar with the *Symposium*, what he says of the process and experience of glimpsing the Divine strongly resembles what Diotima has described. And, consistent with Diotima's account, the ultimate goal of the "miraculous vision [*mirabile visione*]," is not itself the beauty of the divine, but the urgency to go beyond, "until I would be capable of writing about her in a nobler way" (Dante 1973, p. 42), resulting in an achievement that has brought Dante immortality as a poet.

Diotima's doctrine, linking immortality either to reproduction or to the creation of noble works, raises what C. J. Rowe terms "the standing puzzles" about the *Symposium* (Plato 1998, p. 185): Diotima asserts that only the gods have immortality and that humans and other animals share in it through procreation (208a–b). How does this fit with the repeated claims in the *Phaedo*, *Phaedrus*, and the *Republic* that the soul is immortal? See, for instance, Luce (1952, pp. 137–141), Dover (Plato 1980, pp. 148,150), O'Brien (1984, pp. 198–205), and Corrigan (2004, pp. 159 and 224–234). The puzzle is especially perplexing because scholars tend to date the *Symposium* as roughly contemporary with the *Phaedo*, *Phaedrus*, and *Republic*. It would seem odd that Diotima should not mention anything about the immortality of the soul, or the separation of the body and the soul. Indeed, she never speaks of the soul apart from the body. How is this to be understood or explained? Is it proof that Plato rejects the immortality of the soul? Is this evidence that Diotima's speech does not reflect Plato's position? Does it mean that the *Symposium* actually dates earlier than the other dialogues, before Plato has formulated his doctrine? Or, is there some way of reconciling Diotima's notion of immortality with Plato's immortal soul?

While these questions cannot be definitively resolved there are several responses. First, we must keep in mind that it is logically problematic to draw any conclusions from Diotima's silence on the question of a mind-soul dualism. J. V. Luce points out that the doctrine of the immortality of the soul in the *Phaedo* is predicated on the theory of Forms that remained a hypothesis: "immortality in the *Phaedo* remains logically hypothetical, even if morally certain" (Luce 1952, p. 138). Plato believes in the immortality of the soul, but recognizes the inadequacy of his argument to prove it. Luce and others also argue that in Plato's dualism, humans are composite beings, combining both body and soul. That being the case the mortality of the human would mean the death of the body, but not necessarily the death of the soul. Diotima's claim that humans and animals share in immortality only through procreation, would relate only to the bodily side of our being. Similarly the immortality contingent on the recollection of our words and deeds, is also contingent on the bodily side of our being, in that moral agency requires the existence of a physical moral agent in this world. Physical deeds are performed by physical beings.

Does Diotima reflect Plato's position? Socrates claims to believe in Diotima, even as he also acknowledges that she can sometimes resemble a sophist. At the risk of relegating the matter to the vexed issue of the relationship between Plato and Socrates, I would refer this question back to the many-layered frame narrative that Plato has constructed. Put another way, where is Plato in the *Symposium*? We might equally analogously ask where Shakespeare is in *King Lear*? In the context of a dramatic genre the short answer is everywhere and nowhere. It is a question that cannot be answered unless we are dealing with a playwright such as George Bernard Shaw who glosses his plays with extended prefaces that instruct us how and what to think. Otherwise, by its very nature, a dialogue (in effect a play), or any work of literature, is speculative. The text pushes and manipulates us in various directions, but we cannot unambiguously and categorically assert the authorial intention with regard to specific content. In part we may be looking at the exigencies of what happens to have survived over time, but in terms of what has come down to us, we may say unambiguously and categorically that Plato has chosen to rely on the resources of literature rather than those of analytical discourse. Plato is not Aristotle. He has felt that the resources of literature are more effective at expressing the inexpressible. To extract a precise doctrine from a work of literature is to deny literature exactly what it does best, to deny its evocative and suggestive power. Ultimately I agree with the Victorian critic and classicist Walter Pater: "Platonism is not a formal theory or body of theories, but a tendency, a group of tendencies—a tendency to think or feel, and to speak about certain things in a particular way, discernible in Plato's dialogues as reflecting the peculiarities, the marked peculiarities, of himself and his own mental composition" (Pater 1968, p. 150). Another way to put this is that the dialogues are not so much about the exposition of a doctrine, but a series of provocative thought experiments. It is exactly this that marks the enduring fertility of Plato's thought, more than any specific doctrine that he might articulate.

Turning to the next area of inquiry, we should consider the function of Diotima. Halperin (1990, pp. 119–140) and Corrigan and Glazov-Corrigan (2004, pp. 111–114) offer convenient summaries and assessments of the prominent explanations. I will mention five. One possibility is that Socrates puts his views in the mouth of Diotima as a way of mitigating the social awkwardness of defeating and then correcting Agathon at his own party. This is certainly not impossible, but as I have suggested above, such "corrections" would be a natural aspect of a *symposion*, so such a social fiction would be unnecessary. Another possibility is that Socrates invents the fiction of Diotima as a way to express his views on Eros while preserving the stance of Socratic irony and ignorance. Corrigan and Glazov-Corrigan suggest that this is a fair, but incidental explanation (p. 112). In the *Phaedrus* and the *Republic*, Socrates is not reticent about expounding his own convictions about things; further, since Socrates expresses his full agreement with Diotima, he shows no great interest in establishing or preserving an ironic distance. Yet another explanation is that making Diotima a seer, associated with mystery cults, lends her speech added authority. Corrigan and Glazov-Corrigan dismiss this as "foreign to Plato's presentation of Socrates" (p. 112). Their view, however, ignores the fact that Socrates does seem to accept the authority of the Delphic Oracle in the *Apology* (21b–c, 23a–b), as well as the recurrent interventions of the *daimonic*. A more interesting explanation of the function of Diotima relates not to Socratic irony, but to Platonic distance.

One of the striking facts about the *Symposium* is that Plato introduces a woman as the authority on love into what is otherwise a very masculine social setting, and in the context of Agathon's party, a highly homoerotic one. Indeed the institution of the *symposion* is exactly the domain for the "reproduction" and "nurturing" of those masculine and homoerotic values. Thus it is argued that in making Diotima the spokesperson for love, Plato is attempting to mitigate the charge that he is self-servingly making homoeroticism the foundation for philosophy. This sort of argument, Halperin contends, is more about male identity than female "difference" (Halperin 1990, p. 116). Rather than representing her function in positive terms, she is simply reduced to a "not-man." With regard to this positive identity, he notes, that Diotima's central metaphor is pregnancy. "The authentic aim of erotic desire, according to Diotima, is procreation (206e)" (p. 117). Elizabeth. E. Pender complains that Plato "fudges" the question of gender roles. Plato deploys two types of spiritual "pregnancy," she argues, a "male" type, playing on the metaphor of ejaculation and begetting, and a "female" type, playing on the metaphor of pregnancy and childbirth, but then silently shifts focus to the more conventional image of the creator of beautiful things as a man fathering his child (Pender 1992, p. 80).

For Halperin the fact of Diotima's gender dramatizes two aspects of Plato's erotic theory. First, in substituting the language and conventions of male society with the extended metaphor engendering, pregnancy, bearing, labor, bringing forth, and nurturing, "Platonic eros becomes not hierarchical, but reciprocal, not acquisitive but creative" (p. 130). Second, "Love is not for the possession of beauty, but for the procreation of it" (p. 137). As the "ascent" passage makes clear, sexual passion is not about physical gratification, but about moral and intellectual creativity. The mutual relationship between the lover and beloved is about the potentialities and energies that lead to the acts of self-expression that aspire to go beyond the self. I would argue that the question of gender difference shifts to the background with the deindividualization of the Diotima's reproductive language. In this way pregnancy, begetting, bearing, labor, and so forth, are no longer bound to gender identity. Therefore, neither the philosopher nor the task of the philosopher belongs to the privileged realm of one gender or another.

I would like to consider one additional possible function of Diotima. What is striking about Diotima's otherness is not merely that she is a woman in a company of men, that she is a foreigner among Athenian citizens, that she is a stranger at a party of friends, but that she represents a strong presence that is absent, or perhaps more precisely, she resides a step removed from the assembled banqueters at Agathon's party. As Corrigan and Glazov-Corrigan point out, Diotima exists only as a "mental image" (2004, p.115). This is reinforced by the fact that we are given no physical portrait of her; we do not really know whether she is young or old, tall or short, whether she is more like Bettie Page or Dame Edna Everage (perhaps in several senses, given the possibility that it is Socrates speaking through Diotima, rather than Diotima through Socrates).[9] Socrates' "image" or "representation" of her is not subject to the Platonic critique of mimetic art. Her "image" rather is signified first by her name and then by her speech. In a sense, she exists like Zeus in Aeschylus' *Agamemnon*: "Whoever, whatever he is, we will, if it please him, /address him as Zeus, a name we speak in awe" (Aeschylus 1998, p. 16). Her presence as a name signifies something real about her existence, but at the same time something outside or beyond a material appearance of the others. Indeed, her lack of an appearance underlines her material difference from Socrates and the banqueters, all of who would have been physically familiar to Plato's immediate Athenian audience. And of course, the particulars of Socrates' physical appearance are a prominent and recurrent motif. Diotima exists as something beyond the physical domain of Socrates and the others, yet capable of exercising an influence on it through the power of her discourse.

Corrigan and Glazov-Corrigan argue that part of Diotima's authority is not that she is a seer or mistress of mysteries, but that she provides Socrates with an "objective" stance (2004, p. 112). To the degree that we willingly grant Plato the suspension of our disbelief and accept the narrative fiction that Socrates is indeed merely recalling and reciting Diotima's speech, and not giving us an interpreted paraphrase, we all, along with Socrates, stand in the same position, equally outside and in the presence of a view of love. While each of the other speeches was mediated by the subjectivity of the speaker, Socrates' recitation is not. This of course does not mean that Diotima's speech is not mediated by her own subjectivity; her conception of love in terms of pregnancy and reproduction reflects elements of her identity as a woman. Nor does her speech articulate an objective truth in a larger sense; rather it dramatizes her difference in relation to all of the other speakers, and by extension, all subsequent readers.

Diotima's "presence" is symbolic of the entire process of immortality and ascent that she describes. Diotima is a presence at Agathon's party because Socrates felt compelled to repeat her words. She exists only because she said something that Socrates recalls, and in this recollection she transcends a specific time and place, achieving an immortality. She has helped a Socrates "pregnant in soul" give birth to beautiful wisdom. By this, Socrates creates his own discourse which is recollected and transmitted first by Aristodemus, then by Apollodorus, and finally by us as attentive readers.

Closely connected to the function of Diotima is the issue of the relationship between the five stages of the "ascent" passage and the five earlier speeches. I have already made some allusion to this above, and will consider this topic in greater detail in the next chapter, once we have added Alcibiades to the mix. Plato's text invites a variety of ways for combining the sequence of speakers. I would here like to look briefly at the "ascent" passage in relation to the narrative frames, that is our recollection of Apollodorus' recollection of Aristodemus' recollection of Socrates' recollection of Diotima's erotic vision of the beautiful. It does not require too much of a stretch to apply the erotic metaphor to the act of reading and interpretation. Each speech stimulates and helps to give birth to beautiful knowledge, just as our act of reading, a form of recollection, helps the "pregnant" readers bring forth words and discourse of their own. They possess the disposition or potentiality to respond favorably to what they hear, and with the proper guidance of the lover of wisdom, they may apprehend insight. Thus, we might trace the ascent up the ladder of love dramatized through the succession of narrators and narrative frames. First, the reader, the unnamed inquirer who initiates the *Symposium* by asking Apollodorus if he can remember the banquet and the speeches, desired to know something about appearances: Were you at the banquet? Can you tell me about it? Second, Apollodorus, who admits that he was not present at the banquet, desired to apprehend Socrates' soul by learning about his customs and practices from various sources, most notably from Aristodemus. Third, Aristodemus desired to apprehend beautiful knowledge by mimicking Socrates' customary behavior, even going about barefoot. Fourth, Socrates himself sought to gain wisdom from the erotic science of Diotima. Finally, Diotima herself gained her erotic science as part of her desire to glimpse a vision of the Beautiful.

In addition to tracing the stages of ascent through the succession of narrators, the nesting of narrative frames also reminds us that we are separated from Diotima's vision, that whatever we know about the beautiful is filtered by a succession of mediators. If we may assume that our mistress of the mysteries of love has herself glimpsed beauty itself, we must realize that we, like the initiates of the first four levels have only apprehended an image or phantom (*eidōlon*) of beauty, not beauty itself. All of this is an important reminder to the reader that though the text takes us to the top of the ladder of love, we should not suppose that we have ourselves glimpsed Diotima's vision of the beautiful. We have only a verbal image. Merely reading is not grasping or understanding. Our methodical study will lead us only through the first four stages of ascent. It will lay the necessary groundwork, nurture the potentiality, but it will not cause the sudden cognitive leap. We must wait for that to happen in its own good time, if at all, independent of our wills and out of our control.

All of this is finally a reminder that we as the readers are at the farthest remove from Diotima's vision; we must begin at the bottom of the ladder, and her vision of an absolute, pure, unconditional, imageless beauty can make the goal seem remote and insubstantial. It is therefore both ironic and appropriate that the philosophical calm represented by the absent and immaterial Diotima is "suddenly" disrupted by the very physical appearance of Alcibiades. If Diotima points to the remote goals of the erotic, Alcibiades reminds us of its very tangible presence, something outside our subjective control that can come crashing it at any moment.

3.3. THE ALCIBIADES, A SATYR PLAY

Moreover is not the style of argument which Socrates uses here one which stuns us equally by its simplicity and its ecstatic force? In truth it is far easier to talk like Aristotle and to live like Caesar than both to talk like Socrates and live like Socrates.

(Montaigne 1991, p. 1196)

"Suddenness" (*exaiphnēs*) marks the appearance of Alcibiades (212c), and "suddenness" (*exaiphnēs*) marks his sight of Socrates (213c), both ironic allusions to the "suddenness" (*exaiphnēs*) that marks Diotima's glimpse of the beautiful (210e). The arrival of Alcibiades opens the last act of the *Symposium*, which may be divided into three parts: the first is a sort of prologue about

Alcibiades' entrance onto the scene; the second is Alcibiades' *encomium* to Socrates; and the third is the conclusion and breakup of Agathon's banquet: It begins with the disruptive crash of revelers and ends with the disruptive crash of more revelers. Socrates sarcastically calls Alcibiades' performance a "little satyr play" (222d), an allusion that links a number of themes and motifs, including Alcibiades' state of intoxication, much in the spirit of the satyrs, half-human and half-goat, and Alcibiades' comparison of Socrates to the satyr king Silenus and then to the flute-playing satyr Marsyas. He also may be alluding to the theatrical convention of following a tragic trilogy with the emotional relief of a farce. It is appropriate that the seven serious contributions on love, especially at the banquet of a tragic poet should be leavened by the humor of a satyr play on love. Or, to play on another metaphor, having risen to the ethereal heights, we now fall back to something more earthly and earthy. With regard to this, many commentators have also noted that the serious speeches on love are framed by the dismissal of an *aulos*-girl (176e) at their commencement and the return of an *aulos*-girl, accompanying and supporting the drunk Alcibiades at the conclusion of Diotima's speech (Plato 1998, p. 135), her presence signaling the return of the raucous spirit of a more conventional *symposion*.

3.3.1. Alcibiades arrives (212c–215a)

Almost immediately after Socrates completes his speech, Agathon's banquet is "suddenly" disrupted by the arrival of a large party of drunken revelers shouting at the courtyard gate (212c). Agathon's sending a slave to investigate is quickly followed by the call of a very drunk Alcibiades, demanding to see Agathon. He makes his entrance supported by several slave attendants and an *aulos*-girl. There is a double irony here. Plutarch reports that the young Alcibiades refused to play the flute (*aulos*), declaring that it was "an ignoble and illiberal thing" (Plutarch 1954, p. 7). Further, some scholars suggest that Plato dramatizes a political irony, that the great politician is literally supported by slaves and flute-girls, a judgment on the political base of a demagogue (Plato 1994, p. 203). He is adorned with a crown of violets and ivy, and ribbons in his hair. Managing to stand on his own, he asks to join the party or at least be allowed to crown Agathon. A loquacious drunk, he explains: "see, I'm wearing the garland myself. I want this crown to come directly from my head to the head it belongs, I don't mind saying, to the cleverest and best looking man in town" (212e–213a). In retrospect his words take on an unexpected irony. He does indeed ultimately crown the man he judges to be the cleverest and best-looking (figuratively speaking), but it turns out to be Socrates rather than Agathon.

Alcibiades essentially invites himself to Agathon's party. Ever the gracious host, Agathon asks him to share a place next to him on his couch, and Alcibiades struggles to remove the garland crown, which has fallen over his eyes. To this point in the dim lamplight, he has not seen Socrates, who is on Agathon's couch. Alcibiades takes a place between Agathon and Socrates, symbolically between the sophistic poet and the philosopher. Kissing Agathon, and putting the ribbons on his head, Alcibiades turns to the other couch-mate, "suddenly" (*exaiphnēs*) seeing Socrates for the first time: "By Hercules, what's going on here? It's Socrates! You've trapped me again! You always do this to me—all of a sudden you'll turn up out of nowhere where I least expect you!" (213c). His words combine a mixture of anger and affection, ridicule and passion. He snidely asks why Socrates is not sitting next to Aristophanes or others, "who want to be laughed at," instead of contriving to be next to "the most beautiful person in the house" (213c)?

In presumably mock fear, Socrates implores Agathon to defend him, explaining that "he hasn't allowed me to say two words to anyone else—what am I saying, I can't so much as look at an attractive man but that gets jealous and resentful, and does extraordinary things, calling me names and scarcely able to stop himself from hitting me" (213d). Playing on the comic incongruity of the effeminate playwright protecting the tough old philosopher from the athletic soldier-politician, Socrates asks Agathon to prevail on Alcibiades to forgive him. "The fierceness of his passion terrifies me!" (213d).

Alcibiades declares that he will never forgive Socrates, promising to pay him back for this presumed infidelity. Then in a sudden change in tone, he asks Agathon to give him back some of the ribbons he has just given him, that he might crown Socrates as well, claiming that Socrates will otherwise make a scene. "He'll be grumbling that, though I crowned you for your first victory, I didn't honor him even though he has never lost an argument in his life" (213e). So saying, he arranges the ribbons on that "wondrous head [*thaumastēn kaphalēn*]" (213e). Alcibiades' words reveal the existence of a history, a prior relationship that still smolders and bursts out. Envious, jealous, possessive, cruel, violent, his passion for Socrates speaks more to the palpable *ode et amo* of Catullus, loving more but liking less (Catullus 72), or to the Petrarchan trope of bitter sweet love than to the remote ethereal love of Diotima. His words paint an uncomfortably realistic portrait of a dangerous and obsessive passion, just steps away from physical violence. At the same time Alcibiades' words also seem to reveal a jealousy and possessiveness on the part of Socrates as well, petulant if his own achievements are not properly acknowledged.

All of this acknowledges that *eros* is not something simple, but complex and contradictory. It cannot be reduced to rational explanation, but embraces an array of contrary emotions, love and hate, possessiveness and selflessness, attraction and repulsion without any sense of inconsistency or incoherence. This love is something both real and outside of our control. On another level, Alcibiades' words also relate to his perplexity, his inability to comprehend Socrates in all his "wondrousness" and all his "strangeness." Socrates is his "problem." His passion derives from inability to explain a passion that falls outside the conventional boundaries of erotic attraction. Socrates, as Alcibiades reminds us, offers neither the attractions of physical beauty nor the charms of seductive love talk. Yet despite Socrates' ugliness and his plain speech, Alcibiades finds himself uncontrollably attracted to him.

In 416 BCE, the setting of Agathon's party, Alcibiades would have been about thirty-four years old. He had survived near-ostracism after a Spartan victory at Mantinea in 418 defeated a coalition he had put together with Athens, Mantinea, and Elis, and it is a little over a year before he would be implicated in the affair of the *hermai* and the disastrous Sicilian expedition of 415. Alcibiades (ca. 450–404 BCE), was an Athenian general and politician, and among the most controversial figures in Athens, famous for his personal ambition and profligate lifestyle. The historian Thucydides, who knew him, reports that "most people became frightened at a quality in him which was beyond the normal and showed itself both in the lawlessness of his private life and habits and in the spirit in which he acted on all occasions" (Thucydides 1954, p. 376). The son of Cleinias, he was brought up in the household of his guardian, Pericles. Charismatic but polarizing, Alcibiades was a potent demagogue, building his power base among the extreme democrats of Athenian society, positing himself as a guardian of the people against the old aristocracy. His physical beauty was as legendary as Socrates' ugliness. Plutarch says, "it is perhaps unnecessary to say ought, except that it flowered out with each successive season of his bodily growth" (Plutarch 1954, p. 5). If we accept Alcibiades' confession in the *Symposium* that he came to know Socrates and tried to seduce him sometime before their service together in the 432 BCE Potidaea campaign, he would probably have been seventeen or eighteen years old. Ten years later on the death of Cleon, Alcibiades became a leading figure in Athenian politics. Shifting allegiances, exiles and recalls marked his turbulent career. Aristophanes expresses Athenian ambivalence toward the exiled Alcibiades in the comedy, *The Frogs* (405 BCE): "She [Athens] loves, and hates, and longs to have him back" (1425). In 404 BCE, he was assassinated in Asia Minor by Persian agents, probably at the instigation of the Thirty Tyrants (of Athens). The setting of Apollodorus' and Aristodemus' recitation of the events about Agathon's party would have been some time shortly after Alcibiades' murder, and perhaps the recent news of his death might have aroused a curiosity about the party.

Much of the enmity against Socrates that eventually culminated in his trial and execution is related to his supposed association with Alcibiades. Xenophon insisted that though Alcibiades was a pupil of Socrates, he was not really a disciple but merely wanted to use an affiliation with Socrates to advance his own career. The Athenian orator Isocrates (436–338 BCE), himself a follower of Socrates, made a similar point (Nails 2002, p. 10). In his *Erotikos* (*Erotic Essay*), the orator Demosthenes claimed "that Alcibiades, though his natural disposition was far inferior in respect to virtue and it was his pleasure to behave himself now arrogantly, now obsequiously, now licentiously, yet, as a fruit of his association with Socrates, made correction of many errors . . ." (Demosthenes 1949, p. 73). A handful of surviving fragments from the *Alcibiades* remain extant, one of seven Socratic dialogues by Aeschines of Sphettus, a close disciple of Socrates, and present at both his trial and death. Trying to exonerate Socrates for his association with Alcibiades, he records Socrates' lamenting his failure: "And I, through the love that I had for Alcibiades, felt just as the Bacchants do. For whenever they are inspired they draw honey and milk where others cannot even draw water." Aeschines' Socrates adds (in terms reminiscent of Phaedrus and Pausanias), "I though knowing no lesson through which I could benefit a man by teaching, nevertheless believed that by being together with the man I could make him better through love" (Aeschines 2003, p. 97). In effect, Aeschines' Socrates failed to give birth to noble deeds and words in Alcibiades. Plato's *Symposium*, as we shall see, seems to make more of the relationship. Alcibiades also appears in Plato's *Protagoras*, the *Gorgias*, the *Euthyphro*, and the eponymous *Alcibiades* I and II, though the authenticity of these last two is debated.

Having crowned Socrates, Alcibiades reclines on the couch between Agathon and Socrates, only to jump up again immediately when he realizes that everyone else at this drinking party is sober. Seizing control, he appoints himself symposiarch, calling for a large cup. He orders that a slave bring him a "wine-cooler" full of wine, almost half-a-gallon.[10] Draining it, he orders it refilled and given to Socrates, though he laments that no one has ever seen Socrates drunk, no matter how much he drinks. Annoyed by this usurpation of the conventions of the *symposion*, Eryximachus intervenes, complaining of the impropriety of just drinking without the appropriate recitation or song. "Eryximachus!" he responds with exaggerated drunken courtesy. "Best of sons of the best and most sensible father, greetings to you!" (214b). When the physician persists in wanting to observe the niceties of tradition, Alcibiades relents: "so give us your instructions" (214b).

The physician explains the plan of delivering speeches praising Love. Since everyone else has already done so, he proposes that Alcibiades take his proper turn and also give a speech praising Love, then according to the rules, he can order Socrates (as the person to his right) to do what he wants. Alcibiades approves this proposal, but demurs that it is not fair for a drunken man to compete against a sober one, adding: "I hope, my fine friend, you do not believe what Socrates just said? The truth is just the opposite! He's the one who will most surely beat me up if I dare praise anyone else in his presence, even a god!" (214d). Whether Alcibiades is simply the bully projecting his own behavior onto Socrates, exaggerating, or actually revealing some intimacy, Socrates tells him to hold his tongue, to which Alcibiades retorts, "don't you dare deny it" (214d). His remarks to Socrates sound like the knowing challenge of one who seems to possess some shared secret, personal or professional, to which the others are not privy. This is similar in tone to Thrasymachus' challenge in the *Republic*: "you know very well that it is much easier to ask questions than to answer them" (336c–d).

To resolve the problem, Eryximachus proposes that Alcibiades offer an *encomium* to Socrates instead; that way he cannot be jealous. Alcibiades warms to this proposal, wondering ominously if he might not unleash himself on Socrates, in order to punish him in front of the others. When Socrates protests that he does not want to be praised simply to be mocked, Alcibiades insists he will only tell the truth, an assertion he reiterates throughout his speech as a point of emphasis: "Do I have your permission?" (214e). Socrates grants it, but remarks with sarcastic irony, "I would certainly like to hear the truth from you" (214e). Alcibiades insists that Socrates can interrupt and make corrections. Then in a disclaimer that curiously echoes Socrates' earlier request to tell the truth "my way" (199b), Alcibiades says, "you can't hold it against me if I don't get everything in the right order; I'll say things as they come to mind" (215a). He then adds, "even a sober and unclouded mind would find it hard to come to terms with your strangeness [*atopian*]" (215a).

Paradoxically what Alcibiades *knows* is that Socrates is *unknowable* to him and to others. *Atopos* means literally "no-place" or "out-of-place," and figuratively "odd" or "strange." It can also mean "outrageousness" or "absurdity," according to Gregory Vlastos (Vlastos 1991, p. 1), citing Callicles' exclamation in the *Gorgias*: "how outrageous [*atopos*] you are Socrates" (494d). Adeimantus' designation of Socrates as "you wondrous man [*thaumasie*]" in the *Republic* (366d), expresses the same experience of Socratic *strangeness* in a higher register. In all these cases, Socrates falls outside the comprehensible in the sense that he is different from everyone else. He cannot be placed; he does not fit any frame of reference that they possess. This "placelessness," argues Corrigan and Glazov-Corrigan, disarms Alcibiades, causing his perplexity and violent emotions (2004, p. 172). He cannot deny the palpable reality of his passion, yet he cannot understand it. Socrates is a great mystery. He is old, not young, ugly, not beautiful, poor, without power, wealth, or influence. He does not fit the pattern of the typical object of love. Conversely he seems impervious to Alcibiades' beauty and sexual advances. Summarizing toward the end of his speech, Alcibiades declares that while all the great statesmen and heroes can be compared with others, Socrates is absolutely unique: "so strange [*atopian*] is he, both in himself and in the things he says, one wouldn't come even close to finding anyone like him if one looked, whether among men now or among those in the past, unless perhaps if one were to compare him to the figures I'm talking about, not to anyone human, but to silenuses and satyrs" (221d). Like the satyrs, he is neither quite human nor animal. Like the *daimonic* he is neither god nor human. Rather, Socrates is Socrates, unique, self-defining, a tautology.

We see in Alcibiades' erotic love of Socrates the opposite of what the others described in the earlier speeches. Shame has made him shameless in his behavior, unrepentant for how his actions will be perceived by others. He feels disharmony between his nature and experience, between what he thinks he knows and what he feels, a discord that leads to slashing, wounding behavior. Instead of nobility and justice, he feels impelled to deceit and treachery. Rather than seeking to give birth to beautiful words and deeds, he pursues sexual gratification. Yet all of this is a common and observable part of the erotic experience and cannot be dismissed as aberrant.

3.3.2. In praise of Socrates (215a–222c)

Alcibiades' speech differs from the others, including that of Diotima, in several striking regards. He speaks, as Richard Hunter points out, in the autobiographical mode of a legal speech (Hunter 2004, p. 104), someone pleading his case before a jury of his peers. In this he is the only speaker at Agathon's party who explicitly claims to tell the truth. The others may certainly believe what they say; Agathon, as we have already noted, offers at least a partial assent in his claim to being "moderately serious as best I could manage"(197e), but they are also speaking under the rhetorical imperative to be eloquent and persuasive rather than necessarily true. Thus, unlike the other speeches, Alcibiades speaks directly about his own experiences, from the perspective of one who is actually in love, accompanied with all of its emotional complexity. In modes both confessional and defiant, the content of his speech comes straight from his own heart. While we have no reason to doubt that Phaedrus and Eryximachus or Pausanias and Agathon love each other, they are not speaking to each other directly from the intensity of their own passions; they are not explicitly drawing on their own direct experiences of love. Rather, each treats love as something abstract and theoretical, their examples borrowed from myth or history. In sharp contrast, Alcibiades speaks of his own personal erotic passion, and more to the point, the object of that erotic passion is sitting next to him as he speaks. There is a concreteness to his account of love that differs from the other speeches. Similarly, there is a marked physicality in Alcibiades' image of Socrates that is missing in Socrates' image of Diotima. Socrates is a palpable presence while Diotima remains remote. As I discussed above, she is a presence who is absent, a mental image with no physical attributes aside from that of her speech at the center of the party. By contrast, Socrates is an absence that is present, absent, at least, in the sense that he is "no place" (*atopos*), not able to be placed, according to Alcibiades.

Second, Alcibiades' speech resonates with the others in that Alcibiades becomes the concrete example, the test case for the various theoretical models of love. Even though his behavior seems to belie what the others claimed about the moral character of *eros*, his love of Socrates reiterates various aspects of what was said by the others, vividly illustrating the strengths and the weaknesses of each. At the same time his disclaimer that because he is drunk, he should not be held responsible for getting everything in the right order indicates that Plato is not necessarily recapitulating the different views of love as they originally unfolded around the table. Alcibiades' ambivalent *encomium* of Socrates can broadly be divided into four parts: the first (215c–216b) focuses on the similes of the silenuses and the satyr Marsyas, and echoes elements of Eryximachus and Aristophanes. The second part (216b–217a) centers on his ambivalent feelings about Socrates, especially shame, and shows links with Phaedrus and Pausanias. The third part (219d–222c) is about Alcibiades' attempt to seduce Socrates. His interpolated dialogue with the philosopher offers parallels with Socrates' conversation with Diotima. Finally Alcibiades offers a series of recollections illustrating Socrates' virtues, his account resonating with aspects of Agathon's speech.

3.3.2.1. (215c–216b)

Alcibiades begins his speech by declaring that he will praise Socrates "through images [*di eikonōn*]" (215a). With this in mind, he offers two extended similes that have since become among the most famous and often cited creations of the *Symposium*:

> The purpose of the image will in fact be to tell the truth, not to be amusing. I declare that he is most like those silenuses that sit in the statuary-shops, the ones the craftsmen make, with pipes or auloi, and when you open them up by taking them apart, they turn out to have statues of gods inside them. I declare, too, that he's like the satyr Marsyas. Now, that you're like them in your physical appearance, not even you, Socrates, would dispute. (215a–b)

Alcibiades' similes are complex and multileveled. First, and most directly, they speak to describing Socrates' appearance. The figures of Silenus, the half-human, half-goat king of the satyrs and the satyr Marsyas evoke the iconic portrait of Socrates found in Xenophon's *Symposium*, Aristophanes' *Clouds*, and a variety of other works. Further tracing the complexity of this trope, we should recall that the satyrs were the companions of the god Dionysus and infamous for their drunkenness and lechery. If the ecstatic madness associated with the god subverts the rational order, transcending existential boundaries, the drunken misrule of the satyrs overturns the norms of life. A tragic vision of life is reiterated as farce. This undercurrent is most evident in the story of Silenus and King Midas.

For Alcibiades' and Plato's audiences, the figure of Silenus would likely produce associations with the story of Silenus and King Midas (Usher 2002, p. 206). Old Silenus is known as the most drunken of the satyrs, but also the wisest. There are several variants, but Midas desires to capture the satyr king that he might gain wisdom about the human condition. The king's servants spike the river with wine, so that Silenus gets drunk, falls asleep, and is thereby trapped. (In another version he simply falls asleep in Midas' rose garden.) In exchange for wisdom, Midas offers to give Silenus his freedom. In other versions, it is the golden touch. Usher quotes the earliest extant version of Silenus' answer, from a poem by Theognis, a work that comes out of the sympotic tradition:

> For men who dwell on the earth, it is best of all not to be born
> Nor to see the rays of the dazzling sun.
> For the man who is born, it is best to enter the gates of Death as soon as he can
> And lie buried under a pile of dirt. (Usher 2002, p. 211)

Usher points out that the story of Silenus and Midas is part of a larger motif about the encounter of a rich man questioning a wise one. He points to the exchanges between Solon and Croesus found in the *Histories* of Herodotus as another example of this traditional motif (Usher 2002, p. 210). In one instance, Solon's answer to one question is that it is better for a man to be dead than alive. In answer to another, that is best to die in one's sleep upon achieving a great goal, citing the cases of Cleobis and Bition. In each case, we have a pessimistic vision of the human condition. The parallels with the rich Alcibiades seeking wisdom from the Silenic Socrates are obvious, though as we shall see, Socrates proves more alert and wary than the old satyr, despite Alcibiades' various attempts to get him drunk or trap him.

Alcibiades' Silenus is here portrayed holding a reed pipe (*aulos*). The mystical figure of Marsyas was also a famous *aulos*-player. It does not take a Freudian to find phallic undertones in the image of *aulos*-playing satyrs. Surviving figurines and vase paintings typically portray the satyrs sporting (comically) grotesque erections. Such images would likely have decorated the drinking vessels at a *symposion*. We might also recall that the *aulos*-girls often provided sexual as well as musical services.

In addition to the erotic implications of the *aulos* and the Dionysian, Alcibiades extends his second simile, focusing on the spellbinding power of the music. "He [Marsyas] used to charm people by means of instruments, by the power that came from his mouth" (215c). In imagery that resonates with Diotima, he notes that Marsyas' melodies could possess those people who are ready for the gods and their rites of initiation [*teletē*] (215c). We might also recall Eryximachus' view on the role of harmony and music in the order of the cosmos. Extending the trope yet a step further, Alcibiades compares his own emotional possession by Socrates' words with the ecstatic frenzies of the Corybantes: "my heart starts leaping in my chest, the tears come streaming down my face . . ." (215e). The Corybantes were devotees of the goddess Cybele, the Great Mother (*Magna Mater*) whose cult came out of Asia.[11] (Some versions of the myth of Marsyas also portray him a follower of Cybele.) Like the *aulos*-player, Socrates uses the power that comes from his mouth to charm and possess his devotees.[12] Thus in the images of Silenus and Marsyas, Socrates is represented in his ugliness, coupled with hints of his erotic character, and his strange, even dangerous power over people.

Alcibiades' similes also speak to Socrates' interiority, trying to represent what falls outside the realm of appearance. Alcibiades' *silenuses* open up to reveal the images of gods.[13] Richard Hunter notes the analogy between the statues of gods inside the statue of Silenus and Diotima's lover pregnant with beautiful words and deeds (Hunter 2004, p. 100). Beneath the appearance of something ugly and dangerous is something beautiful and morally nourishing. In other words, although Socrates may be satyr-like on the outside, he is beautiful and wholesome on the inside. This becomes a recurrent motif in Alcibiades' account of his attempts to seduce Socrates. Appearances that would seem to bode lust reveal something noble. All of this is the visual correlative with Alcibiades' inability to comprehend Socrates. A person who looks like a satyr ought to act like one: a person who drinks ought to get drunk; a person who is exposed to a beautiful body ought to be tempted by lust. At the same time, if Alcibiades' *silenuses* reveal the beauty that he finds concealed under the appearance of Socrates, they also reveal what he finds concealed under his own appearance. Whether a function of his drunken truthfulness, or unintended irony, Alcibiades reveals himself to be the opposite of Socrates in the double sense of beautiful on the outside, but ugly on the inside.

At the end of his speech, Alcibiades recalls another aspect about the motif of interiority and exteriority. Not only does the disparity of ugliness on the outside, beauty on the inside pertain to Socrates himself, but it also applies to his arguments, we might say his "texts." Alcibiades notes that Socrates' arguments seem rude and ridiculous, clothed in the words of craftsmen: "he's always making the same tired old points in the same tired old words" (221e). But if one is attentive, his arguments reveal themselves as serious and divine: "They're truly worthy of a god, bursting with figures of virtue inside. They're great—no, of the greatest—importance for anyone who wants to become a truly good man" (222a). To those initiated into the mysteries of Socrates, his words open up to reveal great beauty. Alcibiades' assessment of Socrates' arguments introduces the metaphor of the Silenic text, crucial to the subsequent influence of the *Symposium* in literature and philosophy.

There is another important, though more implicit dimension in Alcibiades' imagery. Each involves violence and suffering. This is less evident in the simile of the *sileni*. In the mythic account of King Midas and Silenus discussed above, the old satyr is compelled to divulge the pessimistic secret of the human condition, that it is best not to be born, and falling short of that, to die as soon as possible. Thus underlying the themes of drunken merriment, there is an undercurrent of sorrow and human suffering associated with the figure. At the same time violence is an important component to the stories behind Marsyas and the Corybantes. In the mythical account of Marsyas, the satyr challenges Apollo, god of music, to a musical contest. Inevitably losing, he is punished for his hubris by being flayed alive, a popular theme among Renaissance painters, perhaps most famously Titian. Alcibiades does not mention that part of the myth in the *Symposium*, though the Greco-Roman historian Plutarch said that Alcibiades led a schoolboy revolt against instruction in the *aulos*, citing the fate of Marsyas. Plato is certainly familiar with the satyr's fate. In the *Euthydemus*, Ctesippus tells Socrates that he would not mind if he were flayed (figuratively speaking), as long as he did not end up a leather wine bottle, like Marsyas (285c). In a perverse way, the flaying of Marsyas is another version of the theme of interior and exterior. If we may open up the ugly *silenuses* to get at their beautiful interior, then we are invited to remove the skin of Marsyas to get at his inner being. Is the irony implicit in Alcibiades' trope? Much as he is confounded and perplexed by the paradoxical beauty of Socrates' inner being, does he also sometimes wish that he could skin him alive? The violence of some of his retorts suggests this. This is reinforced and elaborated when he compares himself to the Corybantes. It is important to recall that the priests of the Great Goddess were eunuchs, and that the ecstatic frenzy involves self-mutilation. In broader terms, we might also recall the violence associated with the maenads, the devotees of the god Dionysus, famously dramatized in the *Bacchae* of Euripides.[14] Alcibiades' imagery then, also speaks to the emotional abuse directed outwardly at Socrates, as well as to self-mutilation directed against himself.

In passing, the whole motif of the satyr king's statues that could be opened up might also have served to remind Plato's audience of the vandalism done to the *hermai*, so closely linked with the political downfall of Alcibiades.

In summary, the similes about the *silenuses*, Marsyas, and the Corybantes, lay the groundwork for the rest of his speech, playing on variations of the tensions between appearance and reality, between exterior and interior, the spell of Socrates, and the emotional violence evoked by an erotic passion for Socrates, all of these related to the "strangeness" of Socrates. They also pick up or play with elements from the conceptions of *erōs* found in Eryximachus and Aristophanes. I have already alluded to the theme of music and its power over people in connection to Eryximachus' treatment of harmony and concord. Paradoxically, however, being in harmony with the music of the satyrs (or Socrates) can also produce a discord in the soul of Alcibiades. His psychic state needs to be healed; the proper harmony needs to be established by Socrates the physician. He comprehends snatches of the Socratic music, but is tone deaf, unable to harmonize his soul with that of Socrates. In a similar manner, Aristophanes, like Alcibiades thinks of *erōs* in terms of a deep wound, the product of violence against the very being of the individual. But where the drive of love for the comic playwright is to rejoin the divided tissues, to heal the soul and make it whole, Alcibiades sees it in terms of an opening up, a splitting apart, a violent exposing of the interior. It is exactly the awareness of profound differences, and incomprehensible separateness that characterizes the nature of his passion.

3.3.2.2. (216b–217a)

Trying to explain the power that Socrates exercises over him, Alcibiades notes that none of the great orators moved or upset him the way that Socrates did. Incredulously, Socrates has made him feel that his own life is no better than that of a slave's (215e), even though he is handsome, wealthy, a member of the aristocracy, a successful politician at the top of his game, and by all conventional measures a success. He laments that "[Socrates] makes it seem that my life isn't worth living" (216a). To complete the thought, we should recall Socrates' famous declaration in the *Apology* that the unexamined life is not worth living (38a). Turning first to Socrates, he accuses: "you can't say that isn't true, Socrates," then turning to the group as a whole, he explains: "He always traps me, you see, and he makes me admit that my political career is a waste of time, while all that matters is just what I most neglect" (216a). Socrates, he explains, is the only person who makes him feel ashamed.[15] However, contrary to what had been described by Phaedrus and Pausanias, Alcibiades does not seek to mend his desires, but rather to avoid his lover altogether. He even admits that there are times when he might wish that Socrates were dead, at the same time also admitting that his grief would be even greater. "So I just don't know what to do with this man" (216c).

Thus far his behavior stands in complex relation to the moral conceptions of love described by Phaedrus and Pausanias. On one hand his love for Socrates had made him feel regret at shaming himself in the eyes of his lover, yet this shame was not strong enough to modify his behavior. Ironically, his response is to avoid Socrates' presence rather than live up to his expectations. Erotic passion has not made him better. More exactly, though he knows better, or at least cannot counter Socrates' arguments, and even feels shame at not doing what was agreed between them, he nevertheless persists in returning to his old bad habits. Knowing is not the same as doing.

Alcibiades now proposes to describe the powerful effects of this satyr's music (216c), declaring that he will expose Socrates and reveal to everyone what he is really like (216d), to get past appearances to the authentic Socrates: Like Silenus, "he is in love [*erōtikōs*] with beautiful boys; he constantly follows them around in a perpetual daze" (216d), claiming to know nothing about his appearance. He does not care if the boy is rich, beautiful, or famous "in the eyes of ordinary people" (216e), considering all of this as beneath contempt. But like the silenuses this is all an elaborate show. He may be acting like a drunken, lustful satyr in his apparent bewilderment, but the deep dark secret is that behind this façade of erotic passion Socrates is the model of sobriety and temperance. In mock denunciation, Alcibiades declares: "In public, I tell you, his whole life [is] playing and ironizing [*eirōneuomenos*]" (216e). He then adds that he once beheld (*eidō*) the god-like figures hidden within the silenus: "they were so god-like, so bright and beautiful, so utterly amazing [*thaumasta*]" (217a), that he felt compelled to do whatever Socrates told him.

3.3.2.3. (217a–219d)
Supposing that Socrates was attracted to his beauty and wanted him sexually, Alcibiades decides that all he has to do is let Socrates have his way with him, "and he would teach me everything he knew. Believe me, I had a lot of confidence in my looks" (217a). Paradoxically, Alcibiades' views are confused. On one hand he sees in Socrates' attraction to him the recognition of some nobler qualities. For this he feels gratitude. But on the other hand, he also easily confuses this honorable love of inner nobility with worldly love and its external attractions. He supposes that Socrates possesses some secret knowledge that will give him benefits. "All I had to do was to let him have his way with me, and he would teach me everything he knew" (217a). He thinks of Socratic wisdom as though it were a fungible commodity. Ironically, he is correct that the love of Socrates will make him a better person, but he has not understood what it means to be a better person, supposing it is about worldly successes or some other material benefit.

Alcibiades describes a series of plots to seduce Socrates, or more precisely to provide Socrates with the opportunity to seduce him. On one occasion he sent the attendants away so that he and Socrates could meet alone, assuming that he would naturally take advantage of the opportunity to seduce him. To his chagrin, Socrates' behavior was no different from normal. On another occasion he arranged that they exercise and wrestle together, conventionally in the nude, at the gymnasium, hoping that the physical contract might tempt Socrates. Xenophon records Socrates saying that when his nude shoulder happened once to press against that of young Critobulus, he felt as though he had been bitten by a wild animal: "and for over five days my shoulder smarted and I felt as if I had something like a sting in my heart" (4.28). Whatever Socrates may have felt literally and figuratively wrestling Alcibiades, his behavior remained exemplary. Alcibiades therefore determines to take an active role, reversing the erotic polarity between lover and beloved. "I was the lover [*erastēs*] plotting to have his way with his darling boy [*paidikois*]" (217c). In so doing, he in effect admits to the group at Agathon's party that as the inferior member assuming the active role, he has violated the rules of the erotic decorum; he could be accused of being a *katapugōn* or *kinaidos*.

Setting the context for what follows, Alcibiades appeals to his immediate audience that only other people who have been bitten by a snake can truly understand the pain of snakebite. So only those present, addressing each of the guests at Agathon's party by name, who have also been bitten by philosophy can really appreciate what he is saying, and therefore forgive his shameful behavior. He explains that he feels a profound pain in his heart (*kardian*) or soul (*psuchēn*), "whatever one's supposed to call it" (218a). The qualification points to his concern to be true to the spirit of philosophical precision, at the same time acknowledging his uncertainty about the actual nature of what he is talking about beyond the fact that he feels something real and profound. He quickly explains that he has been, "bitten by the words that philosophy brings with her [*tōn en philosophia logōn*]" (218a). Looking around, he observes that everyone present has some inkling of the experience he is describing: "You've all shared in the madness [*manias*] and the Bacchic frenzy [*bakcheias*] of philosophy" (218b). Echoing themes developed in the Socrates/Diotima speech, and from the *Phaedrus*, philosophy is conceived not so much a calm discourse, but a manic drive. Further, picking up Diotima's language of higher mysteries, he asserts that only the uninitiated or profane (*bebēlos*) could not appreciate what he says and forgive his behavior.

With this qualification in mind, Alcibiades unfolds an account of how he attempted to seduce Socrates. He has finally gotten Socrates alone late one night. The lamps are out, the servants sent away, and Alcibiades and Socrates are stretched out on adjoining couches. In a manner both ingratiating and arrogant, he opens himself up to the philosopher, observing that Socrates was the only worthy lover [*erastēs*] he had ever had (218c). He declares that it is pointless not to gratify Socrates as a lover, and to grant him anything he might desire with regard to material benefit or influence. Playing on the rules that the true beloved will thereby benefit from the gratitude of the lover, he adds, "there is nothing more important for me than my becoming as good a person as possible, and no one can help me more that you to reach that aim" (218d). Responding to this offer, Socrates initially takes Alcibiades at his word that he wants to be a good person, that such a desire reveals a nobility of character on his part that sees past the ugliness of surface to the beauty beneath: "If you are right in what you say about me, you are already more accomplished than you think" (218d–e). He goes on to explain, "if I really have in me the power to make you a better man, then you can see in me a beauty that is really beyond description and makes your own remarkable good looks pale in comparison" (218e). In other words, if Alcibiades has truly understood the benefits that Socrates as a lover has to offer, then he also realizes that the corresponding benefits of physical beauty, material good, or influence are trivial by comparison; Alcibiades would seem to be offering bronze in exchange for gold (219a). He further suggests that perhaps Alcibiades has misread him. "The mind's sight becomes sharp only when the body's eyes go past their prime" (219a).

Alcibiades persists in his conviction that it is for Socrates to guide him in the manner of a mentor/lover. The philosopher acquiesces, saying, "in the future, let's consider things together. We'll always do what seems the best to the two of us" (219b). Thinking that he has nearly achieved his erotic goal, Alcibiades slips next to Socrates, putting his arms around him, "this truly superhuman [*daimoniō*, literally *daimon*-like] and amazing [*thaumastō*] man, and lay there all night long" (219b). At this point in his story, Alcibiades turns back to his audience at Agathon's, rhetorically seeking sympathy and accusing Socrates of arrogance, insolence, and pride: "He spurned my beauty" (219c), framing this in terms of a change brought before a jury: "you're here to sit in judgment of Socrates' amazing arrogance and pride" (219c). The crime: "be sure of it [*eu gar iste*], I swear to you by all the gods and goddesses together, my night with Socrates went no further than if I had spent it with my own father or older brother!" (219c–219d). Ironically Alcibiades affirms and underlines the truth of his claim by the same sophistic verbal formula Diotima uses with Socrates: *eu iste* (208c). In a comic inversion, the dark and shameful secret of the *katapugōn* or *kinaidos* turns out to be that his relationship with Socrates was entirely virtuous, despite his best efforts to the contrary.

Alcibiades explains that this seeming rebuff has left him humiliated, shamed, and in his perplexity, guilty. At the same time, he is drawn all the more strongly to Socrates, awed by his character, his moderation and his fortitude: "here was a man whose strength and wisdom went beyond my wildest dreams! How could I bring myself to hate him? I couldn't bear to lose his friendship. But how could I possibly win him over?" (219d). With characteristic self-regard, he assumes that resistance to his own attractions must represent an act of profound strength. In short, Socrates humiliates him, but for that very reason he cannot help being drawn to him. The irony that Alcibiades fails to grasp is that in his resistance to sexual consummation, Socrates is in fact honoring him, offering him the benefits of a true lover. That Socrates has kept his composure is not an expression of disinterestedness, but exactly his erotic passion. Were he to give in and physically consummate his relationship with Alcibiades, he would be like the non-lover described in the speech by Lysias in the *Phaedrus*. It is the measure of Socrates' true erotic attachment that he has resisted the strong physical power in Alcibiades for the sake of the spiritual.

In acknowledging his humiliation and shame, Alcibiades indicates at least an intuition of the distinction between heavenly love and earthly love that Pausanias took as the jumping-off place for his views of *erōs*. He recognizes that the honorable lover is drawn to what is noble and good in the beloved, a heavenly love that is "by nature stronger and more intelligent" (188c). Socrates has been an honorable lover (*erastēs*) to the beloved (*erōmenos*) Alcibiades consistent with the terms laid out by Pausanias. In resisting Alcibiades' advances, Socrates is acting in terms of the heavenly love rather than the earthly. While on the surface this refusal to acquiesce to Alcibiades' desire for sexual union seems contrary to Pausanias' claim that "the lover's total and willing subjugation to his beloved's wishes is neither servile nor reprehensible" (184c). In fact Socrates exemplifies it. In sublimating his own erotic desires, he affirms the higher character of the beloved. In not "having his way" with Alcibiades, Socrates treats him as one who possesses nobility, as one who is worthy of respect—in Diotima's terms, one pregnant with beautiful words and deeds.

3.3.2.4. (219d–222c)
Alcibiades next illustrates Socrates' character by recounting their subsequent experiences on the Potidaea campaign (432–430 BCE) and the Delium expedition (424 BCE). Each episode illustrates both Socrates' virtues and his incomparable strangeness. The first relates to Socrates' fortitude and endurance. During the Potidaea campaign, when he and Socrates were tent mates, Alcibiades recalled that no one stood up to hunger like Socrates, yet could enjoy a feast, when it was available. Similarly he noted that no one could out drink Socrates (220a), reiterating his earlier remark that no one had ever seen Socrates drunk (214a). Similarly, despite the bitter cold, Socrates went around barefoot dressed only in his usual light apparel, while others wore fur-lined boots. On another occasion he recalled Socrates' propensity for spells of persistent abstraction, and concentration. Thinking about some problem, he simply stood attached to the same spot all day, through the night, until the following morning, when he finally resolved his problem and then went on with his business (220c–220d). Some even moved their bedding outside to watch the spectacle.

Alcibiades now turns to Socrates' behavior in battle, offering a tribute to his courage, his calm, his grace under fire. He explains how Socrates saved his life, and even his armor, when Alcibiades had been wounded in battle. (His story picks up and echoes elements of the story of Patroclus and Achilles.) Ironically, for this gallantry, it was Alcibiades who was awarded a decoration for bravery, a matter he himself attributes to the generals' desire to ingratiate themselves with his aristocratic family. While Socrates, in his modesty, enthusiastically endorsed Alcibiades' receipt of this award, Alcibiades contends that it really belonged to Socrates: "I must say, you [Socrates] were more eager than the generals themselves for me to have it" (220c). During the disastrous retreat from Delium Socrates further showed his courage and prudence. From the relative safety of the cavalry Alcibiades was able to watch the deportment of Socrates, a foot soldier, during the disordered retreat. Recalling a line by Aristophanes about a man walking "with swaggering gait and roving eye" (221b), he watched a cool and collected Socrates walk with a deliberation that discouraged any of the enemy from approaching too close to him. Plato's dialogue *Laches* also celebrates Socrates' courage at Delium (181b).

While Alcibiades heard none of the earlier speeches at Agathon's party, and may not have comprehended the full significance of what he himself has just told the group, we can see how Socrates' behavior plays with the various effects of love described by both Phaedrus and Agathon. Consistent with what Phaedrus says (178e–179a), we can explain Socrates' noble and virtuous behavior under the eye of his beloved in terms of, "seeking honor in each other's eyes" (179a), "For a man in love would never allow his loved one, of all people, to see him leaving ranks or dropping weapons" (179a). Socrates' consorting with the young and beautiful in the form of Alcibiades has given birth to the virtues of moderation, bravery and wisdom (196c–d).

Trying finally to assess Socrates, Alcibiades declares that he is at a loss to compare him to anyone. He falls outside all of the usual standards of measure. The great heroes of antiquity and history share some parallel features; only Socrates seems to stand alone (221c–d). There is nothing human about him. This brings Alcibiades back to Silenus: "The best you can do is not to compare him to anything human, but to liken him, as I do, to Silenus and the satyrs and the same goes for his words [*logous*]" (221d). Finally, he concludes his speech with a warning. He has praised Socrates, but he has not spared him either. Alcibiades insists that Socrates has treated him horribly, and furthermore he has done so to others as well. "He has deceived us all. He presents himself as your lover [*erastēs*], and before you know it, becoming more a beloved [*paidika*] himself instead of a lover" (222b). Thus beware: "I warn you Agathon, don't let him fool you! Remember our torments; be on your guard: don't wait, like the fool in the proverb to learn your lesson from your own misfortune" (222b–c).

READING THE TEXT

What are we to make of Alcibiades' speech? Looking at Plato's notion of love in general, especially set against the case of Alcibiades, Gregory Vlastos speaks for many when he complains that Plato's account of love is too narrow. With its focus on virtue and the ascent to wisdom, schematized by Diotima's "Ladder of Love," "we are to love the persons so far, and only insofar, as they are good and beautiful." Elaborating, he adds, "the problem is that it does not provide for love of whole persons, but only for love of that abstract version of persons which consists of the context of their best qualities" (Vlastos 1981, p. 31). Responding to this position, Martha C. Nussbaum rightly argues that we must take the *Symposium* as a whole and that the meaning emerges from the arrangement of the parts: "I believe that a deep understanding of the *Symposium* will be one that regards it not as a work that ignores the pre-philosophical understanding of *erōs*" (Nussbaum 1986, p. 167). By pre-philosophical understanding, she means the positions articulated by everyone but Socrates/Diotima. She then goes on, however, to argue that it is "all about that understanding, and also about why it must be argued and transcended, why Diotima has come once again to save Athens from a plague" (Nussbaum 1986, p. 167). With this in mind, Nussbaum terms Alcibiades' speech a "counter example" to Diotima's. I would argue, rather, that the idealized erotic of Diotima is mapped onto the actual erotic of Alcibiades. While in the end, Alcibiades falls short of Diotima's ideals, approaching only a tentative approximation of the plateau of the fourth level, and never achieving the final level of insight, his speech is not the "counter example" but the concrete example. His case completes Diotima's picture of love by putting it into the context and full complexity of actual human relationships, not just the "complex of desirable qualities." The erotic relationship between Socrates and Alcibiades illustrates what Diotima's love looks like in the realm of appearances.

Put another way, we might ask how one knows he is in love with beautiful ideas? There will inevitably be periods of confusion and transition, false starts and infatuations. In Diotima's account one really knows only in retrospect that one has progressed to the higher level, because one's older views seem lacking by comparison. In a manner consistent with the Socratic dialectic,

I know love only in the sense that I know what love is not. Thus in the transition from the first and second levels, "he must think that this wild gaping after just one body is a small thing and despise it" (210b), or in the transition between the second and third levels, "he will think that the beauty of bodies is a thing of no importance" (210c). And in general, once one has grasped beauty itself, "it won't occur to you to measure beauty by gold or clothing or beautiful boys and youths" (211d). But only when I have reached that stage of the inadequacy of the others will I know.

The steps in Alcibiades' account of his attempts to seduce Socrates echoes the stages of the erotic mysteries of Diotima, a concrete example of the five stages of love, especially the transitions between the stages. Aptly, we might notice that like Diotima, Alcibiades frames his confessions in the language of the mystery religions. Only those who have been "bitten" by philosophy and feel its pain, both in their awareness of the inadequacy of what one used to value, and in their longing for what they have not yet achieved, will understand what they say and feel. Only those who have been "initiated" at least into the lower mysteries of the love of wisdom are competent to listen: "as for the house slaves and for anyone else who is uninitiated [*bebēlos*], my story's not for you: block your ears" (218b). It is also significant that Alcibiades concludes his speech with the warning that it is difficult to pin down whether Socrates is a lover or beloved. Is he guiding the object of his erotic desires to virtue and wisdom, or is he seeking wisdom himself through his love?

Alcibiades' first attempts at seduction, like the transition from the first and second levels in Diotima's account of love, focused on beautiful bodies. Socrates seems to have been drawn to Alcibiades, presumably recognizing beauty in the true sense of a beauty that is pregnant with beautiful ideas. Alcibiades also seems to sense something, but initially understands it only in terms of the physical attraction of bodies. Thus he attempts to seduce Socrates by making his own body physically available, assuming that Socrates is drawn to a physical beauty and will take the hint, first when he has sent away his guardians, then when he wrestles with him at the gymnasium. Socrates' failure to respond in the right way, frustrates him, enhances his dissatisfaction, and leads to a more direct approach.

The second stage of Alcibiades' seduction resembles something of the transition between the second and third levels of love in Diotima, the move from the manifestation of a beautiful soul to an awareness of beautiful knowledge. He declares that Socrates is the only worthy lover he has had, and that it would be pointless not to show his gratitude by giving him whatever he wants, adding that his aim is to become the best man he can. "I'd feel much more shame towards people of good sense if I didn't gratify such a man than I'd feel, towards the many who have no sense, for doing it" (218d). When Socrates replies that if that is what Alcibiades really believes, he has accomplished more than he realizes, his words echo Diotima's description of the second stage of love, the move from the valuing of beautiful bodies to valuing the beautiful souls beneath the realm of appearances: "even though he is scarcely blooming in his body, our lover must be content to love and care for him and to seek to give birth to such ideas as will make young men better" (210b–210c). While Alcibiades possesses a beauty that is certainly still blooming, Socrates, who is indifferent to appearances, seeks to care for his beloved in a way that nourishes the claim that he wants to become the best man he can. In a similar fashion, Alcibiades himself has seen in Socrates the beauty beneath a body that is by contrast no longer blooming, indeed famously the opposite of beauty. That Alcibiades has recognized something in the soul of Socrates suggests something commendable in his own character. By way of corroboration it is useful to recall Socrates' words in the *Phaedrus*, "that everyone chooses his love after his own fashion from among those who are beautiful" (252d). If Alcibiades is drawn to the ugly Socrates, it is because he recognizes an inner beauty that mirrors the potential of his own inner beauty. Advancing toward Diotima's third level, he expresses the belief that Socrates will make him a good man, that this beauty beneath the surface will lead to good practices or customs. Correspondingly, Socrates' expressed willingness to guide Alcibiades, followed by their entirely virtuous night underlines his own commitment to seeking beautiful customs from beauty, and his hope to guide him from noble customs to beautiful knowledge.

Alcibiades' subsequent rage, shame, and guilt point to the transition from Diotima's third to the fourth level, the move from beautiful customs to beautiful knowledge. Though Alcibiades has failed to comprehend the real significance of Socrates' restraint, attributing it to unnatural perversity, his erotic feelings have nevertheless wakened feelings of shame, leading him to avoid Socrates, or be furious when Socrates "traps" him. That he should respond with feelings of anger, shame, or avoidance, underlines the fact that he somehow "knows" better, that he has engendered some sense of beautiful knowledge that conflicts with his baser impulses. If he did not possess such knowledge, he would not have cared what Socrates thought, or felt anger and guilt in his presence. He has recognized that the beauty of Socrates' customary behavior points toward a beautiful knowledge. Again recalling the *Phaedrus*: "from the outlandish mix of these two feelings—pain and joy—comes anguish and helpless raving" (251d).

Alcibiades' account of Socrates during the campaigns at Potidaea and Delium further suggests the transition from Diotima's third to fourth level, from the contemplation of beautiful knowledge to an awareness of the "great sea of beauty," in the "unstinting love of wisdom [*philosophia*]" (210e). While he himself still has a long way to go, still very much at the third level, he has come to recognize in the behavior of Socrates all of the virtues: endurance, self-discipline, courage, modesty, and prudence. In Socrates' desire that Alcibiades receive the award for bravery, we can see Socrates' own modesty, but also his hope as the lover that the recognition of virtue in the beloved will nurture further virtue.

While admitting that Socrates shares specific accomplishments with others, Alcibiades concludes that he is something that goes beyond all specific instances: "he is unique; he is like no one else in the past and no one in the present" (221c). We might shift to Diotima's metaphor: Socrates is a "sea of beauty," giving birth "to many gloriously beautiful words and theories, in unstinting love of wisdom" (210e). Alcibiades' description of Socrates' uniqueness, his inability to be localized or compared to anything else, is analogous to the horizontal movement described in Diotima's first four levels of love, a movement that embraces more and more instances of beauty, until it is beyond any localization or particularity. To the degree that Socrates' virtues seem to be detached from the web of interests or material benefits, they start to take on an independent character, pointing towards the forms. In all of this Socrates is *daimônic*, something between the human and the divine. Because his erotic object is still attached to Socrates, Alcibiades has not reached the comprehension of Diotima's ultimate of Beauty itself, "absolute, pure, unmixed, not polluted by human flesh or color or any other great nonsense of mortality" (211e). Yet at the same time, Socrates' beauty is beyond human comprehension, at least in the sense that it is not contingent on anything else.

The Socrates whom Alcibiades describes is at the fourth level, unstinting in his love of wisdom, building strength. While by the end of his account neither he nor Socrates has apparently achieved the final fifth level, the highest of the mysteries, the sudden [*exaiphnēs*] catching sight of something "wonderfully beautiful in its nature" (210e), Socrates persists, while Alcibiades guiltily falls by the wayside. He has intimations of the beauty only when he is "trapped" or "surprised" by Socrates, encounters that reveal a glimmering of the beauty, giving birth to feelings of shamefulness for his behavior, producing feelings of guilt, followed by frustration and anger. If he has not yet quite given birth to beautiful words and deeds, he is nevertheless cognizant of the inadequacy of his old words and deeds, and in that awareness, he has advanced up Diotima's ladder.

Love is messy. In the *Phaedrus*, after all, Socrates describes it in terms of longing, pain, suffering, and madness, a complex of emotional responses that also characterize Alcibiades' feelings. Thus, while Diotima's "Ladder of Love" offers a simple schema, there is no reason to assume that she, Socrates, or Plato wish to imply that the actual experience of the erotic stages are simple, unambiguous, or automatic. Arguments are not as neat and tidy as presented, as Socrates reminds us in the *Republic*: "Thrasymachus agreed to all of this, not easily as I am telling it, but reluctantly and after being pushed" (350c). We may gain additional insight into Alcibiades' seduction narrative by drawing parallels with the "Parable of the Cave" in the *Republic*, and the "Parable of the Charioteer" from the *Phaedrus*.

In the "Parable of the Cave," we might recall, Socrates imagines a realm of cave dwellers whose entire knowledge of the world is based on shadows projected on the back of the wall of the cave (allegorically, the world of appearances derived from sense perception). He further imagines the process in which one of these dwellers was forced to turn one hundred eighty degrees and confront the artificial source of light that produces the shadows, and the further difficulty that he would face if he were forced up and out of the cave and into the "enlightenment" of the sunlight (allegorically the world of forms or ideas that shape our capacity to know things). The cave dweller's forced ascent strongly resembles the agonies of Alcibiades' erotic progress up Diotima's ladder:

> And if one were to drag him thence by force up the rough and steep path, and did not let him go before he was dragged into the sunlight, would he not be in physical pain and angry as he was dragged along? When he came into the light, with the sunlight filling his eyes, he would not be able to see a single one of the things which are now said to be true. (515e–516a)

All of this illustrates the fact that Plato is well aware that the pursuit and achievement of wisdom is not something cool and dispassionate, but in many regards something painful, agonizing and even violent, especially as one's old habits of thought are torn inside out; so too is the course of love.

The "Parable of the Charioteer" also speaks of the pain and suffering as well as the joys associated with erotic madness. The charioteer struggling to control and harmonize the competing obedient and good horse with the restive and bad one, is like Alcibiades struggling with his own conflicted erotic desires, one seeking the beauty in Socrates, the other seeking the base. Alcibiades resembles the weaker type of soul described by Socrates in the *Phaedrus*. "[The soul] rises at one time and falls at another, and because its horses pull it violently in different directions, it sees some real things and misses others" (248a). In the end, if the driver is crippled by the incompetence of the charioteer, the soul may give up: "After so much trouble, they all leave the sight of reality unsatisfied, and when they have gone they will depend on what they think is nourishment, their own opinions" (248a). The tragedy at the core of Alcibiades' farce is that though he had apprehended a beauty within Socrates, which also mirrored a beauty within himself, he lacked the patience and persistence to prepare and wait for the "sight of something wonderfully beautiful in its nature" (210e). Failing to achieve immediate gratification, he has abandoned the struggle and returned to the cave.

The failure of Alcibiades serves to dramatize the limits of Socrates and Socratic wisdom. Socrates offers a process, not a doctrine. Wisdom is not a body of information, but a way of thinking and a comprehension. The erotic guide can facilitate and nurture, but it is the beloved who must experience the sudden revelation that takes the initiate to the fifth level, and this revelation in turn follows its own course. The process of the Socratic lover, the Socratic midwife, or the Socratic master of mysteries cannot impart understanding; he or she can only guide, point, encourage, and hope that insight will eventually come to the patient beloved, disciple, or initiate. This is the difference between knowing something and actually understanding it, between the recitation of some memorized piece of information, and the comprehension of it. This is the situation we have with Apollodorus' memorizing and reciting the speeches reported by Aristodemus. It is perhaps even the situation with Socrates' recitation of Diotima. Each has glimpsed enough of something beautiful to believe in what he says, but none has the full assurance of understanding. If Socrates is not finally able to help Alcibiades bring forth noble words and deeds, he can claim the consolation that, like Diotima, he delayed the plague in Athens for the ten years that he tried to guide him, from that late night around 432 BCE until Alcibiades entered politics in 422. And perhaps, as long at Alcibiades is still in love with Socrates, there remains a "beautiful hope."

3.3.3. The party is over (222c–223d)

Alcibiades' speech provokes much laughter from the party, "especially since it was obvious that he was still in love with Socrates" (222c). Socrates is the first to speak. Picking up the motif of the difference between interior and exterior, he accuses Alcibiades of being perfectly sober, that until his final warning to Agathon, he had skillfully concealed his true motive, namely that he is doubly jealous of both Agathon and Socrates, and that he would make trouble between them: "you think that I should be in love with you and no one else, while you, and no one else, should be in love with Agathon" (222d). Socrates chides him for his "little satyr play" (222d), an accusation that picks up the motif of the satyrs, at the same time reprimanding Alcibiades for his outrageous and seemingly drunken behavior. It also hints at the nature of the relationship of Alcibiades' speech to those of the others and the structures of the *Symposium* as a whole.

Socrates asks Agathon not to let Alcibiades come between them, punning on the fact that the three are currently sharing the same couch together. Agathon concurs, joking that he will come over and lie down next to him, a move that provokes Alcibiades to complain: "how I suffer in his hands! He kicks me when I am down; he never lets me go." Then asking if Agathon might not lie down between them, he implores, "Come, don't be selfish, Socrates" (222e). Here Socrates demurs, evoking the convention of the *symposion* that the speeches must move from left to right. Since Agathon is on Socrates' right, it is Socrates' turn to praise Agathon, while if Agathon were to move to Socrates' left, it would be his turn to praise him. Delighted by this prospect, Agathon declares that he will certainly not move. "It's the same old story," Alcibiades responds in a gesture of (presumably) mock despair: "when Socrates is around nobody else can even get close to a good-looking man. Look how smoothly and plausibly he found a reason for Agathon to lie down next to him" (223a).

These turn out to be his last words. Moments later the party is "suddenly [*exaiphnēs*]" disrupted by the influx of a large group of drunken revelers who had found the outer gates open and invited themselves in. Order gives way to chaos amid the noise and drinking. Eryximachus, Phaedrus, and others take their leave. Similarly Alcibiades apparently disappears from the scene without further ado, gone as suddenly as he had initially appeared. Aristodemus reports that he himself soon fell asleep not to be awakened until near dawn by the crowing of a rooster. He notices that only Agathon, Aristophanes, and Socrates are still awake, talking and drinking together from a large cup that they pass from left to right. They are in deep discussion, though because he is still half asleep; he discerns only that Socrates is trying to argue that the same person should know how to compose comedy and tragedy, that the skilled (*technē*) tragic poet (*tragōdopoion*) is also a comic poet (*kōmōdopoion*) (223d). Before the matter is resolved, however, both the tragic and comic poets have themselves nodded off, leaving Socrates the last man awake.

Thereupon he rises and leaves, followed as ever by the dogged Aristodemus. Washing at the Lyceum, Socrates proceeds to spend the rest of the day as he always did, finally returning home to rest as evening was falling. And so we might say that the *Symposium* concludes with Socrates going about his business, preparing with his "unstinting love of wisdom," waiting patiently for the "sudden" glimpse of "something wonderfully beautiful in its nature."

Plato closes the *Symposium* on the paradoxical note of an open-ended wholeness. On one level the party has ended, and Socrates' survival as the last person awake, and his subsequent departure marks a closure, just as his arrival marked a beginning. Thus we feel that we have experienced the whole party at Agathon's house. The series of speeches have carried the topic of *erōs* through a series of levels culminating with the rhetorical climax of Diotima's "Ladder of Love", followed by the comic reiteration of these themes in Alcibiades' speech. We leave Plato's text with a feeling that we have worked through a comprehensive treatment of *erōs*, that we have achieved some sense of completeness or wholeness with regard to the argument. Yet of course, the party was disrupted rather than concluded, and the question of love remains finally open. Socrates spends the rest of the day, just "as he always did" (223d), pointing to the completion of a repetition of the same rather than the closure of an ending. He disposes himself for the possibility of understanding or enlightenment, for the intervention of the *daimônic*, but it has not yet happened. The question of open-endedness brings us back to the nature of Plato's *Symposium* as a whole, both as philosophy and literature.

Socrates' characterization of Alcibiades' performance as a satyr play, as well as Aristodemus' recollection of Socrates arguing that a dramatic poet should be able to write both tragedy and comedy draws our attention to two issues. First, it invites us to read the *Symposium* and its component parts in terms of a dramatic cycle. Second, it brings us back to the larger questions about frame narratives, the generic nature of the *Symposium*, and the problem of truth and writing. With regard to the first, we might recall that classical Athenian drama, especially the Spring festivals at the City Dionysia were in the form of a competition between three tragedians each of whom would contribute a cycle of three tragedies followed by a satyr play.[16] The three tragedies dramatized successive episodes from a single myth story, while the satyr play dramatized some related myth. While most of the classical Greek tragedies that survive were part of trilogies, only the *Oresteia* (458 BCE) of Aeschylus, featuring the *Agamemnon*, the *Choephori* (*Libation Bearers*), and the *Eumenides*, survives as a complete trilogy, the dramatic arc of the component plays developing a thematic whole. This was accompanied by the *Proteus*, a satyr play that has not survived. The *Cyclops* of Euripides, playing off the episode from *Odyssey* 9.105–566, is the only complete satyr play that comes down to us, and is tentatively dated around 408 BCE. We do not know what trilogy it belongs to, but it is roughly contemporary with Euripides' *Trojan Women*.

It is important to keep in mind that since the tragedies were meant as units of an interconnected cycle of plays, we cannot judge the nature of tragedy from any single play. Rather we must see how the thematic tensions are worked out and resolved, as they are in the *Oresteia*, which traces the shift from a concept of justice based on blood feud and vendetta to one based on democracy and litigation. It would be like trying to judge Shakespeare's *Hamlet* on the basis of reading one act. Similarly, we must not be misled by Aristotle's famous definition of tragedy in the *Poetics*, in terms of "incidents arousing pity and fear, wherewith to accomplish its catharsis of such emotions" (1449b25), into assuming that tragedies must have unhappy endings. His concern is about the strategies that a playwright uses to effectively manipulate the emotions of the audience. He is not *per se*, concerned with the development of themes, aside from an overall tone of seriousness. Indeed, he notes that many criticize the tragedies of Euripides exactly because he gives many of them unhappy endings (1453a15–25). Thus, although the traditional stories that provide the raw material for the great tragedies typically involve the misfortunes of their heroes, and it is our sympathy with the heroes' plight that connects us emotionally with the play, the tragedies themselves are not about human misery, but working through and coming to some understanding of the human condition.

With these dramatic conventions in mind, Socrates' designation of Alcibiades' speech as a satyr play invites us to think about the earlier speeches praising love in terms of the tragic trilogy, and how the component speeches contribute to our understanding of the whole. As I have suggested above, the tragic signifies not misfortune, but a serious attempt by means of drama, to come to grips with the issues of love, working through the tensions to some resolution. In broad terms, then, we may briefly summarize what we have seen in the following manner:

The first installment of Plato's trilogy can be characterized as "Love and the individual," joining the *encomia* of Phaedrus and Pausanias into a contrasting pair that brings them together as dialectical complements to each other. Thus each focuses on relationship between love and the individual, whether it is the benefits of love on the beloved or on the lover. At the same time they contrast in Phaedrus' privileging of the beloved and Pausanias' privileging of the lover.

The second installment might be called "Love and nature." Here Eryximachus and Aristophanes form a dialectical complement. They are similar in that both differ from Phaedrus/Pausanias in their move to take love to a more general level, and not to favor homoerotic relationships over others. In turn both see *erōs* in terms of a unity, and in terms of some notion of health. They contrast, however, in that Eryximachus sees the unity in terms of harmony, and the health in terms of the physical, while Aristophanes sees the unity in terms of wholeness, and the health a spiritual healing. They also differ in that Eryximachus sees nature as a whole as the domain of *erōs*, while Aristophanes centers it in human nature.

The third and culminating installment of the trilogy might be called "Love in itself." Agathon and Socrates/Diotima form the dialectical complement. Each states the desire to turn from the benefits of love to the nature of love itself. Plato has Socrates signal this association by way of explicit contrast. In a move that underlines both their similarities and differences, Agathon and Socrates/Diotima playfully offer allegorical representations of Love that are contrasting self-portraits. Thus the youthful Agathon says Love "is youngest, then, and most delicate; in addition he has a fluid, supple shape" (196a). In direct contrast, Diotima through Socrates says "[Love] is always poor, and he's far from being delicate and beautiful," adding that "he is tough and shriveled and shoeless and homeless . . . always living with Need" (203c), a portrait that strongly resembles Socrates. Both Agathon and Socrates/Diotima see Love drawn by beauty, the erotic object. They contrast, however, in that Agathon understands it in terms of the desire to be with the similar, the beautiful Love drawn to beautiful acts, while Socrates understands it in terms of the desire for what is absent, finding its fullest resolution in the metaphor of Diotima's "Ladder of Love."

The "satyr play" of Alcibiades takes up the various themes developed during the course of the first three installments, translating them from the realm of the heroic and mythic into the living realm of humans. The effect is not to ridicule *Erōs*, but to put it into the perspective of the human condition. M. D. Usher notes that the surviving satyr play, *The Cyclops*, echoes elements of the situation between Socrates and Alcibiades (Usher 2002, p. 219). The story of Odysseus and the Cyclops Polyphemus forms the backdrop of the play, forming a "mock" *symposion* between the drunken Silenus and a sexually aggressive Polyphemus. Set against *The Cyclops*, the story of the Silenic Socrates and the drunken and lustful Alcibiades becomes a comic and ironic inversion of "Beauty and the Beast" that lends a living humanity to the otherwise unclassifiable Socrates (Usher 2002, p. 226). Alcibiades' speech touches bases with all three parts of the trilogy, thus dramatizing the erotic economy of the individual lover and beloved, taking love as something beyond the individual, and finally transforming it to a philosophical pursuit of wisdom. The overall effect of Plato's satyr play is to remind his audience that the erotic wisdom sought by Diotima and the "Ladder of Love" is not something remote, but ever present, waiting to be glimpsed.

Ultimately Socrates' argument that the dramatic poet should be able to compose both tragedy and comedy points to something that is more than the sum of tragedy and comedy. We have the dramatic trilogy and satyr play at the center of the *Symposium*, but we also have the larger narrative contexts signified by the roles played by Aristodemus, Apollodorus, and ultimately Plato. In the words of Michel Despland, "philosophy claims to rise above the division of genre and show everything that is beyond language in language. The fragmented truths of tragedy and of comedy are restored to wholeness" (Despand 1985, p. 242). In this line of thought, Jean-Yves Chateau argues that historically speaking tragedy and comedy come together to made philosophy possible (Chateau 2005, pp. 200–202): The tragedies made us as human beings conscious of our condition and the limits of our power to act or our ability to alter those conditions. Tragedies elicit from us a wonder, awe, and fear that violently confront us with a strong sense of our limitations. For these very reasons, they also nourish a hunger for understanding. Comedy offers a counter-message. Living human beings eat, drink, carouse, and make love. The repetitive pursuit of these basic pleasures creates a constancy that puts the larger problems into perspective. Above all, the lesson of comedy is that we should not take ourselves too seriously. Philosophy, by contrast, claims to rise above the division of genre. In the first part of the *Symposium*, the speeches from Phaedrus to Diotima, Plato presents us with the tragic awareness of our limits. In the final part, the speech of Alcibiades, we are shown the comic dimension of Eros that puts the first part into human perspective.

Following similar lines of thought, the Spanish philosopher Ortega y Gasset sees the novel as a synthesis of tragedy and comedy, with both at play in Plato's *Symposium*. "If we prolong the gesture made by Socrates from the *Symposium* in the pale light of dawn, it will seem as if we come up against Don Quixote, the hero and the madman" (1957, p. 40). Ortega y Gasset's interest is thematic rather than generic, focusing on the madness and obsession of *erōs* set against a backdrop of realism. The Russian philosopher and literary critic M. M. Bakhtin also sees the *Symposium* as a proto-novel. His concern, however, is with the nature and workings of literary genre and their relation to thought. Following a hint from Friedrich Schlegel, he finds in the Platonic dialogues an important source for the modern form of the novel (Bakhtin 1981, p. 22). For him the novel is dialogic, bringing together competing voices and layers of language, at the same time resisting making them conform to any one single view. As a result these competing voices and languages "become dialogized, permeated with laughter, irony, humor, elements of self-parody and finally—this is the most important thing—the novel inserts into these other genres an indeterminacy, a certain semantic openendedness, a living contact with unfinished, still-evolving contemporary reality" (Bakhtin 1981, p. 7). Unlike the epic, which represented a closed and absolute past, transmitted without change through memory and oral recitation, the novel is a genre that invites reinterpretation with every reading.

Bakhtin's conception of the novel, inspired by the Platonic dialogue, offers us in retrospect, insight into the workings of the *Symposium*. If in the *Phaedrus*, Socrates complains that, "written words go on telling you just the same thing forever" (275e), then the *Symposium* gives an answer. The deliberate ambiguities that Plato inserts into his work by means of the successive narrative frames and the foregrounding of textual transmission raise the issue of authority in the minds of the attentive reader. Made conscious of the limits of the text, the reader is invited to rethink and reinterpret what he or she has read. Whether it be the mad obsessiveness of Apollodorus' narrative, the limits of Aristodemus' memory, or the disagreements, ironies, and humor among the various speakers at Agathon's party, the *Symposium* challenges Plato's readers to engage actively and passionately with the text, not just accept it as a repetition of "the same thing forever." In this way, Plato breaks out of his hermeneutic bind. The markings on the page may be fixed, but not their subsequent readings. In the end, the text of the *Symposium* itself becomes *daimônic*, neither divine nor human, but the messenger between them. The reader's understanding of Diotima's wisdom may be separated by five levels of mediation: that of Diotima, that of Socrates, that of Aristodemus, that of Apollodorus, and finally that of Plato. Nevertheless the love of wisdom is an erotic passion that can nurture the perseverance and patience for an act of reading that gives birth to beautiful words and noble deeds. The point is perhaps less the final resolution than the willingness to keep trying, no matter how many times one fails. As Socrates exhorts Theaetetus, "start again and try to explain what knowledge is. Never say it is beyond your power; it will not be so, if god [*theos*] wills and you take courage" (151d). Living up to Socrates' challenge demands true love and devotion, but that is what it means to be a philosopher.

READING THE TEXT

DISCUSSION QUESTIONS 3.1

1. Among the first five speakers, whose conception of love seems most plausible or true to experience?
2. Does love make us better persons as each of the speakers' claims? If so, does each speaker provide an adequate account of the perversity, violence, or unhappiness that often seems associated with the experience of love?
3. How in practical terms do we distinguish different kinds of love? On what basis do we judge one better than another? How would (or could) each of the speakers distinguish love from some perversion or fetishism?
4. Does love always have an object? Would it be meaningful to speak of love-for-its own sake?

DISCUSSION QUESTIONS 3.2

1. How do questions of gender identity shape the different models of love? Could Diotima's conception of love accommodate Phaedrus'?
2. Among the various speakers are gender differences a function of social context, nature, or transcendent forms?
3. Is the ethics implicit in Diotima's conception of love consequentialist or non-consequentialist?
4. Many commentators note that Diotima's conception of the soul is different from the tripartite model that Socrates describes in the *Republic* and *Phaedrus*. Does that make what she says about the soul and love incompatible with what is in the *Republic* and *Phaedrus*?
5. For Diotima would it be possible to reach the just and the good without love?

DISCUSSION QUESTIONS 3.3

1. Is Plato developing a unitary model of love? How does he account for the complexity and contrary emotions that we often attribute to love?
2. How would (or could) each of the speakers at Agathon's party explain Alcibiades' behavior in terms of his respective conception of love?

3. Does Alcibiades turn out to be a tragic or comic figure? Is it possible for Socrates to be a tragic figure, or is his philosophical vocation inconsistent with the nature of tragedy?
4. Is Plato better as a poet or a philosopher?

CHAPTER 4

RECEPTION AND INFLUENCE

> [W]e do not believe that there exists, in all rigor, a Platonic text, closed upon itself, complete with its inside and its outside. Not that one must then consider that it is leaking on all sides and can be drowned confusedly in the undifferentiated generality of its element. Rather, provided the articulations are rigorously and prudently recognized, one should simply be able to untangle the hidden forces of attraction linking a present word with an absent word in the text of Plato.
> *(Derrida 1981, p. 130)*

> [T]he myths, when they have taught us as well as they can, allow the man who has understood them to put together again that which they have separated.
> *(Plotinus 1967, 3. 5. 9. 28, 9)*

With its various narrative games and textual ambiguities as well has its profound discussion of love, Plato's *Symposium* has invited a wide variety of interpretations and found its way into many diverse places. It has enjoyed a number of adaptations, including the 1965 BBC Television play, *The Drinking Party*, directed by Jonathan Miller and featuring actor Leo McKern in the role of Socrates, and a 1989 version, *La Banquet*, directed by Marco Ferreri, and featuring Irene Papas as Diotima. More recently German playwright Benno Boudgoust adapted it in his 2007 production *Das Grandiose Leben*. Few works of philosophy can boast providing the inspiration for both modern classical music (such as Erik Satie's 1918 *Socrate (Drame Symphonique)*, Leonard Bernstein's 1954 *Serenade: After Plato's Symposium* and Luigi Nono's 1980 quartet *Fragmente-Stille, an Diotima* which reads Plato through Hölderlin), and a rock-opera (John Cameron Mitchell's and Stephen Trask's 1998 *Hedwig and the Angry Inch*).

It is possible to touch on only a handful of later writers and thinkers in order to indicate the richness and variety of the *Symposium*'s reception since Plato, ranging over philosophy, theology, literature, psychoanalysis, and gender studies. Many of those who are influenced by the *Symposium* draw on it selectively, deploying one or more themes or motifs rather than the whole. With this in mind, I will organize this brief survey in terms of seven frequently used themes or motifs, fully cognizant that many overlap. In several cases, I will also go into a more detailed excursus with regard to specific thinkers or writers.

4.1. PHILOSOPHICAL BANQUET

It is a measure of the influence of Plato's version of the *Symposium* that the genre of the *symposion* was transformed from a site for the transmission of masculine traditions to a vehicle for philosophical discourse, engendering a host of subsequent literary and philosophical banquets. Some of these were serious, some playful. Many authors were less concerned with developing a thesis or unfolding a coherent plot than providing the occasion for displaying their erudition. Some of interest include Athenaeus' *Deipnosophistae* (*The Learned Banqueters*, literally *The Dinner-Sophist*), Plutarch's *Tōn epta sophōn sumposion* (*Banquet of the Seven Sages*), Tacitus' *Diologus de Oratoribus* (*Dialogue on Oratory*), and Macrobius' *Saturnalia*. I will dwell briefly on two symposia that share both an explicit debt to Plato and possess significant literary or philosophical merit: the *Satyrica* of Petronius Arbiter (ca. 27–66 CE), commonly known as the *Satyricon*, and the *Symposion he peri hagneias* (*The Symposium: On Chastity*) by Methodius of Olympus (died ca. 311 CE). Together they display the wide spectrum of ancient responses.

Described by Tacitus as a "refined voluptuary" (*Annals* 16.17–20), Petronius was the arbiter of taste in the court of the Roman emperor Nero. The *Satyricon*, a sort of novel, survives only in fragments.[1] While its basic shape parodies the conventions of the ancient Greek romance with its misadventures of innocent boy-girl lovers, Petronius consciously refers to Plato and the *Symposium*. Here the main action centers on the not-so-innocent sexual adventures among the narrator, Encolpius, his former lover Ascyltus, and Giton, a fickle boy both are trying to woo. The surviving fragments open with Encolpius delivering a tirade against rhetoric, complaining that no one can be sensible on such a diet of "honey-balls of phrases" (Petronius 1969, 1). "I certainly do not find that Plato or Demosthenes took any course of training of this kind" (2). Rather their style "rises supreme by virtue of its natural beauty" (2). Later, the text refers explicitly to Plato when Giton sarcastically thanks the impotent Encolpius for loving him, "as true as Socrates [*Socratica fide*]. Alcibiades never lay so unspotted in his master's bed" (128). Elsewhere, a lecherous poet named Eumolpus tells the tale of the Pergamene Boy, an ironic inversion of the story of Socrates and Alcibiades, explaining how he had secretly plotted to seduce his young charge: "the boy's mother in particular looked on me as a philosopher above the sensual pleasures of the world" (85). Eumolpus soon discovers that the boy is as eager to be seduced as he is to seduce him. In fact, this inversion of a Socrates figure into drunken lecherous master is a frequent comic motif in a number of sympotic dialogues, for instance in Athenaeus' *Deipnosophistae*.

The most famous episode of the *Satryicon* is known as the *Cena Trimalchionis*, the *Dinner of Trimalchio* (26–79). Encolpius, Ascyltus, and Giton attend a banquet hosted by the wealthy freedman, Trimalchio. A perverse parody of the *Symposium*, this banquet is a grotesque and drunken celebration of Trimalchio's self-love, culminating in the staging of his funeral, that he might enjoy a succession of eulogies delivered by the guests. Like Agathon's party, it dissolves in chaos, in this case when the fire brigade, hearing the mourning trumpets, comes crashing in, believing that the house is on fire. In an earlier episode (65) directly modeled on Alcibiades' entrance, Habinnas, Trimalchio's drunken architect arrives, his head adorned with wreathes, supported by his wife (Cameron 1969, p. 368). In all of the references and allusion to the *Symposium*, Petronius is not satirizing Plato, but using the comparisons with Plato to underscore the unphilosophical nature of his "heroes" (Cameron 1969, p. 368), a comic strategy akin to the mock heroic.

At the opposite extreme is the *Symposium* of Methodius. Little is known about Methodius of Olympus, also known as Eubulius. A saint in both the Western and Eastern Church, his feast day is September 18 in the Western liturgical calendar, and June 20 in the Orthodox liturgical calendar, where he is designated by the title of *Hieromartyr* (clergyman martyr). He possessed a comprehensive philosophical education, which he applies to a Pauline Christology, unified under the concept of chastity. Methodius' *Symposium* lacks the narrative and dramatic tautness of Plato's, often giving way to long digressions on the exegesis of dietary, botanical, etymological, and numerological symbolism as well as the allegorical interpretation of scripture. Nevertheless, he offers a sophisticated parody, transforming Plato's account of a male drinking party into the festal banquet of women in a garden. He deploys an elaborate series of correspondences: Plato's party is hosted by Agathon (nobility), the topic under discussion love (*eros*), while Methodius' is hosted by Arete (virtue), the topic under discussion chastity or purity (*hagnos*).

In a metaphor that suggests the silenus, one speaker, Marcella, talks of the importance of keeping one's body undefiled: "just as we should not display our temples as more important than the statues in them; but we must also care for our souls, the images within our bodies" (1958, p. 42). The speech by Agathe reconfigures the Heavenly and Earthly Aphrodites described by Pausanias into the Parable of the Wise and Foolish Virgins (Matt. 25:1–13). Agathe sees the division in terms of a proper attraction to incorporeal beauty, and a false one to corporeal beauty.

Among the most interesting speeches is that of Thecla, according to patristic tradition the companion of Saint Paul.[2] In a symbolic inversion of gender roles, she corresponds to Socrates and by extension Paul, the absent teacher of divine mysteries, corresponds to Diotima. Arguing that only those initiated into the "pure mysteries" of word symbolism (a technique inspired by Plato's *Cratylus*), she contends that *parthenia* (virgin) is etymologically linked to *par[a]theia* (next to the divine), supposedly demonstrating that chastity is fundamental to heavenly ascent. In imagery that conflates the soul from the *Phaedrus* with Diotima's pregnant soul, Thecla declares, "[g]reater good than this it is impossible to find, dwelling apart from either pleasure or pain: and the wings of the soul, impregnated with it, truly become firmer and lighter, accustomed daily to fly from the interests of men" (1958, p. 105). The goal of this moral ascent is the divine realm in which there is justice, love, truth, and prudence in itself (p. 107).

4.2. SILENIC TEXTS

Inspired by Alcibiades' trope, many subsequent writers seize upon the figure of the silenus, something that seems ugly or ridiculous on the surface, but beautiful underneath. By extension it becomes a popular metaphor for the allegorical or symbolic reading of a text, and more specifically that a text that seems to be about something comic, playful, or grotesque might be serious. Much of the popularity for this trope derives from the Dutch humanist Erasmus of Rotterdam (ca. 1469–1536), whose collection, *Adages*, was popular throughout European intellectual circles, growing from 818 entries when first published in 1500 to 3260 in the Aldine edition of 1508. The *Adages* is a compilation of Greek and Latin proverbs and sayings, such as *Festina lente* (make haste slowly), *Herculei labores* (the labors of Hercules), and *Dulce bellum inexpertis* (war is sweet to the inexperienced). Each was accompanied by a commentary, many of which grew into essays expounding humanist doctrine.

Among the most cited of the adages was *Sileni Alcibiades* (the Sileni of Alcibiades). Erasmus first traces the classical sources, citing Athenaeus, Xenophon, Athisthenes, and Plato, then glosses the conventional reading of the figure: "But once you have opened out this Silenus, absurd as it is, you find a god rather than a man, a great, lofty and truly philosophic soul" (Erasmus 1967, p. 78). He quickly elaborates a series of analogies by which he links the Platonic motif with Christianity. "But is not Christ the most extraordinary Silenus of all?" (1967, p. 79), pointing to Christ's humble life, his affiliation with the poor, his rejection of pleasure, and ultimately the "mockery of the cross." "But if one may attain to a closer look at this Silenus-image, that is if he deigns to show himself to the purified eyes of the soul, what unspeakable riches you will find there" (p. 79). Following this line of thought, he proceeds to make similar points about the prophets, John the Baptist, and the Scriptures themselves: "if you remain on the surface, a thing may sometime appear absurd; it you pierce through to the spiritual meaning, you will adore the divine wisdom" (p. 82). Reversing the trope to posit a Reformationist critique, he asks rhetorically about priests concerned with wealth or popes with pomp and secular power.

In addition to the political reformist message, Erasmus' use of the silenus motif introduces the humanist concern for rhetoric and the resources of literature as a means of conveying religious truths, part of a conviction that the rational focus of Scholasticism, (which he often clothes in the guise of Stoicism), is inadequate to comprehending or expressing the unique nature of Christianity. Rather, it requires an (ecstatic) insight of those initiated into the spiritual reading of the text. In this we see early developments of the ecstatic theology that underlies Erasmus' most popular work, *In Praise of Folly* (*Moriae Encomium* 1511), that shows its affinities to Plato and the *Symposium* by its Silenic character, and its form, an encomium delivered by Folly (*Stultitia*), praising herself.[3] In an elaborate wordplay Erasmus links religious ecstasy, mysticism, the mantic, madness, and drunkenness (Screech 1980, pp. 51–61).[4] The result is a vision of Christianity as divine folly, deeply influenced by a Platonic version of love. "Christ too, though he is the wisdom of the Father, was made something of a fool himself in order to help the folly of mankind" (Erasmus 1971, p. 198).

The "Preface" to François Rabelais *Gargantua* draws inspiration from Erasmus and invokes Plato, Socrates, and the *Sileni* to justify the grotesque fun of his text. Taking the metaphor a step further, he compares the act of reading and interpreting his Silenic text to that of a philosophical dog's trying to crack a marrowbone: "Following that example it behooves you to develop a sagacious flair for sniffing and smelling out and appreciating such fair and fatted books, to be swift in pursuit and bold in the attack, and then, by careful reading and frequent meditation, to crack open the bone and seek out the substantifical [*sustantificque* (sic)] marrow"(Rabelais 2006, p. 207). The dog image points both to Diogenes the Cynic, whose epithet derives from *kunikos* (dog-like) and Socrates' favorite oath, "*ma ton kuna* (by the dog)."

One of the most original manifestations of the Silenic text motif comes from the Danish philosopher and theologian Søren Kierkegaard (1813–1855).[5] Assessing the significance of the *Symposium* as a whole, he wrote in his journal, "It's an indescribably wonderful presentation of the power of love to ennoble man, or of man's rebirth through Eros, that we find in the *Symposium*" (1996, p. 134). *Either/Or* (1843) is Kierkegaard's first significant contribution to literature and philosophy. Drawing inspiration from both Plato and the Northern Humanists, he creates a host of pseudonymous authors. *Either/Or* unfolds around the narrative of one Victor Eremita (Victor the Hermit, the herm, or possessor of secret [hermetic] knowledge). Victor finds a writing desk in a shop, buys it, but finding that he cannot open it, breaks it open with a hatchet, thereby discovering an assortment of documents, which he divides into two groups, *Either* (*Enten*) and *Or* (*Eller*). The first group comprises a series of seven discourses on aspects of aesthetics, love and despair composed by an aesthete, a romantic ironist identified as "A," and extracts from the diary by Johannes the Seducer (*The Diary of a Seducer*, *Forførerens Dagbog*). The second group consists of two long letters addressed to "A" by an older married friend identified as Judge Wilhelm, celebrating the virtues of a mature marriage. To these are appended a sermon by a Jutland pastor. *Either/Or* is rich in both its allusiveness and elusiveness, playing on works as diverse as Mozart's *Don Giovanni*, Goethe's *Wilhelm Meister*, and Hegel's *Phenomenology*. Nevertheless the resonance with the *Symposium* is evident even in the most superficial outline, from the hermai, the Silenic desk/texts, the succession of aesthetic essays, and the account of a seducer.

Much of the *Either* section can be read as an ironic inversion of the *Symposium* in which the erotic is conceived in terms of the aesthetic rather than the other way. In the second essay, "The Inmmediate Erotic Stages or the Musical Erotic," "A" characterizes musical experience as a three-stage hierarchy of the erotic, Diotima's Ladder in reverse: The lowest is that of Cherabino (of Mozart's *Figaro*), who possesses an awakening of erotic desire, but without an object; the second Papageno (of Mozart's *Magic Flute*), possessing an erotic desire for an object, but no fulfillment; and finally Don Giovanni (of Mozart's *Don Giovanni*), possessing an erotic desire that passes through a succession of objects without satisfaction. In Diotima's terms, we are left with lovers who are forever dissatisfied, never able to get past the love of individuals. The *Diary of a Seducer* follows a similar pattern of inversion, in which Johannes encloses the beauty and spirit of his "beloved," Cordelia, reducing her to appearances, ignoring her interiority.

4.3. PLATONIC LOVE

The expression "Platonic love" (*Amore Platonico*) was first coined by the Florentine philosopher Marsilio Ficino (1433–1499) in a letter to his friend Alamanno Donati to signify the intellectual love between friends that in turn united the members of the Platonic Academy into a community, and ultimately led to God (Kristeller 1964, pp. 285, 6). From this we get the more conventional modern usage that defines Platonic love in terms of a disinterested and spiritual love without the implications of the physical. At the same time many readers and writers associate it with the strong sympathy for homoeroticism expressed in both the *Phaedrus* and the *Symposium*. Indeed, Ficino himself dedicated *De amore* (1469), his commentary on Plato's *Symposium*, to his friend and companion the poet Giovanni Cavalcanti (1444–1509), whom he frequently addressed, "Giovanni amico mio perfettismo." Plato's homoeroticism is "purified" into a chaste relationship among male friends with a shared devotion to God. Ficino's views were popularized, recast into heterosexual terms by Pietro Bembo in his *Gli Asolani* (1505) and Baldesar Castiglione in his *Il libro del cortegiano* (*The Book of the Courtier*, 1528).

Nevertheless, the homoerotic and the legitimization of the homoerotic passion remains an important current. Oscar Wilde's famous defense of the "Love that dare not speak its name" expresses the view of many: "[It is] a great affection of an elder for a younger man as there was between David and Jonathan, such as Plato made the very basis of his philosophy, and such as you find in the sonnets of Michelangelo and Shakespeare." He adds, "It is beautiful, it is fine, it is the noblest form of affection. There is nothing unnatural about it. It is intellectual, and it repeatedly exists between an elder and a younger man, when the elder man has intellect, and the younger man has all the joy, hope and glamour of life before him" (McKenna 2005, p. 391). In *De Profundis*, Wilde suggests that his erotic letters could be properly understood only by "those who have read the *Symposium* of Plato, or caught the spirit of a certain grave mood made beautiful for us in Greek marbles" (Wilde 2000, p. 702). André Gide's 1925 *Corydon*, a philosophical dialogue in defense of homosexuality, cites Plato and the guests of his *Symposium* as among the few serious theorists of love (Gide 2001, p. 32). Similarly Roland Barthes' *A Lover's Discourse* (1977) draws on a number of passages from the *Symposium* in his meditations of a lone lover. In terms that echo and add insight to Alcibiades' frustration at Socrates' unknowability (*atopia*), Barthes writes:

> Or again, instead of trying to define the other ("What is he?"), I turn to myself: "What do I want, wanting to know you?" What would happen if I decided to define you as a force and not as a person? And if I were to situate myself as another force confronting yours? This would happen: my other would be defined solely by the suffering or the pleasure he affords me. (1977, p. 135)

4.4. THE GOOD AND THE BEAUTIFUL

While Plato was not entirely lost during the Middle Ages, remaining a name and a presence in the works of Plotinus (205–270 CE), Gregory of Nyssa (ca. 335–ca. 398), St. Augustine (354–430), Proclus (410–485), the Pseudo-Dionysus (late 4th, early 5th century), Marsilio Ficino played a crucial role in reintroducing him to Western thought and culture, translating the dialogues and letters, and composing a number of commentaries, as well as his important *Theologia platonica* (1474). He sought to Christianize Plato, bridging classical pagan thought with Christianity, arguing that the concepts of love in Plato and Saint Paul were the same. He further sought to identify the value of beauty with truth and goodness, thereby justifying the humanist interest in rhetoric and poetry. Finally he helped to reintroduce the allegorical mode of interpretation that permitted a Christian reading of the visual and literary arts (Trinkaus 1983, pp. 30, 1). The overall effect of his influence was to help transform the naturalistic conception of love found in the Aristotelian (Scholastic) mindset, characteristic of the Middle Ages, to the spiritual conception of love as desire for ideal beauty, characteristic of the Renaissance. Among those influenced by Ficino's Christian Platonism were Erasmus and John Colet (ca. 1467–1519).

Ficino's *De amore*, his commentary on the *Symposium*, is in the form of a fictionalized philosophical banquet, inspired partly by Plato and partly by Dante's *Convivio* (itself indirectly inspired by the Platonic banquet). After the meal, each of the seven banqueters, who include Ficino himself, Cavalcanti, and the poet Cristoforo Landino, delivers a commentary on one of the speeches of the *Symposium*. The result is less a commentary, *per se*, than a vehicle to survey a variety of ideas about love, and finally Ficino's own philosophical views. Landino, for instance, ostensibly commenting on Aristophanes, argues that since the body is in a perpetual state of flux, Plato must signify the eternal and unchanging soul when he refers to man (Ficino 1985, p. 75). In the sixth speech, Tommaso Benci links Pausanias' Earthly and Heavenly loves (Venuses) with Diotima's Penia and Poros, a move inspired by Plotinus (Ficino 1985, pp. 115–118). The final speech rehearses the levels of madness described in the *Phaedrus*, but concludes, "the most powerful and most excellent of all [madness] is the amatory; most powerful I say, on account of the fact that all the others necessarily need it. For we achieve neither poetry nor mysteries, nor prophecy without vast zeal, burning, and sedulous worship of divinity," or echoing the rhetorical rhythm of Saint Paul (1 Cor. 13.13), "But what else do we call zeal, piety, and worship except love?" (Ficino 1985, pp. 171, 2).

4.5. EARTHLY LOVE AND HEAVENLY LOVE

Pausanias' division between Earthly Love and Heavenly Love, often conflated with Diotima's allegorical account of the birth of Eros from Penia (poverty) and Poros (Plenty) caught the imaginations of a number of thinkers, providing a handy way of negotiating the ambiguities of love and human psychology. Middle Platonists, such as Lucius Apuleius and Plutarch equate Eros with the physical cosmos.[6] In his essay *On Iris and Osiris*, an extended exercise in syncretizing mythography, Plutarch identifies Eros with the Egyptian god Horus, linking both as the symbolic representation of the nature. Eros/Horus is the product of Penia, matter, and Poros, form or logos. The Neoplatonism of Plotinus, on the other hand, rejects this view, asserting the immateriality of Eros and the soul. See, for instance Hadot (1993, pp. 48–63).

In *Ennead* 3.5, Plotinus (205–270 CE) engages in an extended and often opaque exegesis of Diotima's allegory of Penia and Poros. First recalling Pausanias' distinction between the Heavenly Aphrodite (daughter only of Uranus or Kronos—Intellect) and the Earthly (daughter of Zeus and Dione), he argues that it is the Heavenly Aphrodite who appears in Diotima, meaning that Aphrodite, and by extension Eros is something pure and transcendental, unmixed with anything material. The earthly soul of the cosmos possesses a mixed nature. Penia participates in the nature of the intelligible, contemplating the *Nous* (mind, for Plotinus the emanation of the Divine) directly, but as an unformed soul, animated only by a vague desire for self-fulfillment. The result of this is that "Love is not a pure rational principle, since he has in himself an indefinite, irrational, unbounded impulse; for he will never be satisfied, as long as he has in him the nature of the indefinite" (Plotinus 3.5 7.15ff.). The irrational, allegorically represented by the drunkenness of Poros, "arouses a desire demanding external fulfillment," contends John M. Dillon, which he argues is central to Plotinus' account of the origins of the physical world, and indeed the explanation of the impetus for the transcendent *Nous* to create a lower order of Being: "The results are twofold: simultaneously a flood of energy is let loose which imposes Form, through Soul, on Matter, to create the physical world; and the divine force, Eros, is born which creates in each being a capacity, and an urge, to strive upwards" (Dillon 1969, p. 38). This would seem to be something akin to Diotima's "giving birth in the beautiful" projected onto the cosmic.

The distinction between Heavenly and Earthly Love performs an important role in the moral psychology of the Russian novelist, Leo Tolstoy (1828–1910). By his own admission Tolstoy was deeply influenced by Plato and the *Symposium*. He began a close study of the dialogues around 1848, drawn especially to the *Symposium* and the *Phaedo* (love and death), working from the French translations of Victor Cousin (Orwin 1983, p. 501), returning to them in the 1870s, working with the Greek (Gutkin 1989, p. 85). In honor of Plato, Tolstoy includes a minor, but significant character named Platon Karataev in *War and Peace* (1865–1869), and Platon Fokanych in *Anna Karenina* (1873–1877).[7] In an apt metaphor, Tolstoy describes his own philosophy as a "circle" or "ball" with no end, middle or beginning, terms reminiscent of both Plato's Aristophanes and Eryximachus: "the persuasiveness of the truth of this outlook depends on its inner agreement, its harmony" (Orwin 1983, p. 511). In a diary entry from November 1852, he records his views on love. "For me, the main sign of love is the fear of giving offence to or of not being liked by the beloved—really a fear." He even admits a homoerotic dimension. "I was falling in love with men before

I had any understanding of the possibility of pederasty, but even after having learned of it, the thought of the possibility of intercourse never entered my head" (Orwin 1983, p. 502). This is a conception of Platonic love marked by, "a voluntary moral self-restraint on the part of the lover" (Orwin 1983, p. 504n8). In addition to conceptions of Platonic love, Tolstoy was drawn to Plato's moral psychology, and his views on art and aesthetics. The *Symposium* plays important roles in *Anna Karenina*, and the late novella *The Kreutzer Sonata* (1889).

The *Symposium* enters *Anna Karenina* directly. The goodhearted Konstantin Levin has come to Petersburg to propose to his beloved Kitty Shcherbatsaya. Early in the novel, he has dinner with his friend, the dissolute Stiva Oblonsky, the brother of Anna Karenina and the brother-in-law of Kitty. They meet at an elegant restaurant, a sort of symposium, where they eat, drink, and share philosophical conversation. The conversation centers on Levin's belief in the perfection of his love for Kitty, set into the context of a discussion between earthly and heavenly love. Levin explicitly recalls Plato's *Symposium* and the two types of love: "both kinds of love serve as a touchstone for men. Some men understand only the one, some only the other. Those who understand only the non-platonic love need not speak of tragedy. For such love there can be no tragedy" (Tolstoy 1970, p. 38).

Irena Gutkin traces a succession of banquets and synoptic meals through the course of the novel that develop the theme of the tension between body and spirit, and between earthly and heavenly love (1989, pp. 88–90). Indeed, this dichotomy is one of the defining patterns of *Anna Karenina*, Tolstoy playing on the dialectical parallel and contrast between the unhealthy and worldly love of Anna and Vronksy and the healthy, but passionate eros of Kitty and Levin.

The Kreutzer Sonata makes subtler and more complex use of the *Symposium*. The occasion of the novella is a conversation recollected by the narrator among a group of interlocutors on a long train ride. When the conversation turns to modern love and marriage one person argues that love should be about spiritual affinity, while another, "a daddy of the old style!" declares, "the female sex must be curbed in time or else all is lost!" (Tolstoy 1978, p. 528). An intense and increasingly more agitated man named Pózdnyshev soon dominates the conversation, however.

Eventually he confesses that he had killed his wife in a fit of jealous rage, but had eventually been released on the grounds that he had acted under the strain of mental duress. Over the course of the night, drinking strong tea (instead of the sympotic wine), he proceeds to confess his story. Pózdnyshev complains that all relations between the sexes is physical, that everything about modern middle-class culture encourages men and women to seek material and sexual gratification. He holds out for special indictment the power of music to excite unhealthy emotions. "Music carries me immediately and directly into the mental condition in which the man was who composed it. My soul merges with his and together with his pass from one condition into another" (Tolstoy 1978, pp. 582, 3). He especially singles out Beethoven's *Kreutzer Sonata* for stimulating erotic feelings, and indeed it was Pózdnyshev's wife's playing this music that convinced him of her infidelity.

Liz Knapp argues that Pózdnyshev's discussion of music relates to Tolstoy's own struggles to work out the aesthetic theories that come to fruition in *What Is Art?* (1897). She sees Tolstoy drawing on the critique of art from Plato's *Republic* (Knapp 1991, 27). That said, we should not overlook the obvious parallels between Pózdnyshev's confession and that of Alcibiades, who expressed his own mistrust of music, as well as his bewitchment at the sound of Socrates' voice. The erotic for both Pózdnyshev and Alcibiades is associated with music and the manic, and is capable of stimulating violent emotions.

4.6. DIOTIMA, ABSENSE, AND SUBTITUTION

The theme of substitution, especially in context of Diotima's absent-presence has intrigued a number of contemporary thinkers. The influential French psychoanalyst Jacques Lacan (1901–1981) draws significantly on Plato's *Symposium*, finding a variety of motifs resonating with psychoanalytic theory: an unmappable desire-space, splitting (*Spaltung*), *aporia*, the dialectic of love, *agalma*. Among other works, he devotes the entire eighth seminar (1960–1961) of his famous cycle of *séminaire*, to an extended, if idiosyncratic, commentary on the *Symposium*, using this as a jumping-off point to a discussion of psychological transference. I will limit myself to two themes in order to give some sense of Lacan's interest in the *Symposium*.

For Lacan, the figure of Diotima is ripe for thematizing the nature of the symbolic order of language. Thus, looking at Diotima's myth of Poros and Penia, Lacan sees a symbolizing of the nature of desire. Since Poros means "resource" and Penia "poverty," then Penia might also be called *aporia* (literally "without resource"), a term used to label a philosophical impasse (Lacan 2001, p. 149). From a Lacanian-Freudian perspective, Aporia-Penia has "nothing to give except her constitutive lack, *aporia*." To this he adds, "it is a question of giving a discourse, a valid explanation, without having it" (Lacan 2001, p. 150). This closely relates, Lacan suggests, to Socrates' move from *episteme*, predicated on self-evident knowledge to *mythos*. Love can only be articulated around a lack (*manqué*). Structurally speaking this relates to the Freudian discovery of the unconsciousness, explaining how what Lacan terms the symbolic order creates the subject out of language rather than reference to something. From this perspective, Diotima's "Ladder of Love" illustrates the metonymical function of desire, the open-ended and successive substitution of one name or word for another. In Lacan's view, desire emerges from the gap or disparity between need and the demand for love, and the discrepancy between desire and the ability to satisfy the desire (Bowie 1991, p. 136). Inevitably the asymmetry of the relationship between the lover and beloved, the subject and the Other, means that the subject will be disappointed: "That which is thus given to the Other to fill, and which is strictly that which it does not have, since it too, lacks being, is what is called love, but it is also hate and ignorance" (Bowie 1991, p. 136). This aptly describes Alcibiades' relationship with Socrates.

In the relationship between Socrates and Alcibiades, Lacan finds exemplified the "profound," "radical," and "mysterious" relationship between subjects, out of these emerge the phenomenon of psychological transference (Lacan 2001, p. 203). In the *Symposium*, Socrates is in the position of the analyst while Alcibiades is in that of the analysand. "Alcibiades shows the presence of love, but only insofar as Socrates, who knows, can be deceived by it and accompany him only by being deceived about it. The lure is reciprocal" (Lacan 2001, p. 198). Alcibiades desires Socrates because he believes that Socrates possesses the *agalma*—literally "ornament," Lacan's gloss of the beautiful object hidden in the silenus, a possession that Socrates rejects in his claim of ignorance (Lacan 2001, pp. 167–182). From the Freudian perspective the *agalma* is the object of desire, the phallus. "It is because he [Alcibiades] has not seen Socrates' prick," Lacan writes in his *Écrits*, "that Alcibiades the seducer exalts in him the *agalma*, the marvel that he would like Socrates to cede to him in avowing his desire: the division of the subject that he bears within himself being admitted with great clarity on this occasion" (Lacan 1977, p. 322).

The Belgian-born philosopher and psychoanalyst, Luce Irigaray (1932–) offers a poststructuralist feminist take on Diotima and the *Symposium* in her 1982 lecture "Sorcerer Love" ("L'amour sorcier"). Deploying a mixture of deconstruction and *écriture féminine*, Irigaray contrasts Diotima's use of dialectic with that of Socrates (Plato). While the Socratic argument in her view moves linearly, each step predicated on the refutation of the previous, Diotima's dialectic uncovers but preserves: "The mediator is never abolished in an infallible knowledge. Everything is always in movement, in a state of becoming. And the mediator of all this is, among other things, or exemplarily, *love*. Never fulfilled, always becoming" (Irigaray 1993, p. 21).

Dwelling on Diotima's assertion that the union of man and woman is divine, "the presence of immortality in the living mortal," Irigaray argues that love is always prior to any procreation, that it is a "fecundity," a potential that is "mediumlike" or *daimonic*. Love is a beautiful harmony, and without such harmony there can be no procreation. "It is not procreation that is beautiful and that constitutes the object of love. Love's aim is to realize the immortal in the moral between lovers" (Irigaray 1993, p. 26). It is a non-teleological end-in-itself.

In a deconstructive move, however, Irigaray contends that Diotima's method "miscarries," that the division between love of bodies and love of souls reintroduces a metaphysical hierarchy that blurs the divinity in mortality, the equality of opposites between lovers. Instead love becomes teleological. "A beloved is a will, even a duty, and a means of attaining immortality, which the lovers can neither attain nor aspire to between themselves" (Irigaray 1993, p. 27). Irigaray situates love and sexuality in terms of a Lacanian symbolic order, leading Andrea Nye to quip that she judges Diotima as if she were "a lapsed French feminist struggling to maintain the 'correct method' against philosophical orthodoxy" (Nye 1994, p. 200). Critiquing Irigaray's position, Nye suggests that the ahistorical character of Irigaray's methodology blinds her to what distinguished Diotima from philosophers such as Aristotle, Plato, and Kant. "In Diotima's thought, there is no hierarchical logic to expose, no masculine/presence, feminine/absence to deconstruct" (Nye 1994, p. 203). In this she misses exactly the way that Plato has reconstructed her (Nye 1994, p. 212).

4.7. PHILOSOPHER POETS AND POET PHILOSOPHERS

"The Platonic style," wrote Marsilio Ficino, "is more poetic than philosophical" (Ficino 1985, p. 17). Given Plato's praise of poetry and beauty in the *Phaedrus* and *Symposium*, in contradistinction to the charges leveled in the *Republic*, it is not surprising that many poets with a philosophical disposition, or philosophers with a poetic sensibility, are drawn to them. I will focus on four.

The English Romantic poet Percy Bysshe Shelley (1792–1822) explicitly characterized himself a Platonist, a view that informs his conception of the poetic vocation: "Every man in the infancy of art observes an order which approximates more or less closely to that from which this highest delight results: but the diversity is not sufficiently marked, as that its gradations should be sensible, except in those instances where the predominance of this faculty of approximation to the beautiful . . . is very great. Those in whom it exists in excess are poets, in the most universal sense of the word" (Shelley 1992, p. 517). In effect, the true poet is the person most capable of climbing Diotima's Ladder. A standard starting point for Shelley's Platonism is Notopoulos (1969); see also David O'Connor valuable essay (2006, pp. 360–375).

The *Symposium* is prominent among Shelley's inspirations. Not only did he do his own translation of it, his love poetry is thick with imagery and themes drawn from it. It is sufficient to consider one example from the love poem "Epipsychidion" which combines elements of the *Symposium* with Shakespeare's sonnets:

True Love in this differs from gold and clay,
That to divide is not to take away.
Love is like understanding, that grows bright,

Gazing on many truths; 'tis like thy light,
Imagination! Which from earth and sky,
And from the depths of human fantasy,
As from a thousand prisms and mirrors, fills
The Universe with glorious beams, and kills
Error, the worm, with many a sun-like arrow
Of its reverberated lightning. (160–169)

We see the division between Heavenly and Earthly Love, the role of love as the route to enlightenment, and the gaining of truth by grazing on the many truths that point to the universal truth.

The *Les Dialogues Antiques* of poet, philosopher and essayist Paul Valéry (1871–1945) comprise seven prose poems inspired by the Platonic dialogues. In playing off Plato, Valéry articulates a vision in which form and thought are unified by action, a position not unlike that implicit in William Butler Yeats' rhetorical question, "How can we know the dancer from the dance?" Several *Dialogues* resonate with the *Symposium*. "Socrate et son médecin" (1941) centers a conversation between Socrates and Eryximachus, and "L'Ame et la danse" (1921) is a *sympotic* exchange among Socrates, Eryximachus, and Phaedrus as they watch a young female dancer, Athikte, whirling in an ever faster pirouette until she collapses in exhaustion: "In a sonorous world, resonant and rebounding, this intense festival of the body in the presence of our souls offers light and joy," says Socrates (Valéry 1989, p. 59). "Eupalinos, ou l'architecte" (1921) is generally considered the masterpiece among the *Dialogues*. This features an encounter between the ghosts of Socrates and Phaedrus in the underworld. "You, whom of all men I admire," says Phaedrus, "you, more beautiful in your life, more beautiful in your death, than the most beautiful of visible things; great Socrates, adorable ugliness, all-powerful thought that changest [sic] poison into an elixir of immortality," expresses his despair that beauty is inseparable from life (Valéry 1989, p. 79). Socrates posits a three-fold division among the body, which constrains us to desire the useful, the soul, which demands the beautiful, and the world, which obliges us to seek "solidity" or "lastingness," arguing that only in fabricating, in architecture do we discover the form and shape to these laws (Valéry 1989, pp. 128, 9). In terms that anticipate Heidegger, Socrates admits that rather than seek God in the mind, "it is in acts, and in the combination of acts that we ought to find the most immediate feelings of the presence of the divine . . ." (Valéry 1989, p. 145).

Plato and the *Symposium* was important to the thought and work of the German Romantic poet Friedrich Hölderlin (1770–1843).[8] On a personal level, he developed an intense and mutual "Platonic" relationship with Susette Gontard, the wife of his employer, referring to her as Diotima in a number of poems and letters (Kranz 1926, p. 327). And, indeed, a character named Diotima is the object of love in his epistolary novel *Hyperion, oder Der Eremit in Griechenland* (1797–1799). Thematically, *Hyperion* is deeply influenced by Plato: "Without poetry," declares the eponymous hero, "[the Athenians] would in fact never have been a philosophical people!" (Hölderlin 2008 p. 108). Only the person who has felt the effects of pure beauty can be conscious of its discrepancy with human limits and flaws in human thought. It is the intuition of "the harmony of flawless beauty" that makes him a philosophical skeptic. "He disdains the dry bread that well-meaning human reason offers him only because he feasts in secret at the table of the gods" (Hölderlin 2008, p. 109).

Hölderlin's short poem, "Sokrates und Alcibiades" directly addresses the *Symposium*: The first quatrain asks Socrates why he looks so lovingly at such a person as Alcibiades. The second quatrain answers:

> Who the deepest has thought loves what is most alive,
> Wide experience may well turn to what's best in youth,
> And the wise is the end will
> Often bow to the beautiful. (Hölderlin 2004, p. 105) [9]

Hölderlin's hymn, "Der Rhein," represents a complex response to the *Symposium*. Here he develops the trope of the Rhine river as a *daimon* (*der Halbgott*—demigod), situated between its origins in the Alps, the self-sufficient divine, and mortal humans. He reverses the direction on Diotima's Ladder, however. Instead of humans climbing up to the transcendent, it is the gods who need to descend. Because of their immortality the gods need humans to feel. (Interesting comparisons might be drawn with Rilke's *Duino Elegies* and Keats' later odes.) "The most Blessed in themselves feel nothing / Another . . . Vicariously feel in the name of the gods, /And him they need . . ." (Hölderlin 2004, p. 505). In its intermediary position the *daimon*s move us, a "sweet gift." "Like the wine-god foolishly, divinely/ And lawlessly he gives it away. / The language of the purest, comprehensible to the good" (p. 507). Such divine gifts are difficult for all but the most profound to comprehend.

> For hard to bear
> Is misfortune, but good fortune harder.
> A wise man, though, was able
> From noon to midnight, and on
> Till morning lit up the sky
> To keep wide awake at the banquet. (Hölderlin 2004, p. 511)

Socrates stands as the daimonic thinker. The German philosopher Martin Heidegger (1884–1976) glosses "Der Rhein" in a 1934/1935 lecture series: The river is central to human being (*Dasein*): "its flowing as land forming first creates the possibility of the grounding of the dwelling of human beings. The river is not just by way of comparison, but is as itself a founder and poet" (Davis 2006, p. 236). All of this leads us to Heidegger's notion of the philosopher as a sort of poet and poetry (at its profoundest) as a mode of thinking, themes that resonate with the *Symposium*. See, for instance Heidegger's *An Introduction to Metaphysics* (1961, p. 12) and "Why poets" (2002, pp. 200–241).

Confessing his own strong passions in a 1950 letter to his wife Elfriede, Heidegger explains: "The wing beat of [Eros's] touches me always when I take a substantial step forward in my thinking and venture into untrodden territory. It touches me perhaps more strongly and mysteriously than others, when what has been long surmised has to be brought into the sphere of the sayable and when for a long time what has been said must be left in solitude" (Heidegger 2005, p. 264). Although Heidegger cites Parmenides' authority that Eros is the oldest god in this letter, the presence of the *Symposium* is evident. Generally Heidegger's references to the *Symposium* tend to be indirect, mediated by his readings of Hölderlin, or tangential in relation to his extended discussions of other dialogues, especially the *Phaedrus* and the *Republic*, part of his lifelong engagement with Plato (Heidegger

1979, p. 167). I will focus on three points of intersection of Heidegger's thought with the *Symposium*: what Michael Gelven terms the "erotics of understanding," the parallels between *eros* and "care" (*Sorge*), and "poetic dwelling."

Heidegger claimed that his philosophical goal was to "overcome" the metaphysics of Plato, that Plato had grounded truth in metaphysical entities (forms/ideas) rather than in the uncovering of being (*Dasein*) as such. Where Plato thought that "being" was eternal and unchanging, and that "truth" (*aletheia*) was an idea that could be discovered, Heidegger contends that "being" (*Dasein*, literally "being-there" or being-in-the-world), is a relationship, a disposition or comportment between human beings and the world around them. In this regard "truth" is about "uncovering" or "disclosing" our various modes of existing: how do these modes present themselves in a structure by which we make intelligible what we understand of what it means to exist? In other words, Being is bound with the revelation of beings to human awareness. I wish to foreground two points. First, for Heidegger this revelation of human awareness involves an interpretive act that is linguistic: "Discoursing or talking is the way in which we articulate 'significantly' the intelligibility of Being-in-the-world" (1962, p. 204). Since language is the way we make ourselves aware of what we understand, language both reveals and conceals the nature of things. The nature of these disclosures makes language constitutive of *Dasein*'s existence, and since languages are conditioned by time and place, *Dasein* has an historical character unlike Plato's eternal forms. Second, for Heidegger *Dasein* reveals itself most fully in terms of "care" (*Sorge*). Being-in-the-world is essentially care; it is my concern for others, my care for the "ready-to-hand," and most fundamentally my care for the presentness of Being itself (1962, pp. 244–256). Care, writes George Steiner, is what "makes human existence meaningful, that makes a man's life signify." Parodying Descartes Steiner adds, "I care, therefore I am" (Steiner 1978, p. 101). With this background, we are ready to turn more explicitly to Heidegger and the *Symposium*.

Both Plato and Heidegger, argues Gelven, are both concerned with how we understand rather than the knowledge *per se*, in each case predicated on a principle of discrimination. In Plato this is the ability to distinguish between something done well and something done poorly, the ideal perfection against which I distinguish actuality from possibility. In Diotima's account of the erotic, it is the pursuit of the beautiful that makes the lover aware of both what something is and what it might or ought to be. The lover is driven by the awareness of an absence and need. Analogously, Gelven suggests, we know our modes of existing by projecting various possibilities. These possible projects either reveal or conceal existence, according to whether the projection allows us to understand ourselves authentically or inauthentically, between existing in a way that makes existence meaningful or not. "Since meaning cannot be derived solely from the realization that something exists," writes Gelven, "it must entail going beyond the actuality of the object. For Heidegger this is accomplished by the projection of possibilities; for Plato through idealizing" (1973, p. 131). Both the erotic and the projection suspend us between what is and what might be.

Eros, for Heidegger is the most authentic striving for being (Heidegger 2004, p. 155). It is this very striving that "provides the measure and law for the striver's comportment to beings, enabling existence from the ground of beings in the whole" (2004, p. 155). The lover holds himself as an existing being in the midst of beings. The lover does not seek to possess. Rather, "beings are referred to him in his *Dasein*, and he is referred to them, so that in authentic striving for being he strives for his own *Dasein*, wherein it occurs that beings come to be and not to be" (2004, p. 156). In turn, "only to the extent that Being is able to elicit 'erotic' power in its revelation to man is man capable of thinking about Being and overcoming oblivion of Being" (Heidegger 1979, p. 194). Elsewhere he writes, "[w]hat is most loved and longed for in *eros*, and therefore the Idea that is brought into fundamental relation, is what at the same time appears and radiates most brilliantly," that is, the beautiful (1979, p. 167). In this regard the beautiful is exactly that which draws us toward a luminous glimpse of Being and thereby most draws us on and liberates us (Heidegger 1979, p. 194). Summarizing: "That which truth essentially brings about, the unveiling of Being, that and nothing else is what beauty brings about" (1979, p. 198). All of this sounds a bit like Diotima's "giving birth in beauty" (206b). It is not hard to draw parallels between the erotic and care, or to see the erotic as a sort of care, structuring the comportment of the lover toward the beloved. While rejecting Plato's or Diotima's positing of the beautiful as a something eternal and self-sufficient, Heidegger agrees with Plato that eros causes us to orient ourselves and pursue something beyond the actuality of the present.

In ancient Greek culture, Heidegger contends, we may distinguish three conceptions of art (1979, pp. 164, 165): the first is having masterful know-how, expressed by the word *technē*. The second is an acquired capacity (*meletē*) or a notion of "carefulness of concern" (*epi-meleia*), marked by "the mastery of a composed resolute openness to beliefs; it is 'care'" (p. 164). The third is what is brought forward in a "process of bringing-forth" which he relates to *poiēsis*. When Plato discusses the relationship of art and truth, Heidegger suggests, he is primarily concerned with the third kind, the relationship of what has been brought forth by words and its relationship with the ideal. His own view of art and poetic thinking more closely resembles the second kind of art, the composed resolute openness to beliefs, or what he elsewhere terms "poetic dwelling." The poets, understanding the spatial-temporal limits of language, are not concerned with representing, but in the words of John Caputo instituting a world, "the uncovering of the matrix of meaning in which an historical age lives and dwells" (Caputo 1978, p. 235). For Heidegger, poets such as Hölderlin and Rilke engage in "thoughtful poetizing" (1975, p. 12), an act of standing back and poetizing out of his experience of the truth of Being, a process of orienting and disclosing of our place of human dwelling. While Heidegger does not notice, a strong case can be made for the similarity between the "mastery of a composed resolute openness to beliefs" that undergirds poetic dwelling and Diotima's call to gaze on the "great sea of beauty" in unstinting love of wisdom, "until having grown and been strengthened there, he catches sight of such knowledge, and it is the knowledge of such beauty" (210d–e).

While the nature of the knowledge differs, the act is the same. Indeed, Heidegger admits that the enduring power of Plato's works is in the "openness" and "care" that acknowledges the limits of language and forces the would-be reader to become a poet-philosopher, to engage and seek to uncover how we understand. "A dialogue of Plato is inexhaustible" writes Heidegger, "not only for posterity and the changing forms of comprehension to which posterity gives rise; it is inexhaustible of itself, by its nature. And this is forever the mark of all creativeness—which, of course, comes only to those who are capable of reverence" (Heidegger 1968, p. 72). It is exactly this mixture of inexhaustibility, creativeness, and reverence that makes Plato's *Symposium* one of the enduring works of philosophy and literature.

NOTES

1. CONTEXT

1 Many leap to the bemused conclusion that the vandalism centered on the phalli of the *hermai*. In Aristophanes' *Lysistrata* the chorus warns a group of comically tumescent ambassadors: "If you are wise, wrap up, unless you wish one of those Hermes-choppers to catch sight o' you" (Aristophanes 1923, p. 1094). The situation, however, is more complicated. Thucydides reports that it was the faces of the statues that were damaged (Thucydides 1954, p. 383). Plutarch makes a similar claim (Plutarch 1954, p. 49), and modern archaeological evidence supports them (Davidson 1997, p. 296). The symbolism would seem to pertain more to youth trimming the "old" beards than to penis power, the beard being a more visible sign of masculinity than the phallus. Because of their ubiquitousness, "the herm did not stand simply as a mark of former piety, the record of a past transaction between man and god, in the way that a religious dedication might; the herm re-presented the individual Athenian to himself" writes Robin Osborne (1985, p. 65). While the vandals may have knocked off the phalli in the process, it was the destruction of the face that was the real sacrilege.

2 The typical krater holds from ten to fourteen gallons. (We should keep in mind that the practice was to dilute wine with water; only barbarians drank their wine neat.) In an extant fragment by the comic playwright Eubulus (405–335 BCE), the god Dionysus proposes that *symposia* limit themselves to three kraters of wine: "One for health, the second for love and pleasure, and the third for sleep; when this has been drunk up, wise guests make for home." He then warns, "The fourth krater is mine no longer, but belongs to hubris; the fifth to shouting; the sixth to revel; the seventh to black eyes; the eighth to summonses; the ninth to bile; and the tenth to madness and people tossing the furniture about" (quoted Davidson 1998, pp. 47, 48).

3 G. M. A. Grube glosses the riddle of the eunuch and the bat as something like: What is a man who is not a man, who saw and did not see a bird which was not a bird, sitting on a bough that was not a bough, and pelted it with a stone which is not a stone? The answer is that the man is a eunuch with poor eyesight, mistook a bat for a bird, which clung to a reed rather than a bough, and threw a pumice stone (Plato 1974, p. 139).

4 On the rules of the *encomium* see Hunter (2004, pp. 34–37). See also Nightingale's survey of the multiple manifestation of the discourse of praise (1995, pp. 94–106).

NOTES

5 The courtly love tradition centers the erotic ideal on heterosexual relations, not the homoerotic ones envisioned by Pausanias. While Andreas Capellanus was not directly familiar with the *Symposium*, he was, nevertheless, indirectly influenced by Plato, through Arabic poets who contributed significantly to the troubadours of Provençal Occitan and *trovères* of Northern France (Nykl 1946, pp. 371–411). Particularly influential was *The Ring of the Dove* by the writer and statesman Ibn Hazm, who lived in Islamic Spain from 994–1064 CE. Inspired by Plato, he saw true love as the recognition of self in the other. "[I]t is evident that the soul itself being beautiful, it is affected by all beautiful things, and has a yearning for perfect symmetrical images; then, if it discerns behind that image something of its own kind, it becomes united and true love is established" (1953, p. 28).

6 The term *katapugōn* most fully implies sexual obsession and insatiability, and could be applied to women and animals (e.g. lascivious mice) as well as men (Davidson 1968, pp. 172, 173). Aristophanes' Lysistrata accuses the women of Athens of being "*pankatapugōn* [wholly-*katapugōn*]" (1924, p. 137). See also Dover (1980, p. 143). Plato uses the term *kinaidos* similarly in *Gorgias* 493a–494e. Michel Foucault's analysis distorts the picture, focusing too literally on the penetrator penetrated binary: "The consequence of this was that on the one hand the 'active' and dominant role was always assigned positive values, but on the other hand it was necessary to attribute to one of the partners in the sexual act the passive, dominated, and inferior position" (Foucault 1990, p. 220). The problem is that the negative *katapugōn/ kinaidos* are playing an active role (c.f. Dover 1980, pp. 100–109 and Halperin 1990, pp. 34, 35). In the logic of gender, the *katapugones* or *kinaidoi* are overcome and controlled by their sexual drives rather then controlling them. It is less a matter of sexual plumbing then that their wills or reasons are passive to the active dictates of their appetites.

3. READING THE TEXT

1 Aristotle attributes this argument to the Pythagorean philosopher and physician, Alcomeon of Croton (*De Anima* 405a29). The Latin *anima* embraces the multiple senses of soul, breath, vital force, and animation. Thomas Aquinas' account of the soul is not irrelevant. See *Summa Theologiae* [1266–73], part 1, question 75, article 1–6.

2 The Eleatic philosopher Parmenides (ca 515–ca 450 BCE) declared that Eros was the first of all the gods devised by the "divinity who steers everything" (Wheelwright 1966, p. 100).

3 Some anthropologists classify societies according to whether they are "shame cultures" or "guilt cultures," the difference often taken to imply a moral progression. Ruth Benedict offers an explanation. "True shame cultures rely on external sanctions for good behavior, not, as true guilt cultures do, on an internalized conviction of sin. Shame is a reaction to other people's criticism. A man is shamed

either by being openly ridiculed and rejected or by fanaticizing to himself that he has been made ridiculous. In either case it is a potent sanction. But it requires an audience or at least a man's fantasy of an audience. Guilt does not. In a nation where honor means living up to one's own picture of oneself, a man may suffer from guilt though no man knows of his misdeed and a man's feeling of guilt may actually be relieved by confessing his sin" (1967, p. 223).

4 Blind to the ironies of the situation, Mann's Aschenbach explicitly and wistfully fantasizes that he is Socrates to Tadzio's Phaedrus.

5 Hippocrates goes on in his account of the "sacred disease" to suggest that the designation is fraudulent: "My own view is that those who first attributed a sacred character to this malady were like the magicians, purifiers, charlatans and quacks of our own day, men who claim great piety and superior knowledge. Being at a loss, and having no treatment which would help, they concealed and sheltered themselves behind superstition, and called their illness sacred, in order that their utter ignorance might not be manifest" (Hippocrates 1959, vol 2, p. 141). In other words, Hippocrates sees those who call the disease sacred as the medical equivalent of those Plato indicts of sophistry.

6 In Xenophon's account of Socrates' court defense (*Apology*), Socrates complains that his little voice does not represent the creation of a new god, that there is nothing different between his experience and those who read the omens of birds or oracles. "The only difference between them and me is that whereas they call the sources of their forewarning, 'birds,' 'utterances,' 'chance meetings,' 'prophets,' I call mine a 'divine' thing [daimonion]; and I think that in using such a term I am speaking with more truth and deeper religious feeling than do those who ascribe the gods' power to birds" (Xenophon 1923, p. 14).

7 Aristodemus reported that at the end of Socrates' speech, Aristophanes tried to respond to something Socrates had said about his own speech, but could not be heard over the applause (212c). Unless Diotima and Aristophanes share some common source about the androgynes, Diotima could not have alluded to Aristophanes' speech. Since we possess no knowledge about such a source, Diotima's allusion is taken as evidence that Socrates is inventing Diotima's speech as he goes along to respond to the various interlocutors at Agathon's party. Aristophanes seems to have noticed this, but cannot get a word in edgewise. Part of this can be taken as one of Plato's winks at the reader to underline the fictional character of the dialogue.

8 Compare Diotima's description of self-identity with that of Hume: "For my part, when I enter most intimately into what I call *myself*, I always stumble on some particular perception of other, of heat or cold, light or shade, love or hatred, pain or pleasure. . . . I may venture to affirm of the rest of mankind, that they are nothing but a bundle or collection of different perceptions, which succeed each

NOTES

other with an inconceivable rapidity, and are in a perpetual flux and movement" (*A Treatise of Human Nature*, vol 1, part 4, section 6).

9 Bettie Page is the infamous black-haired pinup girl of the 1950s and Dame Edna is the lilac-haired *grande dame* created by the Australian comedian Barry Humphries.
10 A "wine-cooler" (*psyktēr*) is the name for a fat-bellied vessel with a long narrow base rather than a beverage. It is so called, because it could be put into a krater of cold water or ice to keep its contents cool.
11 The priests of the cult were eunuchs. The narrative poem, "Super alta uectus Attis celeri rate maria" (LXIII) by the Roman poet Catullus shows a worshipper of the Great Goddess caught up in a state of ecstatic derangement castrating himself. (Attis was the consort of Cybele.)
12 In the "Reed Flute's Song," Persian poet and mystic philosopher Rumi (Mowlana Jalaloddin Balkhi, 1207–1273), imagines the sound of the reed-flute as a lament for the lost reed-bed from which he was cut: "Love's fire is what makes every reed-flute pine/ Love's fervour thus lends potency to wine; /The reed consoles those forced to be apart . . ." (Rumi 2004, 10–12). It is not hard to find echoes of the *Symposium* with the incantatory power of the silenic flute, the themes of the mantic and the drunkenness, and the notion that love grows out of a violent separation or splitting. Indeed, for Rumi, language and music is the result of our emptiness, a function of our homelessness, our longing to return to our source. Rumi adds, "Be joyful, love, our sweetest bliss is you,/ Physician for all kinds of ailments to, /The cure for our conceit and stubborn pride/ Like Plato here with Galen, side by side; /Through love the earthly form soars heavenward/. . ." (21–25).
13 Although there are various figurines and other representations of satyrs, there is no archaeological evidence for the sort of statue that Alcibiades describes that can be opened up to reveal another figure inside. Kenneth Dover speculates that there might have been a brief fashion for such objects, but admits that none have survived, and all textual references postdate the *Symposium*, and so may be attributed to it (Plato 1980, p. 166 b1).
14 In the *Bacchae*, King Pentheus rejects the power of Dionysus (Bacchus). For this hubris, he is torn to pieces by the maenads (the worshipers of the god), when he accidentally falls among them while trying to watch their ecstatic worship.
15 A favorite topic in 18th and 19th–century history paintings features Socrates dragging a reluctant Alcibiades away from the arms of temptation: Jean-Baptiste Regnault's (1791), "Socrates," Félix Auvray (1833), "Alcibiades with the courtesan," and Jéan-Leon Gérôme's (1861), "Socrates seeking Alcibiades in the house of Aspasia."
16 The Winter Lenaean Festival generally featured a competition between two tragedians, each contributing two tragedies.

NOTES

4. RECEPTION AND INFLUENCE

1 While Petronius is playing with the form of the Greek Romance, the *Satyricon* is often described in terms of Menippean satire, a literary hybrid marked by a mixture of prose and verse, often displaying a wide range of register in its diction. In his *Academia*, Cicero has Varro quip: "in my imitation of Menippius . . . I treated with a certain amount of merriment, a copious mixture of elements derived from the inmost depths of philosophy, and logical utterances" (1.2.8). Some theoreticians see in the Menippean satire the prototype of the novel (Bakhtin 1984, pp. 113–121). See also Frye (1971, pp. 309–312).
2 Widely venerated in the Eastern Church, Saint Thecla was reportedly a follower and companion of Paul in the 1st century CE, inspired by his "Discourse on Virginity." She does not figure in the New Testament, her story appearing in the apocryphal *Acts of Paul and Thecla*, which is the probable basis of the claim for her existence by a number of early church fathers, including Gregory of Nyssa, Ambrose, Chrysostom, and Eusebius.
3 The title, *Encomium Moriae*, is a multilingual pun, implying in Greek a speech of praise by Folly (*Moria*), and in Latin a speech in praise of Sir Thomas More (*Moriae*).
4 Ecstasy, *ekstasis* derives from the preposition *ek* "from" and *stasis* "standing position," meaning literally "displacement" and figuratively "entrancement" or "astonishment." *Ekstasis manikē* can signify "madness," "fear," "rapture," or "drunkenness" depending on the context.
5 In 1841 Kierkegaard defended a thesis titled, *The Concept of Irony, with Constant Reference to Socrates*. In this he attacks the use of irony by the Romantics, especially Fichte, Tieck, and Schlegel, as negating for the sake of negating, resulting in a relativism that renders all knowledge meaningless. Socrates, however, exemplifies the true ironist. While rejecting the actuality of his world, he does not reject actuality altogether. In this way the true ironist opens the way for a new actuality, even though he does not know what it is.
6 In his *De Deo Socratis*, Lucius Apuleius cites the *Symposium* in his discussion of the *daimones*, which he defines as "living beings in kind, rational creatures in mind, susceptible to emotion in spirit, in body composed of the *aer* [a clear element between matter and *aether*], everlasting in time" (Apuleius 2001, p. 205). In his "novel" the *Metamorphoses* known also as *The Golden Ass*, Apuleius offers an alternative to Diotima's allegory by imaging the love and tribulations of Cupid (Eros) and Psyche (Soul), and Psyche's struggle with the trials imposed on her by her mother-in-law Venus (Aphrodite).
7 Robert L. Jackson sees a possible allusion to Plato's Parable of the Cave in the episode in the flickering light of Platon Karataev's shed in *War and Peace*, though it raises the problem of whether we are to

NOTES

take Karataev's realm as a self-sufficient ideal or illusion (1978, p. 542).
8 Hölderlin had been a roommate at the Lutheran seminary in Tübingen with Hegel and Schelling, both destined to be the leading figures in German Idealist philosophy. Because of his religious doubts, Hölderlin never took orders, subsequently supporting himself as a tutor, translator, and poet. His fervent admiration for ancient Greek culture helped him to negotiate his complex religious doubts with his deeply felt sense of divinity. He eventually suffered a mental breakdown and was institutionalized in 1806 until his death.
9 Heidegger comments on this poem in his discussion of "thinking": Truth, for Heidegger, means the disclosure of what keeps itself concealed, and what we call the beauty is poetic truth: "The beautiful is not what pleases, but what falls within the fateful gift of truth which comes to be when that which is eternally non-apparent and therefore invisible attains its most radiantly apparent appearance" (Heidegger 1968, p. 19).

FURTHER READING

PRIMARY TEXTS AND TRANSLATIONS

Aeschylus (1998), *The Oresteia*, trans by D. R. Slavitt. Philadelphia: University of Pennsylvania Press.
Apuleius (2001), *Rhetorical Works*, trans by S. Harrison, J. Hilton, and V. Hunink. Oxford: Oxford University Press.
Aristophanes (1923), *The Lysistrata, the Thesmophoriazusae, the Ecclesiaszusae, the Plutus*, trans by B. B. Rogers. Cambridge: Harvard University Press.
— (1924), *The Peace, The Birds, The Frogs*, trans by B. B. Rogers. Cambridge: Harvard University Press.
— (2007), *Fragments*, trans by J. Henderson. Cambridge: Harvard University Press.
Aristotle (1960), *The Rhetoric of Aristotle*, trans by Lane Cooper. New York: Appleton-Century-Crofts.
— (1983), *Rhetorica ad Alexandrum*, trans by H. Rackham. Cambridge: Harvard University Press.
— (1985), *Nicomachean Ethics*, trans by T. Irwin. Indianapolis: Hackett Publishing.
Capellanus, Andreas (1960), *The Art of Courtly Love*, trans by J. J. Parry. New York: Columbia University Press.
Dante Alighieri (1973), *Vita Nuova*, trans by M. Musa. Bloomington: Indiana University Press.
— (1986), *The Divine Comedy of Dante Alighieri: The Paradiso*, trans by A. Mandelbaum. New York: Bantam Books.
Demosthenes (1949), *Demosthenes VII: Funeral Speech LX, Erotic Essay LXI, Exordia, Letters*, trans by N. W. and N. J. DeWitt. Cambridge: Harvard University Press.
Diogenes Laertius (1972), *Lives of Eminent Philosophers*, trans by R. D. Hicks. Cambridge: Harvard University Press.
Dionysius of Halicarnassus (1985), *Critical Essays*, vol 2, trans by S. Usher. Cambridge: Harvard University Press.
Erasmus (1967), *Erasmus on His Times: A Shortened Version of the Adages of Erasmus*, trans by M. M. Phillips. Cambridge: Cambridge University Press.
— (1971), *Praise of Folly and Letter to Martin Dorp 1515*, trans by B. Radice. London: Penguin Books.
Ficino, Marsilio (1985), *Commentary on Plato's Symposium on Love*, trans by S. Jayne, 2nd ed. Dallas, TX: Spring Publications.
Gorgias of Leontini (2003), "Encomium of Helen," in *The Greek Sophists*, trans by J. Dillon and T. Gergel. London: Penguin Books, pp. 76–84.

Hesiod (1988), *Theogony* and *Works and Days*, trans by M. L. West. Oxford: Oxford University Press.
Hippocrates (1959), *Hippocrates*, 4 vols, trans by W. H. S. Jones. Cambridge: Harvard University Press.
Hölderlin, Friedrich (2004), *Poems and Fragments*, trans M. Hamburger. Oxford: Anvil Press.
— (2008), *Hyperion*, trans by R. Benjamin. Brooklyn: Archipelago Books.
Homer (2003), *The Homeric Hymns*, trans J. Cashford, notes by N. Richardson. London: Penguin.
Ibn Hazm (1953), *The Ring of the Dove: A Treatise on the Art and Practice of Arab Love*, trans by A. Arberry. London: Luzac Oriental.
Johnson, D. M. (2003), *Socrates and Alcibiades: Four Texts*. Newburyport, MA: Focus Publishing.
Kahn, C. H. (1981), *The Art and Thought of Heraclitus: An Edition of the Fragments with Translation and Commentary*. Cambridge: Cambridge University Press.
Kierkegaard, Søren (1992), *Either/Or: A Fragment of Life*, trans by A. Hannay. London: Penguin Books.
— (1996), *Papers and Journals: A Selection*, trans by A. Hannay. London: Penguin Books.
Methodius of Olympus (1958), *The Symposium: A Treatise on Chastity*, trans by H. Musurillo. Westminster, MD: The Newman Press.
Mirandola, Giovanni Pico della (1986), *Commentary on a Poem of Platonic Love*, trans by D. Carmichael. Lanham, MD: University Press of America.
Montaigne, Michel de (1991), *The Essays of Michel de Montaigne*, trans by M. A. Screech. London: Penguin Press.
Petronius (1969), *Petronius*, trans by M. Heseltine, ed by E. H. Warmington. Cambridge: Harvard University Press.
Phillips, M. M. (1967), *Erasmus on His Times: A Shortened Version of the "Adages" of Erasmus*. Cambridge: Cambridge University Press.
Pindar (1969), *The Odes of Pindar*, trans by C. M. Bowra. Baltimore: Penguin Books.
Plato (1901), *Platonis Opera* II, ed by J. Burnet. Oxford: Oxford University Press.
— (1961), *The Collected Dialogues of Plato*, ed by E. Hamilton and H. Cairns. Princeton: Princeton University Press.
— (1973), *The Symposium of Plato*, ed by R. G. Bury. Cambridge: W. Heffer and Sons.
— (1974), *The Republic*, trans by G. M. A. Grube. Indianapolis: Hackett Publishing.
— (1980), *The Symposium*, ed by K. Dover. Cambridge: Cambridge University Press.
— (1989), *The Symposium*, trans by A. Nehamas and P. Woodruff. Indianapolis: Hackett Publishing Co.
— (1995), *The Phaedrus*, trans by A. Nehamas and P. Woodruff. Indianapolis: Hackett Publishing.

FURTHER READING

— (1998), *The Symposium*, ed by C. J. Rowe. Warminister: Aris and Phillips.
— (1999), *The Symposium*, trans by C. Gill. London: Penguin Books.
Plotinus (1967), *Plotinus*, 6 vols, trans by A. H. Armstrong. Cambridge: Harvard University Press.
Plutarch (1954), *Le banquet des sept sages*, trans by J. Defradas. Paris: Librarie C. Klincksieck.
— (1954), *Plutarch's Lives*, 11 vols, trans by B. Perrin. Cambridge: Harvard University Press.
— (1957), *Plutarch's Moralia*, 15 vols, trans by F. C. Babbitt. Cambridge: Harvard University Press.
Rabelais, François (2006), *Gargantua and Pantagruel*, trans by M. A. Screech. London: Penguin Books.
Rūmī, Jalāl al-Dīn (2001), *The Pocket Rumi Reader*, trans by K. Helminski. Boston: Shambhala.
— (2004), *The Masnavi* I, trans by J. Mojaddedi. Oxford: Oxford University Press.
Shelley, P. B. (1992), "A defense of poetry," in *Critical Theory since Plato*, ed by H. Adams. New York: Harcourt Brace Jovanovich, pp. 516–529.
— (2002), *The Symposium of Plato: The Shelley Translation*, ed by D. K. O'Connor. South Bend: St. Augustine Press.
Tacitus (1970), *Dialogus*, trans by W. Peterson and M. Winterbottom. Cambridge: Harvard University Press.
Thucydides (1954), *The Peloponnesian War*, trans by R. Warner. London: Penguin Books.
Tolstoy, Leo (1970), *Anna Karenina*, trans by A. Maude, ed by G. Gibian. New York: W. W. Norton.
— (1978), *The Portable Tolstoy*, ed by J. Bayley. New York: Viking-Penguin.
Valéry, Paul (1989), *Dialogues*, trans by W. McCausland Stewart. Princeton: Princeton University Press.
Wheelwright, P. (1966), *The Presocratics*. New York: Odyssey Press.
Wilde, Oscar (2000), *The Complete Letters of Oscar Wilde*, ed by M. Holland and R. Hart-Davis. New York: Henry Holt and Company.
Xenophon (1923), *Memorabalia, Oeconomicus, Symposium, Apology*, trans by E. C. Marchant and O. J. Todd. Cambridge: Harvard University Press.

SECONDARY READINGS

Allen, R. E. (1991), "Comment," in *The Symposium: The Dialogues of Plato*, vol 2. New Haven: Yale University Press, pp. 3–109.
Anderson, D. E. (1993), *The Masks of Dionysos: A Commentary on Plato's Symposium*. Albany, NY: State University of New York Press.

FURTHER READING

Armstrong, A. H. (1980), "Platonic *Eros* and Christian *Agape*," 79, 105–121.
Averil, C. (1969), "Petronius and Plato," *The Classical Quarterly*, 19, (2), 367–370.
Bakhtin, M. M. (1981), *The Dialogical Imagination*, ed by M. Holquist, trans by C. Emerson. Austin: University of Texas Press.
— (1984), *Problems of Dostoevsky's Poetics*, trans by C. Emerson. Minneapolis: University of Minnesota Press.
— (1985), *Rabelais and His World*, trans by H. Iswolsky. Bloomington: Indiana University Press.
Barthes, R. (1977), *A Lover's Discourse: Fragments*, trans by R. Howard. New York: Hill and Wang.
Benedict, R. (1967), *The Chrysanthemum and the Sword: Patterns of Japanese Culture*. Cleveland: Meridian Books.
Berg, S. (2003), "On Socrates' speech in Plato's Symposium," in E. A. Velásquez (ed), *Love and Friendship: Rethinking Politics and Affection in Modern Times*. Lanham: Lexington Books, pp. 1–35.
Bowie, A. M. (1997), "Thinking with drinking: wine and the *Symposium* in Aristophanes," *The Journal of Hellenic Studies*, 117, 1–21.
Bowie, M. (1991), *Lacan*. Cambridge: Harvard University Press.
Burger, R. (2008), *Aristotle's Dialogue with Socrates: On the Nicomachean Ethics*. Chicago: University of Chicago Press.
Burkert, W. (1985), *Greek Religion*, trans by J. Raffan. Cambridge: Harvard University Press.
Burnyeat, M. F. (1977), "Socratic midwifery, Platonic inspiration," *Bulletin of the Institute of Classical Studies*, 24, 7–16.
Cameron, A. (1969), "Petronius and Plato," *Classical Quarterly*, 19, (2), 367–370.
Caputo, J. D. (1978), *The Mystical Elements in Heidegger's Thought*. Athens: Ohio University Press.
Chateau, J-Y. (2005), *Philosophie et religion: Platon* Euthyphron. Paris: J. Vrin.
Chen, L. C. H. (1983), "Knowledge of beauty in Plato's *Symposium*," *Classical Quarterly*, 33, (1), 66–74.
Cornford, F. M. (1950), *Unwritten Philosophy and Other Essays*. Cambridge: Cambridge University Press.
— (1971), "The doctrine of eros in Plato's Symposium," in G. Vlastos (ed), *Plato II: Ethics, Politics, and Philosophy of Art and Religion*. Garden City: Anchor Books, pp. 119–131.
Corrigan, K. and Glazov-Corrigan, E. (2004), *Plato's Dialectic at Play: Argument, Structure, and Myth in the Symposium*. University Park: Pennsylvania State University Press.
Davidson, J. N. (1998), *Courtesans and Fishcakes: The Consuming Passions of Classical Athens*. New York: St. Martin's Press.
Davis, J. A. (2006), "Need delimited: the creative otherness of Heidegger's demigods," *Continental Philosophy Review*, 38, 223–239.

FURTHER READING

Derrida, J. (1981), *Dissemination*, trans by Barbara Johnson. Chicago: University of Chicago Press.
Des Places, E. (1981), "Platon et la langue de mystères," *Etudes platoniciennes, 1929–1978.* Leiden: Brill, pp. 83–98.
Despland, M. (1985), *The Education of Desire: Plato and the Philosophy of Religion.* Toronto: University of Toronto Press.
Dillon, J. (1969), "*Enn.* III 5: Plotinus' exegesis of the *Symposium* myth," *Agōn,* 3, 24–44.
Dobbs, E. R. (1951), *The Greeks and the Irrational.* Berkeley: University of California Press.
Dover, K. J. (1974), *Greek Popular Morality in the Time of Plato and Aristotle.* Berkeley: University of California Press.
— (1980), *Greek Homosexuality.* New York: Vintage Books.
Eliade, M. (1978), *A History of Religious Ideas I: From the Stone Age to the Eleusinian Mysteries,* trans by W. R. Trask. Chicago: University of Chicago Press.
Festugière, A. J. (1950), *Contemplation et vie contemplative selon Platon.* Paris: J. Vrin.
Foucault, M. (1990), *The Use of Pleasure,* trans by Robert Hurley. New York: Vintage Books.
Friedländer, P. (1958), *Plato: An Introduction,* trans by H. Meyerhoff. New York: Harper and Row.
Frye, N. (1971), *Anatomy of Criticism: Four Essays.* Princeton: Princeton University Press.
Gager, J. G. (1992), *Curse Tablets and Binding Spells from the Ancient World.* Oxford: Oxford University Press.
Gelven, M. (1973), "Eros and projection: Plato and Heidegger," *Southwestern Journal of Philosophy,* 4, 125–136.
Gide, André (2001), *Corydon,* trans by R. Howard. Urbana: University of Illinois Press.
Gleason, J. B. (1989), *John Colet.* Berkeley: University of California Press.
Gould, T. (1963), *Platonic Love.* New York: Free Press of Glencoe.
Guthrie, W. K. C. (1969), *A History of Greek Philosophy* III: *The Fifth-Century Enlightenment.* Cambridge: Cambridge University Press.
— (1975), *A History of Greek Philosophy* IV: *Plato the Man and His Dialogues: Earlier Period.* Cambridge: Cambridge University Press.
Gutkin, I. (1989), "The dichotomy between flesh and spirit: Plato's *Symposium* in *Anna Karenina,*" in H. McLean (ed), *In the Shade of the Giant: Essays on Tolstoy.* Berkeley: University of California Press, pp. 84–99.
Hadot, P. (1993), *Plotinus or the Simplicity of Vision,* trans by M. Chase. Chicago: Chicago University Press.
Halperin, D. M. (1990), *One Hundred Years of Homosexuality and Other Essays on Greek Love.* London: Routledge.
Heidegger, G. (2005), "*Mein liebes Seelchen!":* Briefe Martin Heideggers an seine Frau Elfride, 1915–1970.* Munich: Deutsche Verlags-Anstalt.

Heidegger, M. (1961), *An Introduction to Metaphysics*, trans by R. Manheim. Garden City: Anchor Books.
— (1962), *Being and Time*, trans by J. Macquarrie and E. Robinson. New York: Harper and Row.
— (1968), *What is Called Thinking*, trans by F. Wieck and J. Gray. New York: Harper and Row.
— (1975), *Poetry, Language, Thought*, trans by A. Hofstadter. New York: Harper and Row.
— (1979), *Nietzsche I: The Will to Power as Art*, trans by D. Krell. New York: Harper and Row.
— (2002), *Off the Beaten Track*, ed by and trans by J. Young and K. Haynes. Cambridge: Cambridge University Press.
— (2004), *The Essence of Truth: On Plato's Allegory and Theaetetus*, trans by T. Sadler. London: Continuum.
Hunter, R. (2004), *Plato's Symposium*. Oxford: Oxford University Press.
Irigaray, L. (1993), *An Ethics of Sexual Difference*, trans by C. Burke and G. Gill. London: Althone.
Irwin, T. (1995), *Plato's Ethics*. Oxford: Oxford University Press.
Jackson, R. L. (1978), "The second birth of Pierre Bezukhov," *Canadian-American Slavic Studies*, 12, (4), 525–542.
Kahn, C. H. (1996), *Plato and the Socratic Dialogue: The Philosophical Use of a Literary Form*. Cambridge: Cambridge University Press.
Knapp, L. (1991), "Tolstoy on musical mimesis: Platonic aesthetics and erotics in the 'The Kreutzer Sonata,'" *Tolstoy Studies Journal*, 4, 25–42.
Kofman, S. (1998), *Socrates: Fictions of a Philosopher*, trans by C. Porter. Ithaca: Cornell University Press.
Konstan, D. and Young-Bruehl, E. (1982), "Eryximachus' speech in the Symposium," *Aperion*, 16, 40–46.
Kranz, W. (1926), "Diotima," *Die Antike*, 2, 313–227.
Kristeller, P. O. (1964), *The Philosophy of Marsilio Ficino*, trans by V. Conant. Glouchester, MA: Peter Smith.
Lacan, J. (1977), *Écrits: A Selection*, trans by A. Sheridan. New York: W. W. Norton.
— (2001), *Le séminaire*, book 8, *Le transfert, 1960–1961*, ed by J.-A. Miller. Paris: Éditions du Seuil.
La Charité, R. C. (1984), "Rabelais and the Silenic Text: the Prologue to *Gargantua*," in Raymond C. La Charité (ed), *Rabelais's Incomparable Book: Essays on His Art*. Lexington, KY: French Forum Publishers, pp. 72–86.
Lissarrague, F. (1987), *The Aesthetics of the Greek Banquet: Images of Wine and Ritual*, trans by A. Szegedy-Maszak. Princeton: Princeton University Press.
Luce, J. V. (1952), "Immortality in Plato's Symposium," *The Classical Review*, 2, (3/4), 137–141.
Lukinovich, A. (1990), "The play of reflections between literary form and the sympotic theme in the *Deipnosophistae* of Athenaeus," in

FURTHER READING

O. Murray (ed), *Sympostica: A Symposium on the Symposion*. Oxford: Clarendon Press, 1990, pp. 263–271.
McKenna, N. (2005), *The Secret Life of Oscar Wilde*. New York: Basic Books.
Miles, L. (1962), *John Colet and the Platonic Tradition*. London: George Allen & Unwin.
Moravcsik, J. M. E. (1971), "Reason and Eros in the "ascent"—passage of the *Symposium*," in J. P. Anton, G. L. Kustas (eds), *Essays in Ancient Greek Philosophy*. Albany: State University of New York Press, pp. 285–302.
Morgan, M. L. (1990), *Platonic Piety: Philosophy and Ritual in Fourth-Century Athens*. New Haven: Yale University Press.
Nails, D. (2002), *The People of Plato: A Prosopography of Plato and Other Socratics*. Indianapolis: Hackett Publishing.
— (2006), "Tragedy off-stage," in J. Lesher, D. Nails, F. Sheffield (eds), *Plato's Symposium: Issues in Interpretation and Reception*. Cambridge: Harvard University Press, pp. 179–207.
Neumann, H. (1965), "Diotima's concept of love," *American Journal of Philology*, 86, (1), 33–59.
Nightingale, A. W. (1995), *Genres in –Dialogue: Plato and the Construct of Philosophy*. Cambridge: Cambridge University Press.
Notopoulos, J. A. (1969), *The Platonism of Shelley: A Study of Platonism and the Poetic Mind*. New York: Octagon Books.
Nussbaum, M. C. (1986), *The Fragility of Goodness: Luck and Ethics in Greek Tragedy and Philosophy*. Cambridge: Cambridge University Press, pp. 165–199.
Nye, A. (1994), "Irigaray and Diotima at Plato's Symposium," in N. Tuana (ed), *Feminist Interpretations of Plato*. University Park: The Pennsylvania State University, pp. 197–215.
Nygren, A. (1953), *Agape and Eros*, trans by P. S. Watson. Philadelphia: Westminster Press.
Nykl, A. R. (1946), *Hispano-Arabic Poetry and its Relations with the Old Provençal Troubadours*. Baltimore [printed by J. H. Furst Co].
O'Brien, M. C. (2002), *Apuleius' Debt to Plato in the* Metamorphoses. Lewiston: Edwin Mellen Press.
O'Brien, M. J. (1984), "Becoming immortal in Plato's *Symposium*," in D. E. Gerber (ed), *Greek Poetry and Philosophy: Studies in Honour of Leonard Woodbury*. Chico: Scholars Press, pp. 185–205.
O'Connor, D. K. (2006), "Platonic selves in Shelley and Stevens," in J. Lesher, D. Nails, F. Sheffield (eds), *Plato's Symposium: Issues in Interpretation and Reception*. Cambridge: Harvard University Press, pp. 360–375.
Ortega Y Gasset, J. (1957), "The nature of the novel," *Hudson Review*, 10, (1), 11–42.
Orwin, D. (1983), "Freedom, responsibility, and the soul: the Platonic contribution to Tolstoi's psychology," *Revue Canadienne des Slavistes*, 25, 501–517.

FURTHER READING

Osborne, R. (1985), "The erection and mutilation of the *Hermai*," *Proceedings of the Cambridge Philological Society*, 31, 47–73.
Pater, W. (1925), *Plato and Platonism: A Series of Lectures*. New York: Greenwood Press.
Pender, E. (1992), "Spiritual pregnancy in Plato's *Symposium*," *Classical Quarterly*, 42, (1), 72–86.
Ranasinghe, N. (2000), *The Soul of Socrates*. Ithaca: Cornell University Press.
Robin, L. (1929), *Platon: Le Banquet*. Paris: Le Belles Lettres.
Rosen, S. (1987), *Plato's Symposium* (2nd ed). New Haven: Yale University Press.
Rowe, C. (2007), *Plato and the Art of Philosophical Writing*. Cambridge: Cambridge University Press.
Scott, D. (2000), "Socrates and Alcibiades in the *Symposium*," *Hermathena*, 168, 25–37.
Screech, M. A. (1980), *Erasmus: Ecstasy and the Praise of Folly*. London: Penguin Books.
Seigel, J. E. (1968), *Rhetoric and Philosophy in Renaissance Humanism: The Union of Eloquence and Wisdom, Petrarch to Valla*. Princeton: Princeton University Press.
Sheffield, F. (2006), "The role of the earlier speeches in the *Symposium*: Platonic endoxic method?," in J. Lesher, D. Nails, Frisbee Sheffield (eds), Plato's *Symposium: Issues in Interpretation and Reception*. Cambridge, MA: Harvard University Press, pp. 23–46.
Smith, D. E. (2003), *From Symposium to Eucharist: The Banquet in the Early Christian World*. Minneapolis: Augsburg Fortress Press.
Sontag, S. (1966), "Notes on 'Camp'," in *Against Interpretation and Other Essays*. New York: Farrar, Straus and Giroux, pp. 275–292.
Spelman, E. V. (1994), "Hairy cobblers and philosopher-queens," in Nancy Tuana (ed), *Feminist Interpretations of Plato*. University Park: The Pennsylvania State University, pp. 87–107.
Stehle, E. (1997), *Performance and Gender in Ancient Greece: Nondramatic Poetry in its Setting*. Princeton: Princeton University Press.
Steiner, G. (1978), *Martin Heidegger*. Chicago: University of Chicago Press.
Strauss, L. (1978), *The City and Man*. Chicago: University of Chicago Press.
Tecuşan, M. (1990), "*Logos Sympotikos*: patterns of the irrational in philosophical drinking: Plato outside the *Symposium*," in O. Murray (ed), *Sympostica: A Symposium on the Symposion*. Oxford: Clarendon Press, pp. 238–260.
Trinkaus, C. (1983), *The Scope of Renaissance Humanism*. Ann Arbor: University of Michigan Press.
Usher, M. D. (2002), "Satyr play in Plato's *Symposium*," *American Journal of Philosophy*, 123, (3), 205–228.
Vlastos, G. (1981), *Platonic Studies*, 2nd ed. Princeton: Princeton University Press.

FURTHER READING

— (1991), *Socrates, Ironist and Moral Philosopher*. Ithaca: Cornell University Press.

White, F. C. (1989), "Love and beauty in Plato's *Symposium*," *Journal of Hellenic Studies*, 109, 149–157.

Wider, K. (1986), "Women philosophers in the ancient Greek world: donning the mantle," *Hypatia*, 1, (1), 21–62.

Zuckert, C. H. (1996), *Postmodern Platos: Nietzsche, Heidegger, Gadamer, Strauss, Derrida*. Chicago: University of Chicago Press.

INDEX

Agathon's speech 52–5
Alcibiades
  confusion 111–12
  in literature 100
  life of 5, 6, 99–100, 123
  speech 102–16
Apollodorus, narration of 27, 33
Apuleius, Lucius 160 n6
Aristodemus, narration of 27, 33–6, 43, 60, 124–5
Aristophanes 4, 10, 34, 43, 52, 72, 100, 127, 157 n6
  androgynes 26, 48–50
  comic playwright 9, 12, 44, 48, 52
  speech 48–50
Aristotle 2, 58, 157 n1
  definition of tragedy 126
  friendship 22
  happiness 69, 73
  rhetoric 9–10
authority
  establishing 27–32, 64, 92, 94, 130
  questions about 15

Barthes, Roland 140–1
beauty *See also* kalos
  benefits of 34, 36, 80
  itself 83–4
  Love desires 63, 72, 118
  pursuit of as madness 14
  "the sea of beauty" 83, 120
birth 17 *See also* midwifery; pregnancy 17
  as metaphor in philosophy 75–7, 93, 95, 103, 116, 120, 130, 143

Capellanus, Andreas 12, 157 n5
Corybantes 107–9
Creativity 54, 80, 93, 155

Dante Alighieri 89, 141
daimon 39, 89, 158
  as guardian divinity 69
  as intermediary 17, 151
  function of the word 68–70
  love like a 6, 21, 68, 70, 147
  Plato's use of 70, 72
  possession by 35
  Socrates likened to 113, 151
  Socrates' understanding of 24, 70, 92, 158 n6
dialogue
  as literary device 29, 58, 91, 129, 158
Diotima *See also* women's roles
  account of 71, 86
  function of 86, 92–5
  her wisdom expounded 16, 30, 60, 64
  historical prototypes of 65–6
  speech 71–85
divination 46, 65, 70, 158 n6
  See also mantic

encomia 23, 62, 156
  conventions 8, 36
  Gorgias 9, 19, 56
endoxa 13, 16, 29, 57, 58
Erasmus of Rotterdam 135–6
eros 21, 25 *See also* love
  as proper noun 10–11, 34
  Phaedrus 23–6
  Xenophon 21–2
Eryximachus' speech 44–8

Ficino, Marsilio 139–42
Foucault, Michel 157 n6

Gide, André 140

Heidegger, Martin 151–5, 161 n9
hermai 5, 7, 44, 99, 109, 156
  Kierkegaard 139
Hippocrates 44, 46–7, 158 n5

INDEX

homoeroticism 6, 10–12, 21, 42, 92, 140, 143, 157
  Phaedrus 37, 60, 127
  Plato 12, 92
Hölderlin, Friedrich 150–1, 161 n5

Ibn Hazm 157 n5
immortality 76–81, 84, 90–1, 94, 147, 149, 150
  desire for 17
intermediary
  between audience & source 30, 61
  between human and divine 67
  daimon as spiritual 16
  midwifery 51, 67
Irigaray, Luce 147–8

kalos *See also* beauty
  function of the word 21, 34, 76
  lover embodied as 39
  Socrates' efforts to match Agathon's 34
  soul 82
Kierkegaard, Søren 136–8

Lacan, Jacques 145–7
Ladder of Love (ascent passage) 30, 84, 96, 117, 122
  Alcibiades 121
  form of the *Symposium* 95, 96, 121
  Hölderlin 150
  Kierkegaard 139
  Lacan 146
  Parable of the Cave 14, 88
  Shelley, Percy Bysshe 148
  stages of ascent 83
Lie (or fiction), noble 29, 32, 65, 67
Love 21 *See also* eros
  characteristics of 72
  Diotima's explanation of 67–85
  dual nature of (ambivalence) 59, 72, 74
  heavenly and earthly 22, 40–2, 142–4
  hierarchy of types (*Phaedrus*) 38

nature of 13, 38, 47–8, 61, 72, 127
  Socrates' understanding of 16, 19, 22, 23
lover-beloved relationship (*erastēs-erōmenos*) 11, 36, 82

madness 14, 33, 138
  desire for wisdom as 33
  ecstatic 105, 160
  eros as 24–5, 33–4, 121–2, 129, 142
  philosophy as 112
  poetic 25, 54
  positive qualities of 25
Mann, Thomas 39, 158 n4
mantic 24, 65, 70
  See also divination
Marsyas 97, 104–9
memory 7, 28, 78, 130
  cultural 6
  knowledge 30, 31
  the *Symposium* 27
  writing 31
metaphysical realism 17, 70, 89
Methodius of Olympus 132–4
midwifery *See also* birth, pregnancy
  as metaphor in philosophy 20, 51, 66–7, 81
moral psychology 16
mystery religions 14, 43, 67, 82, 92, 118
  Diotima 112, 118, 136

noble conduct *See also* virtue 22, 26, 37, 41, 58, 101, 116, 130

Parable of the Cave 14, 29, 88, 160
Parable of the Charioteer 25, 47, 121–2
Pausanias' speech 39–42
Peloponnesian War 2, 4
Petronius Arbiter 132–3
  Cena Trimalchionis 135–6, 160 n1
Phaedrus 36, 47, 49, 54, 90, 120, 121, 148

later influence 142, 151, 158
love 14, 53, 68, 119
Methodius of Olympus 136
similarities with *Symposium* and *Republic* 4
the soul 47, 72, 90
writing 31, 130
Phaedrus' speech 36–9
philosopher – nature of 2, 7–8, 14, 17, 26, 34, 74–5, 130
different from philodoxoi 8
likened to midwifery 20, 51, 86
physician as 46, 59
Plotinus 141–3
Poros and Penia 71, 142–3, 146
pregnancy *See also* birth; midwifery 76, 80–2, 107

Rabelais, François 138
Republic 3–5, 32, 83, 89, 92, 102
and the Ladder of Love 14
and Tolstoy 145
Myth of Er 85
Parable of the Cave 121
the soul 25, 47
Rumi (Mowlana Jalaloddin Balkhi) 159 n12

shame
holding lovers together 12
in failing to live up to expect 37
in lover's disapproval 37, 79–80, 104
vs. guilt 38, 157–8
Shelley, Percy Bysshe 148–9
Sileni 21, 97, 105, 111, 116, 136–7, 147 n3, 159
Silenic texts 137–9
Silenus (satyr king) 105, 107, 128
Alcibiades 97, 103–6, 110
Cyclops 128
King Midas 105–6, 108
Xenophon 21
Socrates *See also* daimon
acting as heavenly lover 114
as physician 109
his strangeness 99, 102–4, 115

his ugliness 20–1, 105, 107, 149
power over Alcibiades 110
soul 119
speech (first) 61–5
speech (second) 67–71
Sophistry 9, 10, 30, 36, 79, 81, 158
soul 25, 78, 82
tripartite model of 23, 47
symposion (drinking party) 1, 12, 20, 29, 35, 92, 106, 128
Agathon's 1, 36, 86
as literary convention 2, 29, 134
conventions of 6, 7, 56, 67, 101, 124, 156 n2, 159 n10
Plato's reservations about 8
Symposium of Plato
as drama 29–30, 127–8
as proto-novel 129
narrative frame 15, 26–7, 33, 95, 130
Symposium of Xenophon 19–22

theater
comedy 43, 124, 128–9
conventions of parodied 29, 127–8
satyr play 125, 128
tragedy 124–6, 128–9, 159 n16
Thucydides 5, 28, 99–100, 156
Tolstoy, Leo 141–3
truth 30, 57, 64, 152
identified with beauty 141, 153, 161
methods for reaching 14, 57, 62, 67, 149, 152, 161
relationship with appearances 28, 33, 94–6, 107, 109–11, 117, 119–21
relationship with art 154

Valéry, Paul 149–50
virtue 54, 60, 80–2, 85
as goal of love 59
Eros as source 16
foundation 16
Love (god) causes 38, 54
lover and beloved 42
Socrates' 105, 115, 120

INDEX

Wilde, Oscar 41, 140
wisdom 7, 10, 25, 54, 57, 83, 111
  as achievement of excellence 59
  collective *See* endoxa
  Diotima's 30, 64
  imparted by Socratic method 86
  likened to midwifery 66
  love as guide to 55
  lover embodied as 54
  nature of the philosopher 2, 74–5
  of Sophists 30
  poetry a form of 55
  the soul 31

women's roles 1, 11–12, 52–3, 64–6, 92–3
writing
  cognitive power of 32
  role of 31–3, 130
  truth and 125, 130

Xenophon 19
  Socrates 20, 65–6, 69, 100
  Symposium 12, 19–22, 111, 158 n6

www.ingramcontent.com/pod-product-compliance
Lightning Source LLC
Chambersburg PA
CBHW070332230426
43663CB00011B/2287